ETHIC

MW01518094

Demonstrated in Geometrical Order and Divided into
Five Parts, which Treat (1) of God; (2) of the Nature
and Origin of the Mind; (3) of the Nature and Origin
of Effects; (4) of Human Bondage; (5) of the Power
of the Intellect, or of Human Liberty

Benedict de Spinoza

ISBN 1-56459-625-7

PREFACE TO FOURTH EDITION.

In 1899 Professor Freudenthal published his *Lebens-geschichte Spinoza's*, indispensable to every student of Spinoza. It has enabled me to make some additions to the biographical part of the *Preface*. The whole of the remaining part of the *Preface* has been revised and, I trust, improved. Two or three mistakes in the body of the work have also been corrected. I wish particularly to call attention to what has been said on p. xciii that I have not attempted to connect Spinoza with metaphysic before and after him, nor to give an exhaustive account of Spinoza's own metaphysic. I also desire again to remind the reader that Spinoza's aim was ethical, or search, as he says, for that " by whose discovery and " acquisition I might be put in possession of a joy " continuous and supreme to all eternity "; for those " clear and distinct ideas " through which " a passion ceases to be a passion."

W. H. W.

PREFACE TO THIRD EDITION.

In this edition a few mistakes have been corrected. Most of them were kindly pointed out to me by Sir Frederick Pollock and the late Dr. Land.

W. H. W.

PREFACE.[1]

THE second edition of the present translation has been carefully revised by Miss Stirling and myself, and a few improved renderings have been introduced. The object of the translators has been to present a version of the *Ethic* which shall be perfectly literal, and yet be intelligible, so far as they can understand it. Those who complain of obscurity must be reminded that the Latin is often obscure. For example, *modus* at one time means mode, as defined in the fifth definition of the first book, and at another time "manner" or "way." Again, it may often be supposed that the right name has not been given to some of what are called the "affects," and the translation does not apparently always cover everything intended by the Latin word; but individual passages must not be isolated, and we had to select that word which best meets the requirements of all the passages taken together in which a particular affect is mentioned. With regard to the use of the terms "subjective" and "objective," it is to be observed that with Spinoza and Descartes they bear a meaning exactly the reverse of that now assigned to them. Dr. Stirling has been good enough to furnish the following historical note upon this subject.

"Prantl (vol. iii. p. 208) says of these words 'subjective' and "'objective' in Duns Scotus—'In innumerable places from now on to "'the eighteenth century (that is, until Alexander Baumgarten) we find "'this use of the words 'objective' and 'subjective' which relates "' itself to the present one as exactly the reverse: namely, 'subjective' "' then meant what refers itself to the subject of the judgments; con-"'sequently to the concrete objects of thoughts: 'objective' again

[1] This preface is based on the preface to the second edition.

" ' what lies in the mere *objicere*, that is, in the making conceivable or
" ' mentally representable, and falls consequently to the score of the
" ' conceiver—the mental representer.' Trendelenburg (El. Log.
" ' Aristotel. p. 52, note) also observes : 'Thus *subject* during the
" ' Middle Ages has the force of underlying substance, as it has also with
" ' Descartes and Spinoza.' The latter (Princip. Philos. Cartes. p. 11,
" ' ed. Paul.) says,—' Everything in which, as in a subject, there is
" ' immediately any property, whose real idea is in us, is called sub-
" ' stance.' So *esse subjectivum* (to be subjective—subjective Being), quite
" ' contrary to the present usage amongst the Germans, is said by
" ' Occam (Sec. XIV.) to be ' that which, as though a thing in nature,
" ' is placed outside of the forms of the mind, and is not imaged by
" ' thought alone ;' whereas *esse objectivum* (objective Being), on the
" ' contrary, is explained as Cognition itself, and consequently a certain
" ' imaged Being (*esse quoddam fictum*).' (Occam, sentent. lib. I. dis-
" ' tinct. II. quæst. 8.) From which it will be evident what is the
" ' meaning of *objective reality* with Descartes (*e. g.*, in med. 3). Amongst
" ' the Germans, chiefly Kant and then Fichte being the originators of
" ' the change, the use of these words is completely inverted. While
" ' the *subject* is said to be he who knows ; the *object*, on the contrary, is
" ' something which, *while subjected in thinking* (*i. e.*, the subject of
" ' thought), still maintains, nevertheless, its own nature in indepen-
" ' dence of the opinions of him who thinks. Hence it is that *subjective*
" ' is said to be that which lies in the changing condition of the
" ' thinker, and *objective*, again, that which lies in the fixed nature
" ' of the thing itself.' "

It may be added that a blemish which has disfigured previous translations, both French, German, and English, and indeed most Latin editions, has been removed ; for the references to the different propositions, axioms, and postulates have been carefully verified and corrected.

Baruch de Spinoza was born at Amsterdam on the 24th of November, 1632.[1] The name Baruch (blessed) was

[1] Old style. The new style was adopted in the Protestant Netherlands on the 18th of February, 1700, but the year had been reckoned from the 1st of January to the 31st of December since 1586. Auerbach's story, *Spinoza : ein Denkerleben*, although professedly a romance, is well worth reading as a successful and sympathetic attempt by a Jew, thoroughly acquainted with Jewish customs, to make Spinoza and his surroundings real to us.

Unfortunately the English translation is not so correct as it might be.

changed for Benedict, its Latin equivalent, after he
ceased to be a Jew. His father was a Portuguese Jew,
a merchant, living at Amsterdam, and member of a small
Jewish community which had found in Holland a refuge
from the Inquisition. The family was originally Spanish,
and Spanish was Spinoza's mother-tongue. It is worth
while to notice in what directions men's thoughts were
turned about this time. The telescope was discovered
by Jan Lipperhey in 1608: Kepler died in 1630; and
Galileo in 1610 announced the revolution of Jupiter's
satellites, and a little later that Venus presented phases
like the moon; thereby confirming finally the truth of
the Copernican system.

Before Spinoza was twenty-four years old Huyghens
had constructed his larger telescope and had seen
Saturn's ring and his fourth satellite. We know from
Spinoza's correspondence that he took the deepest
interest in these discoveries, and it was impossible that
it should be otherwise, for probably never before in
human history had there been an epoch so revolutionary
and so suggestive. The scientific value of the Copernican
system was immense, but its moral value was perhaps
even greater; and it is really to the mathematicians and
astronomers of the sixteenth and seventeenth centuries
that the overthrow of popular theology is due; it is
they who are answerable for that vast reconstruction of
which we have even now seen but the beginning. The
influence of the new revelation was everywhere, and it
was not a mere accident that Spinoza's philosophy
should have been what it was. What he did in theology
and ethic is parallel to the work which Copernicus,
Kepler, Galileo, and Huyghens did in the science of
worlds, for his main achievements are the enlargement of
the idea of God: the removal of God from the provincial
and petty position He had formerly occupied, and the
introduction of unity into our conceptions of man and

nature. It is noticeable also that the occupation Spinoza selected was that of a maker of lenses. No calling more characteristic or significant could have been chosen. Colerus, the biographer of Spinoza, gives the reasons why Spinoza learned a trade. " As a learned " Jew he well knew the law and the counsel of the old " Jewish teachers that together with his studies a man " must take up an art or a handicraft by which he may be " able to get a living. For thus says Rabbi Gamaliel in " the Talmudic Treatise *Pirke Avoth*, cap. 2, 'the study of " the Law is a noble thing if it be joined with some art, " for occupation with both makes us forget sin, and all " study which is not accompanied by a craft comes at " last to nothing and leads to sin '. And R. Jehuda has " said ' he who teaches his son no craft brings him up to " be a highwayman '. Therefore Spinoza, before he began " his quiet life outside the town, learned to polish lenses " for telescopes and other purposes. He became such a " master herein that everybody desired to buy his work, " and in need he could live by it. Several lenses which " he had polished were found amongst his goods after his " death and fetched a fair price as I myself have seen in " the account of the auctioneer." Spinoza also learned to draw, and Colerus possessed a volume of portraits which he had taken.

Of the character of Spinoza's father and his mother nothing whatever is known.[1] He had two sisters, Rebekah and Miriam. He learned Latin at first from a German master, but afterwards from Francis Van den Ende, a physician in Amsterdam, who not only practised medicine but instructed the children of the richest merchants of the city. Colerus says that Van den Ende taught atheism as well as Latin, and that many of his

---

[1] The father came from Figueira near Coimbra. The family stood high in the Jewish community at Amsterdam. Freudenthal, pp. 241, 242.

pupils " bless every day the memory of their parents who took care in due time to remove them from the school of so pernicious and impious a master." Van den Ende's character was of the insurrectionary type, and he was executed at Paris in 1674 for his share in a conspiracy against the French king; the main object of which, so far at least as Van den Ende was concerned, was to give such employment to that monarch that his forces could not be turned against the United Provinces. Van den Ende had a daughter, who was able to teach her father's scholars in his absence; and, according to Colerus, Spinoza fell in love with her, and often confessed that he designed to marry her. She accepted, however, a rival named Kerkkrinck. Van Vloten, the editor of the last edition of Spinoza, has discovered that Clara Maria Van den Ende was married to Kerkkrinck in 1671, at the age of twenty-seven years. If these dates are correct, she was eleven or twelve years younger than Spinoza. Now the sentence of excommunication was passed on Spinoza in 1656, and about that time, although the date is not certain, he had moved from Amsterdam to the house of a friend on the Ouwerkerk Road. Clara was then about twelve years old and Spinoza twenty-four. It has been therefore assumed that the story of Colerus is without foundation. But Colerus does not say that in 1656 Spinoza had determined to make Clara an offer, and as the marriage did not take place till 1671 there is no reason to conclude that the tale is untrue. While Spinoza was in the Ouwerkerk Road he was close to Amsterdam; he was never throughout his life very far from the city, and we know he visited it frequently.

When he had learned Latin Spinoza gave up what Colerus calls " Divinity " and betook himself to the study of natural philosophy and of Descartes. He must have worked hard at his natural philosophy, for his books and his letters show a considerable knowledge of mathematics, both pure and applied, which helped him largely afterwards in his trade. He now began to forsake the synagogue and the Jewish doctors. They expected that he would become a Christian, but they were mistaken; for, although he abandoned the religion of his fathers, he never professed conversion to any other recognised creed. At the outset the Jews endeavoured to bribe him into conformity. A pension of one thousand florins was offered him if he would remain quiet and appear now and then in the synagogue. The offer was declined, and assassination,[1] which was happily avoided, was attempted. Finally, on the 27th July, 1656, he was excommunicated with a curse, which may be read at length in Van Vloten's *Supplementum.* He was cursed by day and night; in sleeping and rising; in going out and in coming in; with all the curses with which Joshua cursed Jericho and Elisha cursed the children. Van Vloten says that it is known that Spinoza was not present when the sentence was pronounced on him, but that he sent an answer. Unhappily it has been lost. In 1661, as we learn from a letter from Oldenburg, Secretary to the English Royal Society, Spinoza was at Rijnsburg. Oldenburg had called on him there and had discussed with him " God, Extension and Infinite Thought," and he now addresses his friend as *clarissime Domine, Amice colende.*[2] At this time Spinoza's first work, the *Renati des Cartes Principia Philosophiæ,* &c., had not been published, and Oldenburg's attitude towards him is therefore remarkable and may be taken as a proof of his personal power. It is difficult, by the way, to discover what are the dates of Spinoza's changes of residence. Colerus distinctly says that Spinoza went straight from Ouwerkerk to Rijnsburg in 1664; but, as

---

[1] The story of the attempted assassination is doubtful. See Freudenthal, p. 248.

[2] Letter 1. The numbering of the letters quoted is that in Van Vloten and Land's edition.

we have already seen, he was living at Rijnsburg in 1661, and a letter to Oldenburg, dated 17–27th of July, 1663,[1] shows that he moved to Voorburg in April, 1663. In 1670, or the early part of 1671, we know that he made another move to the Hague, and lived there till his death. In 1860 a document was discovered at Delft which shows what Spinoza's reputation was in 1665, five years before the *Tractatus Theologico-Politicus* was published. A dispute had arisen as to the appointment to the pastorate of the Reformed Church at Voorburg and was referred to the administration at Delft which had the authority to nominate. Tydeman, Spinoza's landlord at Voorburg, and some of Tydeman's friends desired a certain Van der Wiele, but strong objection was raised against him and the remonstrants alleged that the memorial (not yet recovered) in Van der Wiele's favour had been drawn up by Tydeman's lodger, reported to be "an atheist, "a mocker against all religion, and a dangerous ' Instru- "ment' in this Republic". Tydeman and the memorialists are denounced as "busybodies acting from pure, wanton "malignity, headstrong in the determination to achieve "their end".

In 1673 Spinoza was invited to Utrecht to meet Lieutenant-Colonel Stoupe, an officer in the service of Lewis XIV, who assured him, apparently not without authority, that a pension might be given to him if he would dedicate a book to the French monarch. Spinoza, however, refused. On his return he found the mob at the Hague greatly incensed against him, as France and Holland were at that time at war. His landlord was alarmed, and feared lest his house should be plundered and his tenant murdered. Spinoza, however, calmed him by the assurance that the reason of his visit to Stoupe was well known, and by a promise that as soon as the least noise was made at the door he would present him-

[1] Letter 13.

self outside, even if he knew he should be killed. He would certainly have done so, for Leibnitz says that, after the massacre of the brothers De Witt, Spinoza was with difficulty restrained from going out on the same night and protesting by written notice, to be affixed to some public place, against the crime. In 1673, after his return from Utrecht, he received through Professor Fabritius, who was also a member of the council of the Elector Palatine, an offer from that prince of a chair at Heidelberg.[1] He was to have the most ample freedom in philosophy, the only condition being that he should

[1] Charles Lewis, Elector Palatine, son of Frederick V, Elector Palatine, "Winter King" of Bohemia and Elizabeth, daughter of James I. of England, was brother consequently to Prince Rupert and Sophia, mother of George L He was born on the 22nd of December, 1617, and educated at Leyden. He fell upon evil times. The Palatinate was occupied successively by Swedes, French, and the Imperial troops, and it is said that the population was reduced to a fiftieth part of what it was in the days of its prosperity. When he was a youth he went to England to seek the assistance of his uncle, Charles I., and fell into dissipation, but when he grew up to be a man he altered his way of life, and became a lover of the sciences. After the peace of Westphalia he came into the possession of that part of the Palatinate which was assigned to him, and proved himself a wise ruler. The devastation and misery were inconceivable, but he gradually restored prosperity. His government was very tolerant, and all sects, even such as the Anabaptists, were protected from persecution. As soon as possible he set up the schools again, and the University of Heidelberg was reopened with much ceremony in 1651. His troubles, however, were not at an end. War broke out once more in 1672 between the Emperor and the King of France, and the Palatinate was again the scene of the usual horrors. The Elector did not live to see the end. He died on the 28th of August, 1680, in his sixty-third year, and, notwithstanding the almost ruinous losses the country had undergone, he left the State free of debt and a considerable sum in the treasury, tolerably good evidence of economical administration. His marriage with Charlotte, daughter of the Landgrave of Hesse, was not particularly happy, and after separation from her, he married again, morganatically, Louisa von Degenfeld.

It is quite in harmony with what we know of his character that he should have invited Spinoza to Heidelberg, and it is clear that the only condition imposed, abstinence from attack on the State religion, was due not to bigotry or timidity but to motives of State policy.

not disturb the established religion. The *Tractatus Theologico-Politicus* was published in 1670. In 1671 we find that the excitement against the book was so great that Spinoza begged his friend Jarigh Jellis to stop its translation into Dutch, so that it might not be placed under interdict. In 1674, after many complaints against it from the Church synods, it was prohibited by the States-General and the Prince of Orange, our William III. It is described in the edict as overflowing with blasphemies against God, his attributes, the doctrine of the Trinity, the divinity of Christ and our salvation by him; it is a dangerous poison, &c.. &c. The *Posthumous Works* were suppressed by the States of Holland and West Friesland in an edict of the 25th June, 1678. The book is alleged to be " profane, atheistical and blasphemous ", seductive of " the innocent reader from the sole and true way of salvation." The Protestants as well as the Roman Catholics had their *Index Expurgatorius* and dealt in epithets. It is true that the *Tractatus* was published without Spinoza's name, but he was well known to be the author, and the liberality of the Elector was therefore singular. Spinoza nevertheless felt obliged to refuse. In the first place he did not know within what limits liberty of philosophising would be permitted, nor how the condition as to disturbing established religion would be interpreted. He feared also lest his professional duties would withdraw him from his studies.

Spinoza's constitution was sickly; "he was unhealthy and lean," according to Colerus, " and had been troubled with a Pthysick above twenty years." Either he did not expect his death, or, expecting it, the anticipation of it did not affect him, for on his landlord's return from church on Saturday, the 20th of February, 1677, at about four o'clock in the afternoon, Spinoza went downstairs and talked to him for some time, chiefly upon the sermon, which, in accordance with the usual custom, had been preached on that day to admonish people to prepare for the Holy Communion to be administered on the Sunday of the last week before Lent. Spinoza smoked a pipe and went early to bed. On Sunday morning before church-time he came down again and conversed with his landlord and his wife. He had, however, sent for his friend Lewis Meyer, a physician at Amsterdam, who came and ordered him at once some fowl-broth. He drank the broth and ate a part of the fowl, but in the afternoon—21st of February, 1677—about three o'clock, he died, Meyer being the only person present at his death. He was buried on the 25th February in what is called a "huirgraft" of the New Church. "Huirgraft" according to Freudenthal is a grave from which after a certain number of years the body is removed in order to make room for another. All sorts of stories were circulated about the manner of his death ; but Colerus, who was strictly orthodox, affirms them to be "mere lies" ; and as to his reported invocations of God when he was ill, "he always expressed in all his sufferings a truly stoical constancy ; even so as to reprove others when they happened to complain and to show in their sicknesses little courage or too great a sensibility." His property was sold by auction, and fetched four hundred and thirty florins and thirteen pence. He was of middle height, dark skinned, his face was delicately cut, and he had black curly hair. His mode of life was that of the student. When he first went to the Hague he boarded with a widow, but his food was often taken into his own room, where he would remain sometimes for two or three days without seeing anybody. Afterwards, thinking he spent too much, he took a room in another house and supplied himself with his own victuals. He was extremely frugal and temperate, not to say abstemious, and his household accounts found after his death show at most two half-pints of wine a month. His conversation was " very sweet and easy ": he was never very melancholy nor very merry, and if he happened to be what he considered unduly affected, he was in the habit of retiring lest he should be betrayed into anything unbecoming. He was no lover of money, and his economies were due rather to a dislike to complications and to a preference for simplicity and the freedom it brings, than to any desire to accumulate. Lucas in his *La Vie de Monsieur Benoit de Spinosa* says that when a man who owed Spinoza two hundred florins became bankrupt Spinoza quietly observed with a smile, " I must economize in order to make up this loss. At " that price I buy tranquillity." Lucas well adds " I " do not relate this action as anything illustrious. But as " there is nothing in which genius is more evident than " in these little things I could not make up my mind to " omit it."

A young medical student, Simon de Vries, was much drawn to Spinoza, his "*amicus integerrimus*," and gave him two thousand florins; but the gift was declined on the ground that so much money would divert him from his studies and occupations. De Vries wished to make Spinoza his heir; but he would not consent and persuaded De Vries to leave his estate to his brother. This was done on condition that a sum should be paid to Spinoza annually sufficient for his support. But when, after the death of De Vries, it was proposed that the annuity should be five hundred florins, Spinoza refused to take more than three hundred, as five hundred were too much. After the death of his father Spinoza handed over to his sisters his own legal share in the estate, with the exception of a bed and its furniture, although they had done all they could, without success, to exclude him as a legatee. As he thought so he lived, and the unity of his life and writings is one reason for the permanence of his influence.

His attitude towards the religion of the day is characteristic. We have the express testimony of Colerus that he put his landlady's children "in mind of going often to church : that he sometimes went to church himself to hear Dr. Cordes, whom he much esteemed ; and that he advised his landlord and the people of the house not to miss any sermon of so excellent a preacher." His landlady asked him once whether he believed she could be saved in the religion she professed. He replied, "Your religion is a good one ; you need not look for another, nor doubt that you may be saved in it, provided, whilst you apply yourself to piety, you live at the same time a peaceable and quiet life." On the other hand he never shrank from the expression of his own creed to his correspondents. His friend Oldenburg was alarmed at the prospect of something dangerous in the *Ethic,* and begged him not to say anything which would in any way loosen *(labefactare)*[1] "the practice of religious virtue ; especially because this degenerate and evil age hunts after nothing more greedily than doctrines of this sort, conclusions from which appear to sanction outrageous vices." This was written in 1675 in England, and Oldenburg might be well excused if he did not desire that anything should be done to accelerate the dissolution of manners and virtue. But Spinoza quietly answered[2] that whatever "is in conformity with reason is most useful to virtue." He then asked Oldenburg to refer him to any passages in the *Tractatus* which were considered objectionable. Oldenburg pointed out that the authority of miracles on which revelation rests was attacked.[3] Spinoza replied,[4] "I am persuaded that the

---

[1] Letter 62.   [2] Letter 68.   [3] Letter 71.
[4] Letter 73.

certitude of Divine revelation can be established solely by the wisdom of the doctrine, and not by miracles; that is to say by ignorance, as I have shewn at sufficient length in Chapter VI. on miracles. Here I will only add that between religion and superstition I recognize the main distinction to be that superstition is based upon ignorance, and religion upon wisdom."

Spinoza was a mathematician, and he had a high opinion of it as an education. He believed that it had powerfully contributed to prevent utter submergence in theological ignorance. He uses the example of two non-concentric circles, one of which encloses the other, to show that number cannot, without contradiction, express all inequalities of distance, and that the true Infinite is not the beyond and beyond of the finite. We find him also begging Oldenburg to tell him whether the movements of two comets confirm Kepler's " hypothesis," and the treatise on the Rainbow is an explanation, following Descartes, of the laws governing the refraction and reflection of the rays of light forming the two bows. Huyghens knew Spinoza, the "Jew of Voorburg," as he calls him, as a maker of remarkably good lenses of small dimensions, and Leibnitz wrote to him expressly to ask an interesting question about Spinoza's own craft. Leibnitz had heard that a young man, Johannes Oltius Helvetius, had promised a lens which would collect all the rays from all points of an object "into so many other corresponding points." [1] " My proposal is," says Leibnitz, "not that the rays from all points should be re-united : this with an object at any distance or of any figure is impossible, so far as we at present know, but that rays from points outside the optic axis may be united exactly in the same way as those in the optic axis, so that the apertures of glasses may be made of any

[1] Letter 45.

size desired without impairing distinctness of vision."
Leibnitz was aiming at the correction of spherical
aberration, but he is obscure, and Spinoza replied that
he could not understand him, nor offer any suggestion.
The great problem was not to be solved until some
eighty years later by an English optician.

Spinoza's works are as follows, the dates being those
of publication:—

    1. "Renati des Cartes, Principiorum Philosophiæ
        Pars I. et II, more geometrico demonstratæ per
        Benedictum de Spinoza Amstelodamensem. Ac-
        cesserunt ejusdem cogitata metaphysica, in quibus
        difficiliores, quæ tam in parte metaphysices
        generali, quam speciali occurrunt, quæstiones
        breviter explicantur." 1663.

    2. "Tractatus Theologico-politicus continens disserta-
        tiones aliquot, quibus ostenditur libertatem philo-
        sophandi non tantum salva pietate et reipublicæ
        pace posse concedi: sed eandem, nisi cum pace
        reipublicæ ipsaque pietate, tolli non posse." 1670.

These are the only books published and printed by
Spinoza during his lifetime; and the second, although
its authorship was well known, did not bear his name.
Other works of his were circulated by him in manuscript
amongst his friends.

After his death there appeared—

    3. B. D. S. Opera Posthuma (1677), containing—
        (*a*) Ethica, Ordine geometrico demonstrata.
        (*b*) Tractatus Politicus; in quo demonstratur quo-
            modo societas, ubi imperium monarchicum
            locum habet, sicut et ea, ubi optimi imperant,
            debet institui, ne in tyrannidem labatur, et ut
            pax, libertasque civium inviolata maneat.[1]

---

[1] Some additional notes by Spinoza are given at the end of Van
Vloten and Land's edition.

(*c*) Tractatus de intellectus emendatione et de via, qua optime in veram rerum cognitionem dirigitur.

(*d*) Epistolæ doctorum quorundam virorum ad B. D. S. et auctoris responsiones; ad aliorum ejus operum elucidationem non parum facientes.

(*e*) Compendium Grammatices Linguæ Hebrææ.

4. Stelkonstige Reeckening van den Reegenboog, dienende tot naedere samenknoping der natuurkunde met de wiskonsten (a treatise on the rainbow). 1687.

5. Korte verhandeling van God, den mensch en deszelfs welstand (a short treatise upon God, man, and man's well-being).

This was discovered in MS., and printed in 1862. An abstract of it had been found and printed ten years earlier.

6. A few letters and parts of letters, not included in the Opera Posthuma, collected and printed in the edition of Spinoza's works by Van Vloten and Land.

The treatises which are most closely connected with the Ethic are the *Short Treatise upon God*, the *Tractatus de intellectus emendatione*, the *Descartes*, and the *Tractatus Theologico-Politicus*.

It would be very interesting if we could discover the dates at which these books were composed. Unfortunately the only evidence is that which is internal or is derived from the correspondence. The date of the composition of the *Short Treatise* is discussed below. We will provisionally assume that it ought to come first.

With regard to the *De Emendatione*, the first notice which we had of it until very recently was in a letter [1] from Oldenburg, dated April 3rd, 1663, in which he asks

[1] Letter 11.

Spinoza whether the little work is finished. But an addition has been recently published[1] to one of Spinoza's letters, undated, but a reply to one of Oldenburg's of October, 1661, and evidently written late in 1661 or early in 1662, in which Spinoza says that he has written an " integrum opusculum de Emendatione Intellectus," and is revising it. He abstains, however, from publication, because he knows that the theologians will attack it, and he has a dread of quarrels—_rixas prorsus horreo._

The _Descartes_ was written in the early part of 1663. In the letter to Oldenburg of July, 1663,[2] Spinoza distinctly says that it was taken in hand in that year in order to oblige some friends, and that he added some reflections which he had dictated to a young man some time before, on the chief points in metaphysics.[3]

In 1665 the _Tractatus Theologico-Politicus_ was in progress. This we learn from a letter[4] from Oldenburg of September, 1665, in reply to one from Spinoza now lost, but we do not know when the book was begun or in what stage it then was. Spinoza had told Oldenburg something about it, and it is a fair presumption, from Oldenburg's reply, that it was nearly complete, although it was not published till five years later.

Of the _Short Treatise_ no direct mention is made in Spinoza's works nor in his correspondence. It was not known that anything of the kind was extant till the year 1851, when Dr. Boehmer, of Halle, found, attached to a manuscript life of Spinoza by Colerus, a little abstract or summary, also in manuscript, and in Dutch, entitled, _A Short Sketch of the Treatise of Spinoza upon God, Man and Man's Well-being._

[1] Letter 6.   [2] Letter 13.
[3] Lucas says that the _Descartes_ was written to show that Spinoza was capable of thoroughly expounding the _Principia_. Descartes was at that time the tyrant of the philosophical world, and Spinoza had been charged with the heresy of disputing his authority.   [4] Letter 29.

Some years afterwards another manuscript was bought at a public sale by a bookseller of Amsterdam, named Muller. It was also in Dutch, and was clearly the Treatise itself, of which Boehmer's MS. was the abstract. A note was appended, stating that it was a translation of a Latin original by Spinoza. About the same time a third manuscript of the same treatise, differing in many readings from the second, was discovered by Herr Adrien Bogaers. A careful collation of the last two has been made by Dr. Van der Linde, and the result of his labours has been published, with an accurate German translation by Dr. Christoph Sigwart. The little book is evidently a kind of preliminary draft of the *Ethic*, and there cannot be the slightest doubt that it is really Spinoza's. No other man could possibly have written it. But there is also other evidence. Mylius, in his *Bibliotheca Anonymorum*, says that the *Ethic* was originally written in Dutch, and afterwards translated into Latin by the author, but that in the Latin version a chapter on the Devil was omitted. This chapter is found in the *Treatise*. The *Treatise*, it is true, professes to be a translation from a Latin original, and it is just possible that it may be so and yet that Mylius may be right. The *Treatise* may have been originally written in Latin and the *Ethic* in Dutch.

It is remarkable that the *Treatise* contains definitions, axioms, and propositions not found as they stand in the *Ethic*, but more nearly in the form in which we find them in the correspondence with Oldenburg. Those which Oldenburg had before him were sent to him in 1661 for his consideration, and may be collected from the letters of that date. For the sake of comparison they are given below with the corresponding definitions, axioms, and propositions in the *Treatise* and in the *Ethic*. The *Treatise* consists of two parts, the *Treatise* proper and two appendices. The quotations in italics under the head "Treatise and Appendix" are from the *Treatise* proper. Those in ordinary type are from the first appendix.

DEFINITIONS.

OLDENBURG.	TREATISE AND APPENDIX.	ETHIC.
I. God, I define as a Being consisting of infinite attributes, each one of which is infinite or absolutely perfect in its own kind.	*God is a Being of whom everything or infinite attributes are affirmed; of these attributes each is infinitely perfect in its own kind.*	By God, I understand Being absolutely infinite, that is to say, substance consisting of infinite attributes, each one of which expresses eternal and infinite essence.
II. By attribute I understand every thing which is conceived through itself and in itself, so that its conception does not involve the conception of another thing. For example, extension is conceived through itself and in itself, but motion is not conceived in this way, for it is conceived in another thing, and its conception involves extension.	Wanting.	By attribute, I understand that which the intellect perceives of substance, as if constituting its essence.
III. Body is not limited by a thought, nor a thought by body.¹		That thing is called finite in its own kind which can be limited by another thing of the same nature. For example, a body is called finite, because we always conceive another which is greater. So a thought is limited by another thought; but a body is not limited by a thought, nor a thought by a body.

¹ What Spinoza really sent to Oldenburg as the 3rd definition we do not know. Oldenburg quotes these words only. We are not sure, in fact, that it was sent as a definition.

DEFINITIONS—*continued.*

OLDENBURG.	TREATISE AND APPENDIX.	ETHIC.
IV. By Substance I understand that which is conceived through itself, and in itself, that is to say, whose conception does not involve the conception of another thing.	Wanting.	By substance, I understand that which is in itself and is conceived through itself; in other words, that, the conception of which does not need the conception of another thing from which it must be formed.
V. By modification or by accident I understand that which is in another and is conceived through that thing in which it is.		By mode, I understand the affections of substance, or that which is in another thing through which also it is conceived.

AXIOMS.

OLDENBURG.	TREATISE AND APPENDIX.	ETHIC.
I. Substance is prior in nature to its accidents.	Substance, by reason of its nature, is prior to its modifications.	Substance is by its nature prior to its affections.[1]
II. Excepting substances and accidents, nothing really exists, or exists outside the intellect.	Things which differ are distinguished either really or modally. Things which are really distinguished have either different attributes, such as thought and extension, or are assigned to different attributes, as, for example, intellect and motion, of which the first belongs to thought, the latter to extension.	Two or more distinct things are distinguished from one another, either by the difference of the attributes of the substances, or by the difference of their affections.[1]
III. Things which have different attributes have nothing in common.	Things which have different attributes, or those which belong to different attributes, have nothing in common.	Two substances having different attributes have nothing in common with one another.[1]
IV. If things have nothing in common, one of them cannot be the cause of another.	A thing which has nothing in itself which is common with another thing cannot be the cause of the existence of that other thing.	If two things have nothing in common with one another, one cannot be the cause of the other.[1]

[1] These all appear in the *Ethic* as propositions to be *proved.*

PROPOSITIONS.

OLDENBURG.	TREATISE AND APPENDIX.	ETHIC.
I. In nature there cannot exist two substances which do not differ in essence totally (or, as Oldenburg puts it, two substances possessing the same attribute).	*Two similar substances do not exist.* To no substance which exists can one and the same attribute be ascribed which is ascribed to another substance, or, which comes to the same thing, there cannot be in Nature two substances which are really distinct.	I. In Nature there cannot be two or more substances of the same nature or attribute.
II. Substance cannot be produced. It belongs to its nature to exist.	*One substance cannot produce another.* One substance cannot be the cause of the existence of another substance. It pertains to the essence of every substance to exist, so that it is impossible that there should be in the infinite understanding an idea of the essence of a substance which does not exist in Nature.	One substance cannot be produced by another substance. It pertains to the nature of substance to exist. (These are two distinct propositions in the Ethic.)
III. All substance must be infinite or absolutely perfect in its own kind.	*There is no finite substance, but all substance must be infinitely perfect in its own kind.* Every attribute or substance is by its nature infinite and absolutely perfect in its own kind.	Every substance is necessarily infinite.
IV. Existence follows, not from the definition alone of anything, but only from the definition or idea of any attribute; that is to say, of a thing which is conceived through itself and in itself. (This is a note or scholium to the three propositions, and is not given as a whole in the correspondence. It cannot, therefore, be completely restored.	*In the infinite understanding of God there is no substance which is not formally in Nature.*	There is nothing exactly corresponding to this in the Ethic. See, however, Prop. viii., Schol. 2. pt. 1. See scholium to Prop. xvii., pt. 1.

It is clear from this comparison that what Spinoza sent to Oldenburg was neither the *Treatise* nor, as has been usually supposed, the *Ethic*, and it seems nearly certain that the *Treatise* proper is earlier than the letters, and that the appendices are much nearer to them. The *Ethic* is of course the final revision. It is to be noticed that the proposition, " it pertains to the "nature of substance to exist," is not in the *Treatise* proper, and that the axioms of the correspondence and the appendices are all considered in the *Ethic* as needing demonstration.

What, then, is the date of the *Ethic?* All we can confidently say is that it must have been completed in its present form in 1675. In his letter[1] of the 22nd of July, 1675, Oldenburg alludes to the " Treatise in five parts," and in the Tschirnhausen correspondence of 1675-6 the propositions are quoted in the order in which we now have them, and substantially in the same words. The first allusion to the *Ethic* is in a letter[2] of the 24th February, 1663, from De Vries. There was a kind of club of young men at Amsterdam occupied in discussing the propositions which Spinoza sent them in sections. When they could not understand them they wrote to the master. In this letter the scholium to the present 10th proposition, part 1, is quoted as the " 3rd scholium, proposition 8,"[3] and De Vries's thanks for the scholium to Prop. 19 cannot refer to the unimportant scholium to the present Prop. 19. In 1665[4] Spinoza promises to send to an unnamed friend the third book of the *Ethic* up to the 80th proposition. The arrangement of the propositions, therefore, must have been altered after this date, if

[1] Letter 62.

[2] Letter 8.

[3] In the correct version of the letter there is no reference to " book i." The editors of the Opera Posthuma added these words. and corrected the reference from Prop. 8 to Prop. 10, intending, no doubt, to assist the reader, but mutilating historical evidence. This is not a solitary case.

[4] Letter 28.

nothing else was altered. The third book contains now only 59 propositions. In a letter[1] to Blyenbergh of the 13th of March, 1665, Spinoza mentions *mea ethica necdum edita*, for the first time giving his book the name of "Ethic." "If you ask, therefore," says the letter, "whether the thief and just man are equally perfect and "happy, I answer, No. For by a just man I understand "one who constantly desires that each person should "possess that which is his own. This desire I demon- "strate in my Ethic, not yet published, necessarily to "arise in the pious from the clear knowledge which "they have of themselves and God. As a thief has no "desire of this kind he is necessarily deprived of a "knowledge of God and himself, that is to say, of the "chief thing which makes us men."[2] The corresponding propositions are 34-37, book iv. In July, 1675, we find from a letter[3] to Oldenburg the *Ethic* was ready for the press. It was not published, for the author's intention had been discovered, and consequently information had been laid before the authorities.

We thus see, and this is a point worth notice, that the *Ethic* was the result of consideration, and recon-sideration during at least twelve or thirteen years; that Spinoza took the unusual course of submitting it to his friends before publication, and that, as it now stands, it is an expression of what his deliberate conviction was after hearing all they had to say. It was not a "flash "of inspiration" hastily reproduced, a representation without correction of what just *occurred* to him, and the mathematical form which was assumed on revision, whether a mistake or not, is at least evidence that he wished his readers to understand that what he offered to

---

[1] Letter 23.

[2] *Quod nos homines beatos reddit* is the reading in Paulus and Bru-der. But the edition of 1677 has *quod nos homines reddit*, and is followed by Van Vloten and Land. The Dutch version agrees also with the edition of 1677.

[3] Letter lost, but Oldenburg's reply is Letter 62, 22nd July, 1675.

them had been reached by careful deduction. It is also clear that he was in no hurry. It did not particularly matter to him whether the *Ethic* was published during his lifetime or not.

We now proceed to a consideration of the four works by Spinoza, which are connected with the *Ethic* and of the *Ethic* itself.

It is a mistake to suppose that the *Short Treatise* is not well worth reading. It has been superseded by the *Ethic;* it is often obscure; there are constant gaps; and it is obviously imperfect, for there are allusions in it to arguments which are no longer there; but it is interesting, not only because it shows how Spinoza worked his way to further development, but because many things which recur in the *Ethic* are presented in the *Treatise* in a new light. There are also many things in it which are true but are omitted in the *Ethic*, apparently for want of room, or because they are not pertinent. A few examples of what is in the *Treatise* are appended, not in order to give any idea of its contents as a whole, but rather for the sake of inducing a study of it.

Dialogue I. 3: "We conceive Nature as infinite; in "which everything is comprehended, and the negation "of the same we call the Nothing." The Nothing; the Void is a mere negation, a figment.

Dialogue II. 13: "So long as we have not a clear idea "of God which unites us to Him in such a manner that "it is impossible for us to love anything except Him, "we cannot say that we are in truth united to God, or "immediately depend upon Him."

Part i. cap. ix. 3: "The understanding is also a Son, "a Work of God, or an immediate creation by Him, "created from all eternity and to all eternity remaining "unchangeable. Its sole attribute is to understand "everything clearly and distinctly at all times. Hence

" unchangeably arises an infinite or absolutely perfect
" contentment (*genoegen*) which cannot omit to do that
" which it does."

Part ii. cap. xviii. 2 : " Hence it follows that we are
" of a truth the servants, or rather the slaves of God,
" and that it is our greatest perfection that it should
" necessarily be so. For if we were handed over to our-
" selves, and not dependent upon God, there would be
" little or nothing which we could accomplish, and con-
" sequently we should grieve. Now, however, on the
" contrary, we see that we depend on that which is most
" Perfect, so that we are a part of the Whole—that is to
" say, of Him—and contribute, so to speak, that which is
" ours to the accomplishment of so many admirably
" arranged and perfect works dependent on Him."

Part ii. cap. xxiv. 6 : " For although men make laws for
" their own welfare, and have no end in view, excepting
" the furtherance thereby of their own well-being, this
" end, as subordinate to other ends, which another Being
" has in view, who is above men, and causes them to
" act as parts of Nature, this end, I say, may be so
" ordered as to concur with the eternal laws which are
" appointed by God from eternity, and so contributes to
" make all things work together. For although, for
" example, the bees in all their work, and with strict
" order which they observe amongst themselves, have
" no other end in view than to make sure provision for
" themselves in the winter, the man, who superintends
" them, has an entirely different end in his nurture of
" them and care for them : to wit, that he may have
" honey. So man, in so far as he is a being by himself,
" has no other end than his limited essence can attain,
" but in so far as he is a part and an instrument of
" Nature as a whole, this end cannot be the final end of
" Nature, for Nature is infinite and employs him as its
" instrument with all other things."

Part ii. cap. xxv. 1, 2 : " If the devil is a thing which
" is entirely opposed to God and has nothing from Him,
" he is absolutely indistinguishable from the Nothing
" of which we have already spoken. But, if we suppose
" with some that the devil is a thinking thing, who
" neither wills nor does anything whatever that is good,
" he is certainly most miserable, and if prayers could
" help him we ought to pray for his conversion."

The *Tractatus de Emendatione* has been left unfinished
and the text is imperfect in places. There are passages
in it which it is very difficult, if not impossible, to understand, and others which the editors of the posthumous
works justly describe as *obscura, rudia adhuc et impolita,*
but nevertheless it is, as Bruder calls it, *aureus libellus.*

At the very beginning we find that the aim which
Spinoza proposed to himself was what we call moral.
There is no satisfaction in ordinary pleasures, and he
desires to discover something which will give him " a
joy continuous and supreme to eternity." It is important to bear in mind that this was the purpose of his
enterprise. His object, therefore, becomes fourfold—to
know himself; to know nature ; to know how it can be
modified, and what power over it man has. The first
thing that he has to do is to purify and strengthen the
intellect, so that it may be free from error.

There are four modes of arriving at truth.

1. Testimony.
2. Loose induction (*vaga experientia*).
3. Determination of the essence of a thing from some
   other thing, but not adequately. When we infer
   a cause from an effect, we can attribute to the
   cause nothing more than the effect contains.
4. Perception through essence, or through knowledge
   of the proximate cause. This is called intuitive
   knowledge in the. *Ethic.* The things which can
   be known in this way, says Spinoza, are very few.

The difference between the third and fourth modes comes out clearly in one of the examples given. We conclude by the third mode that the body and soul are united, and that, as we are conscious of sensation, the union is the cause of it; but what that union is we cannot understand. Under the fourth mode, however, we know that the essence of soul is union with body. The fourth mode is not mere inference. It enables us to see that the meaning of soul is that it and the body are one being. The first and second modes are dismissed as they are not the means of obtaining the intellectual perfection desired, and the third mode *per se* is insufficient. We are promised an explanation of the manner in which things are to be understood by the fourth mode; but in the *Treatise*, as we now have it, the explanation is not forthcoming. We have something answering to it in the *Ethic*. It is clear from the further description of the fourth mode in Schol. 2, Prop. xl., pt. 2, and from Prop. xxiv. and following propositions of Part 5 of the *Ethic*, that Spinoza believed in the possibility of possessing what he calls an adequate knowledge of an attribute of God, by which we arrive at a more intimate knowledge of things. If we could have this adequate knowledge of gravity we should know, not merely what some of its laws are, but what it is, in the same way as we know a circle, and not merely one or two of its properties. Every advance in our knowledge brings us closer to an adequate conception. In the case of light it is nearer to us now that we have the theory of an ether and vibrations than when we knew merely how light behaved when it was reflected or refracted.

The *Treatise* now takes another turn and considers the grounds of certainty, an inquiry suggested of course by Descartes. Spinoza points out that there cannot be a *regressus ad infinitum*. We cannot go on asking why we know and why we know that we know, etc., etc.

Certitude and " objective essence " are the same ; objective essence being the presence of the essence of the
thing *in me.*[1]

Spinoza endeavours to illustrate his meaning by the
example of an idea of an object in the mind ; but it is
necessary to know in what sense he uses the word
"idea." The idea of a circle is, in the first place,
not an actual circle but its intellectual counterpart ;
what we should now call the idea of a circle as distinguished from my personal thought. If we take
Spinoza's own definition of definition, we might say
that in this sense the idea is a complete definition.
But in the second place the idea is something in me ; it
is my idea, notion, conception of a circle. In the first
sense the idea is the formal essence, and in the latter the
objective essence of the circle. Spinoza does not always
keep these two senses distinct ; but in the example he
proceeds to give idea is objective essence. The idea
of any man, Peter, for instance, is a something intelligible, and may therefore be the object of another idea,
which in its turn may be made the object of a third, and
so on. But, in order to understand Peter, it is not
necessary that I should understand the idea of Peter,
and still less the idea of the idea.[2]

What now follows had better be translated.

" But since the relationship between two ideas is the
" same as the relationship between the formal essences of
" their ideas, it follows that the reflective knowledge
" which we have of the idea of the most perfect Being is

---

[1] The full explanation of this is
hardly possible until we have read
the *Ethic.* It must suffice to say
that the thing and the " objective
essence," that is to say the thought
in God of the thing, are the same
thing conceived under two different attributes—those of extension and thought.

[2] What Spinoza understands by
the example of Peter is that there
is no intellectual *regressus ad infinitum* if I have to understand the
fact of Peter's existence. I can
say no more than that I have the
idea. If I begin to ask for its
credentials, I must ask for the
credentials of the credentials.

" more excellent than the reflective knowledge of other
" ideas—that is to say, that method will be the most
" perfect which shows, according to the law of the given
" idea of the most perfect Being, in what manner the
" mind is to be directed. Hence it is easy to see how
" the mind, by increasing its knowledge, at the same time
" acquires other instruments by which it may more easily
" advance in understanding. For, as may be collected
" from what has been said, there must first of all exist in
" us a true idea, an innate instrument as it were ; and if
" this idea be understood, the difference which there is
" between such a perception and all others is at the same
" time understood. Herein consists one part of the
" method. and since it is self-evident that the mind
" understands itself better the more it understands
" Nature, it is clear that this part of the method will
" be more perfect the more things the mind understands ;
" and will be most perfect when the mind attends to, or
" reflects on, the knowledge of the most perfect Being.
" Again, the more things the mind knows, the better
" it understands its own powers, and the order of Nature ;
" and the better it understands its own powers the more
" easily it can direct itself and propose rules to itself ;
" the better also it understands the order of Nature, the
" more easily it can restrain itself from that which is
" useless. In this, as we have said, the whole method
" consists."

In other words, the wider our knowledge of nature,
the more perfect our method becomes ; and the wider
our knowledge of nature, the better we know ourselves.
The true idea, the innate instrument is pre-supposed, and
certainty grows as our acquaintance with Nature increases. Furthermore (and this becomes even more
evident a little later on) it is plain that the " law of the
given idea of the most perfect Being" means simply the
law of what we call the Universe. The continued accu-

mulation of facts therefore results in a rule—a law of the most perfect Being, by which we direct our subsequent research.

The next point is the distinction between a true idea and other ideas, and the fictitious idea is first considered. By fictitious idea Spinoza means any supposition or hypothesis we may choose to imagine which is unsupported by facts. No fictitious idea can be formed of eternal truths—that is to say, we cannot conceive them to be other than they are. Eternal truths are those which, if they are affirmative, could not be negative. I may, however, suppose a thing to be what I know it is not: as, for example, that the sun moves round the earth, or I may imagine a candle burning before me is not burning. These, however, are not really fictitious ideas. In the first case, that of the sun, I recall an actual mistake, or one which I might have made, and in the second case, that of the candle, I imagine the candle before it was alight, or another candle unlighted.

The more distinct and the wider our knowledge becomes the less power we have of forming fictitious ideas. If we know what the mind is we cannot ascribe squareness to it, and if we really know what men are and what trees are we cannot suppose that trees can speak. Perfect distinctness of conception is the test. All confusion arises either from partial knowledge, or because we attend to many things at the same time in an object without separating them. A note reminds us that the imagination never creates anything entirely new, but only combines.

The difference between a fictitious and a false idea is that in the case of the false idea we give our assent. The remedy for falsity is that perfect clearness of conception which also prevents fiction. There is no extrinsic mark distinguishing falsity from truth. If, for example, I say that Peter exists, and I do not know that he exists, the affirmation is false, even though Peter does really exist. Whether a thought is true, or, as Spinoza calls it, the form of true thought, depends upon the thought itself. It is true that a globe is produced by the revolution of a semicircle; but it is also false to assert that any globe is so produced. Simple ideas, such as the simple idea of a semicircle, cannot be false, for there is no affirmation beyond the idea. Spinoza makes the remark that one frequent cause of error is the conjunction of what we imagine confusedly with what we really understand. We thoroughly comprehend some one particular thing and we join to it a half-understood thing, the result being complete untruth. The Stoics knew that there were certain subtle matters or fluids which penetrated everything. They had also a notion of a soul which they imagined to be immortal. They did not understand what a soul is, nor what immortality is; but there seemed to be a certain fitness or connection between this immortal soul and a fluid, and thus we have the doctrine that the soul is a mysterious immortal subtlety pervading the body. The section on the false idea concludes with renewed cautions against the danger of abstractions. They are a fruitful cause of error, if we imagine that they have any real existence; and if we deal too much in them we lose sight of differences.

Doubt and memory are next considered, but not much is said about them. Spinoza observes that no single conception taken by itself can be said to be doubtful. Doubt arises from the presence of a second idea which is not clear and distinct. For example, if we have never considered the liability of the senses to deception, no doubt arises as to whether the sun is larger or smaller than he seems to be. When we know confusedly that the senses deceive us, we doubt his size; when we have a thorough knowledge of the manner in which size diminishes with distance, doubt disappears.

Before proceeding to the Second Part we encounter a difficult passage, which becomes only clear in part after its fuller exposition in the *Ethic.* " But we have shown " that the true idea is simple, or composite of simple " ideas ; and that it shows in what manner and why " anything is or has become what it is, and that [1] its " objective effects in the mind proceed according to the " rule of that which is formal in the object itself. This " is what the ancients said, that true science proceeds " from the cause to the effects, although they have never " conceived, so far as I know, as we do here, that the " mind acts according to certain laws, and, as if, so to " speak, it were some spiritual automaton."

Spinoza goes on to insist, as he does so earnestly in the *Ethic,* that the intellect is not limited by the imagination, and that words deceive us because they are framed by the imagination. Positive realities therefore, like infinity, have negative names because we can only represent them as something contrary to what the imagination can picture.

The object of the Second Part of the *Treatise* is to discover the mode of acquiring clear and distinct ideas which shall be the counterpart of nature ; and to distinguish the products of the intellect from those of the

---

[1] " Et quod ipsius effectus objec-" tivi in anima procedunt ad ratio-" nem formalitatis ipsius objecti." Auerbach gives as usual a perfectly literal translation. " Und dass " ihre objectiven Wirkungen in " der Seele nach Verhältniss der " Formalität des Objects selbst " vorgehen." Saisset, also as usual, shows that he perfectly understands the Latin, so far as grammatical knowledge goes, but is determined at all costs to be lucid. " Que les effets objectifs des choses " dans l'âme s'y produisent à " l'image de ce qu'il y a de formel " dans l'objet lui-même." Sir Frederick Pollock's version is " that the effects of the object, as " represented in the mind, corre-" sponds to the reality of the " object itself." On the whole I am inclined to think that the first *ipsius* refers to the " idea ; " and that the meaning is that the development of the idea is that of the object. What we have here is, in fact, Prop. 7, Book II. of the *Ethic.* " The order and con-" nection of ideas is the same as " the order and connection of " things."

imagination. If we are to have a clear and distinct idea of anything self caused, we must know it through its essence. If it be a created thing, we must know it through its proximate cause. The more complete our knowledge of the effect, in the case of created things, the more complete will be our knowledge of the cause, and hence "we cannot know anything of nature without "increasing our knowledge of the first cause, or of God." Spinoza does not, therefore, intend to say that _before_ we can understand a thing we must completely understand its proximate cause, but, that until we know the proximate cause, we cannot be said to completely understand the effect—that is to say, to have "a clear and distinct idea of it."

Spinoza now presents us with one of those surprises which are not infrequent with him. "The best conclu- "sion," he says, "will be drawn from some particular "affirmative essence—that is to say, from a true and "legitimate definition." At first sight, we are disposed to say that Spinoza, as a mathematician, has his own science and nothing else in view; but, of course, this is impossible. In fact, he expressly refers to "physical "entities and realities" as distinguished from figures; and it is for these physical entities and realities that the true definition is specially necessary. But let us hear what he means by definition. A definition of anything self caused should be such that the object will need for its own explanation no other being but itself. The definition also should imply existence, and should be ultimate—that is to say, without abstract terms. Of these self-caused things Spinoza gives us no example, and we hear nothing more of them in the _Treatise_. We shall meet with them in the _Ethic_. The definition of the created thing ought to include the proximate cause, and to be such that from the definition alone all the properties of the thing can be deduced. Spinoza gives

an example of the false and true definition. If we define
a circle to be a figure, such that all the lines drawn from
the centre to the circumference are equal, we have really
got, not an explanation of the essence of a circle, but of
one of its properties. The true definition is that a circle
is a figure described by a line, one end of which is fixed
and the other moves. Spinoza's theory is that, in some
cases—although probably he would have admitted them
to be very few—it is possible to build up a definition
which shall not be partially descriptive, but wholly ex-
planatory. In fact, definition in this sense answers to
adequate conception, and the illustration I have given
(p. xxxii) of an approach to an adequate conception may
serve the same purpose with regard to definition. We
have no definition of light, but we are certainly nearer
to it since Dr. Young's time, and its "essence" is more
nearly within our grasp than it was when we knew
nothing more than a few facts *about* it. Spinoza thinks
that when once a true definition has been obtained, it
may be used deductively. Undoubtedly it can, and we
have many instances of an "optima conclusio" obtained
from the definition of light as a series of spherical waves
propagated in ether. We ought, perhaps, to be more
cautious than Spinoza in the use of a definition, and we
should not be content if we did not continually attempt
independent verification; but, at any rate, definition as
he defines it is the goal of our research.

The next question is "whether there is any Being, and,
"if so, what it is, which is the cause of all things, so that
"its objective essence may be also the cause of all our
"ideas, and our mind, as we have said, may exactly
"repeat nature." The phrases "Being" and "cause of
"all things" are difficult. There is but little doubt
from the context that what Spinoza meant was what we
should call the uniformity of nature. We have to
remember the Jewish tendency in him which leads him

to describe as *ens* the rigid sequence of cause and effect on the universe.

To ascertain what this *ens* is, " we must deduce all " our ideas from natural objects—that is to say, from " real entities—advancing as much as possible according " to the series of causes from one real being to another " being." Nevertheless, true knowledge is not a knowledge of particulars, but of what Spinoza calls " fixed " and eternal things," on which individual things depend in such a way that, without these fixed and eternal things, individual things cannot be nor be conceived. Furthermore, the fixed and eternal things are a kind of universals, or definitions of things individual and mutable, and are their proximate causes. We are at once reminded of the Baconian Forms. " The Form of a nature is such," says Bacon (*Nov. Org.*, book ii. 4), " that given the Form, " the nature infallibly follows," and " if it be taken " away, the nature infallibly vanishes." They are " eternal and immutable " (*Nov. Org.*, book ii. 9). They " govern and constitute any simple nature " (*Nov. Org.*, book ii. 17). " Their commensurations and co- " ordinations make all this variety " (*De Augmentis*, book iii.). We know that Spinoza had studied Bacon, and the doctrine of Forms would be that which would mainly attract him; but whether they are really his " fixed and eternal things " we cannot positively determine. All we can affirm is, that if they are not, Spinoza and Bacon both thought that it was possible to reach something which Spinoza calls a definition and Bacon a Form, which should be expressive of Essence and the cause of all things.

After a short recapitulation, which seems to show that there are some omissions in the *Treatise* as we now have it, it comes to an end abruptly. The editors of the posthumous works give us no information as to their copy, and there is both internal and external evidence that one more complete must have existed. In the letter[1] to Oldenburg, previously quoted, Spinoza distinctly says he *has* written an *integrum opusculum*, in which he discusses the beginning of things, the manner in which they depend on the first cause, the attributes of God and the union of God with nature, as well as the improvement of the intellect. This description is much too wide for our edition of the *Treatise*.

What is the main drift and purpose of this remarkable fragment, so far as we can ascertain it, notwithstanding its incompleteness and defective arrangement?

The primary object is contentment, satisfaction, peace of mind : in other words, the end is practical and ethical, as it always is with Spinoza. This peace of mind is to be obtained by a knowledge of nature or of individual things, which leads us to the contemplation of a fixed order or of God. The mind undertakes this quest, not as a task, but because it is its native office. Certainty arises when the formal essence of things becomes objective in the mind, and there is no other test. When we are certain, our conceptions are perfectly clear : confusion and error are due to imperfect apprehension. We shall meet with all these propositions in the *Ethic*, altered in form, but unaltered in substance.

The relationship of the *Descartes* to Spinoza himself calls for some explanation. Meyer, who wrote the Preface, is most careful to tell us that, neither in the *Principia* nor in the Appendix, is there anything " except " the opinions of Descartes and their demonstrations as " they are to be found in his writings, or as they are " strictly deducible by legitimate reasoning from his " conclusions." There is really much in the book which not only is not Spinoza's, but is distinctly controverted by him. Such, for example, are the doctrine of the freedom of the will and the extension of the will beyond

[1] Letter 6.

the understanding. Descartes is also adversely criticised in the Scholium to Prop. vii., pt. i.

Spinoza's own account of the *Principia* is as follows. It is to be found in a letter to Oldenburg, 17–27th of July, 1663 [1]:—" When I moved hither (Voorburg), in April. "I went to Amsterdam. There some of my friends "asked me to impart to them a certain treatise contain-"ing, in a brief form, the second part of the Principles "of Descartes, demonstrated in geometrical order, and "the chief points of Metaphysics. This treatise I had "some time before dictated to a youth,[2] to whom I was "unwilling to teach my opinions openly. They then "asked me to treat, as soon as possible, the First Part "by the same method. Not desiring to oppose their "wishes, I immediately addressed myself to the under-"taking, finished it in a fortnight, and handed the "treatise over to them. They then asked me that they "might print the whole of it, and I readily consented, "on the condition that some one of them, under my "supervision, should put it into more elegant language, "and add a preface. in which my readers should be "warned that I do not acknowledge as my own every-"thing which is contained in the Treatise; for in it "I have written not a little which is exactly contrary to "my own belief, as I have once or twice shown by way "of example."

Those who desire to study in detail the relationship of Descartes to Spinoza, and Spinoza's relationship to his predecessors generally,[3] had better turn to Schwegler,

[1] Letter 13.

[2] It was formerly supposed that this youth was Albert de Burgh, who wrote to Spinoza in 1675 a curiously silly and fanatical letter (Letter 67) announcing his conversion to the Roman Catholic Church. This, however, is not certain. It is quite certain that "Casearius" mentioned in Spinoza's letter to de Vries in 1663 (Letter 9), and hitherto identified with de Burgh, was Casearius, a distinguished botanist. See Sir F. Pollock's *Spinoza*, 2nd edition, p. 23.

[3] It is supposed by many that Spinoza was much indebted to

Trendelenburg, and more particularly to Sir Frederick Pollock, whose account of the influence of the Cartesian physics on Spinoza is specially interesting. An additional word or two, however, may not be out of place. The *Meditations* had been published barely twenty years when Spinoza was writing the *De Emendatione*, and it was impossible for him to escape the influence of its author. Descartes, says Schwegler, "is the originator "and father of modern philosophy." . . . "The absolute "protest maintained by Descartes against the accept-"ance of anything for true because it is so given us, or "so found by us, and not something determined and "established by thought, became thenceforward the "fundamental principle of the moderns." Accordingly, at every turn in parts of Spinoza we are reminded of Descartes.

His suggestiveness to Spinoza is manifest in the fruitful distinction between the imagination and the intellect. Descartes insists that it is no argument to say that a thing is unbelievable because it is unpicturable, and this is one of the foundations of the Ethic. Error and imperfection also to Descartes, as well as to Spinoza, are nothing positive, but simply deficiency, and Descartes also affirms that falsity is due to confusion and to the fact that the individual is a part and not the whole. The Substance of Descartes is that which needs nothing beyond itself in order that it may exist, and the distinction between attribute and mode also belongs to him. But it is as a general intellectual stimulus that Spinoza owes so much to Descartes, to such sayings, for example, as that indifference is not freedom, and that we are never more free than when we are impelled to a thing because we know it to be true and good. Spinoza must have

Giordano Bruno, although there is no direct evidence that he ever read Bruno. Some of the most striking parallel passages from Bruno are given at the end of this preface.

been greatly impressed too with that memorable proposition of the Principles that we shall never err if
we give our assent to nothing excepting what we clearly
and distinctly perceive. It was the enthronement of
Reason; the deposition of Obscurantism and the beginning of the new era. It may be remarked, by the way,
that this proposition was announced by a Frenchman,
and is characteristic of the service French thought has
rendered to the world. On the other hand, the diver-
gence of Spinoza from Descartes is as remarkable as his
correspondence with him. The attitude of Descartes
towards established religion and theology is deferential.
Descartes, after taking the greatest pains to free himself
from presuppositions, and to establish a basis in reason
for his beliefs, suddenly halts and protests that not for
one moment does he mean to offer any criticism on
revelation. "We ought." he says (*Principia*, part i.
lxxvi.), "to prefer the Divine authority to our percep-
"tion . . . what God has revealed is incomparably more
"certain than anything else," and, in fact, he overdoes
his submission every now and then so far that we cannot
help suspecting it to be irony or a device to protect
him from theological controversy and give him greater
freedom.

Descartes believes in an extension of the will beyond
the understanding. Spinoza believes that the will and
understanding are coincident. To Descartes God is set
over against His works, and we feel that the argument
is for the existence of a Deity as distinct from creation
as Jehovah. Similarly, thought is set over against
extension and the mind against the body. When we
have got all these entities before us, we ask how they
came there, each separate and independent. There is
also a remarkable difference between the two men, so far
as the doctrine of evil is concerned. Descartes insists
on God's wisdom and goodness, although these attributes

do not *follow :* and are not realised. They are, in fact, merely taken over by him as a supposed necessity. To Spinoza they are something he does not understand as applied to God, and there is no need of any assumption or supernatural supposition in order to reconcile actual facts with our idea of God, for the conception of evil is due to our inadequate way of looking at things, and to God there is no such thing as evil.

The *Tractatus Theologico-Politicus* is, at least from one point of view, the most difficult book Spinoza has written. The reader naturally is prepared for a purely rationalistic treatment of the Bible, but he finds to his astonishment that Spinoza seems to accept much of it, and even of the supernatural part of it, simply as it stands. It is worth while. not only for Spinoza's sake, but as a very interesting problem in itself, to try to find out what his position in the *Tractatus* really is ; more especially as the common opinion both at home and abroad is that the *Tractatus* is simply destructive.

We shall, perhaps, best attain our end if we endeavour to make it as far as possible speak for itself. The result will not be a distinct conclusion, but a distinct conclusion in this case would be misleading. If the reader finds the abstract not consecutive nor satisfactory, he must remember that the book itself is somewhat of a puzzle. Its object, according to the preface, is to prove that liberty of thought and speech may safely be granted by the State to its subjects. Spinoza does not overlook the objection that words are deeds. He deals with that later on. Observing the bitterness of religious hatred and dissension, he determines to examine the Bible and to see what the Bible itself does and does not teach. It will at once be objected that to treat the Bible inductively as a whole is impossible. We now admit that it is made up of separate tracts or collections, and that the authority of each differs. But we must remember that

Spinoza's argument is addressed to the orthodox. He wishes to show them what are the deductions from their own premisses, and to prove that, if they will but be honest in dealing with the Scriptures in the way in which they maintain that we ought to deal with them, a theology and a religion will emerge very different from those which are usually extracted from them.

A beginning is made with Prophecy. " Whatever " may be said about it must be sought from Scripture, " since we have no true knowledge of prophecy, nor can " we explain it through its first causes." Prophetical revelation the Bible attributes either to a real voice— such as that with which God spoke to Moses—or to one which was imaginary. But by what law of nature this happened we are ignorant. " I might indeed say, with " others, that it was done by the power of God; but " I should but chatter; for I should do nothing but " explain by a transcendental term the form of some- " thing which is singular since everything is done by " the power of God. Indeed it is certain that, inasmuch " as the power of Nature is nothing but the power itself " of God, we do not understand the power of God so " long as we are ignorant of natural causes; and there- " fore, if we are ignorant of the natural cause of anything, " it is foolish to have recourse to the power of God; for " Divine power and the natural cause are the same thing. " However, it is not our business now to understand the " cause of prophetic knowledge. As I have already " observed, we here endeavour only to investigate the " documents of Scripture, so that we may draw our own " conclusions from them as if they were facts of Nature. " With the sources of the documents we have nothing " to do."

" It is evident," he goes on to say, " that God used " some kind of real voice, since Moses found God ready " to speak with him whenever he wished." Furthermore, as an instance of external revelation, the story of Baalam is mentioned, and the opinion of Maimonides— that all angelic apparitions appear during sleep, because nobody can see an angel—is declared to be absurd and an attempt to foist upon Scripture Aristotelian quibbles and the figments of commentators. Is Spinoza really speaking here in his own proper person, or has he, for the time being, assumed the character of an interpreter of Scripture? It will be better, perhaps, to postpone an answer until we have read a little further. There can, however, be no mistake when it is declared of Christ that " the ordinances of God, which lead men to salva- " tion, were revealed to Him, not by words or visions, " but immediately ; " that " the voice of Christ may be " called the voice of God like that which Moses heard," and that " in this sense, we may say that the wisdom " of God—that is to say, wisdom which is more than " human—took upon itself human nature in Christ, and " that Christ became the way of salvation."

In the second chapter, which deals with the certainty of prophecy, Spinoza reminds us that the Bible does not recognise prophecy taken by itself as a sign of a Divine mission. Furthermore, not only is the message fitted to the mouth of the prophet, but to his intellect ; just as God is revealed to Moses as living in the heavens and descending to a mountain. We are not bound, therefore, to believe the setting of the prophecies, but only their " end and substance." An example is given : it is Micaiah's prophecy to Ahab (1 Kings xxii.). Micaiah declares he saw the Lord sitting on His throne with all the host of heaven round Him, and that a commission was given to a lying spirit to deceive Ahab. All that it is intended to teach here, says Spinoza, is " that God " revealed to Micaiah the true issue of the battle between " Ahab and Aram, and to this only are we bound to give " credit " (*quare hoc etiam tantum tenemur credere*). The

Bible itself forbids us to believe any more. Here, again,
we are not quite certain whether Spinoza himself, *the
philosopher*, actually believes that Micaiah by some non-
natural assurance was able to foresee Ahab's defeat.
One thing, however, is certain—that Spinoza denies
much that is usually accepted as essential in the Sacred
Writings, and justifies himself in so doing by an appeal
to them alone.

In the fourth chapter we diverge into an explanation
of what is meant by the phrase Divine Law, and we
come close to some of the most characteristic propositions of the *Ethic*. In one sense there is but one law,
for "all things are determined by the universal laws of
" Nature," but we may, for convenience' sake, distinguish
between the law, which is a natural necessity, and
which we call *lex*, and that which is ordained by
man for a purpose, and might be more properly called
jus. Leaving the consideration of physical laws, we
find that the law, which is a method of life (*ratio vivendi*),
may be divided into human and Divine; the former
looking to the preservation of life and the State, and the
latter to the *summum bonum*—that is to say, " the true
" knowledge and love of God." In one half page Spinoza
then presents us with a summary of what he considers
a true philosophical religion.

" Since, then, the intellect is the better part of us, it is
" certain that we ought to endeavour above everything
" to perfect it as much as possible, if we really desire to
" seek what is profitable for us ; for in its perfection our
" chief good must lie. But, since all our knowledge and
" the certainty which really removes all doubt depend
" solely on the knowledge of God—in the first place
" because without God nothing can be nor can be con-
" ceived, and secondly, because we can doubt of every-
" thing so long as we have no clear and distinct idea of
" God—it follows that our chief good and our perfection

"depend solely upon the knowledge of God. Again,
"since nothing can be nor can be conceived without
"God, it is certain that all things which are in nature
"involve and express the conception of God in propor-
"tion to their essence and perfection ; and, therefore,
"the more we understand natural things do we attain
"to a greater and more perfect knowledge of God ; or
"(since the knowledge of an effect through its cause is
"nothing else than a knowledge of some property of the
"cause) the more we know natural things, the more
"perfectly do we know the essence of God, which is
"the cause of all things. Therefore the whole of our
"knowledge—that is to say, our highest good—not only
"depends on our knowledge of God, but wholly consists
"in it, a truth which is also evident when we consider
"that a man is more or less perfect according to the
"nature or perfection of the thing which he loves
"above everything else. He, therefore, is necessarily
"the most perfect and is the chief sharer in the highest
"happiness who loves above everything the intellectual
"knowledge of God, the most perfect Being, and is
"chiefly delighted therewith. In this, therefore, our
"highest good and our happiness are summed up—the
"knowledge and the love of God. The means, therefore,
"which this end of all human actions requires—that is
"to say, God Himself, in so far as the idea of Him is in
"us—may be called the laws (*jussa*) of God, because
"they are prescribed to us as it were by God Himself in
"so far as He exists in our mind ; and so also the method
"of life, which has this end in view, is most fitly called
"the Divine law (*lex divina*). But what these means
"are ; what is the method of life which this end requires,
"and how the fundamental institutions of the best state
"and the method of life amongst men conduce to this
"end, are discussed by universal ethic. Here I shall only
"have to do generally with the Divine law."

d

We shall be able to understand this passage a little better perhaps when we come to the *Ethic.* Meanwhile we may remark that just previously Spinoza had enumerated three classes of proper desire—" to understand " things through their first causes : to govern the pas- " sions or acquire the habit of virtue, and finally to live " in safety and with a sound body." To *know,* to ascend to first causes, to rest in that knowledge without ulterior advantage, pure intellectual activity, as we should call it. is again therefore for Spinoza, as it was in the *Tractatus de Emendatione,* an original end of man, not something *permitted* him, but *necessary.* It would be presumptuous to say what Spinoza intended to its fullest depth ; but there is certainly one interpretation which is true of the proposition that our knowledge depends on our knowledge of God. Our knowledge of natural things, Spinoza affirms here and elsewhere, conducts us to a knowledge of God ; but unless we have a conviction of God—that is to say of an Established Ruler, Order, or whatever we like to call it, of events—we cannot have any knowledge of natural things. Nor is this arguing in a circle. Without the natural things we could not know God : the acquaintance with the law of falling bodies is acquaintance with Him ; but if, at every new inquisition, we had to convince ourselves that order and uniformity exist, science would be impossible.

The highest law, therefore, says Spinoza, is not something external or imposed : it is a self-evident means to an end, and, so far as this law is concerned, ceremonies and institutions are useless—" the natural light requires " nothing which the light itself does not touch " (nihil enim lumen naturale exigit, quod ipsum lumen non attingit). " Denn die natürliche Vernunft erfordert nichts, was die natürliche Vernunft selber nicht berührt " (Auerbach). *But,* secondly, in the Old Testament we are not to look for a law propounded naturally. It is a rule,

a mandate promulgated as the decree of a monarch,
although to many at least of the writers of the Old
Testament the self-sufficient reason was known. "*If
thou criest after knowledge,*" says the book of Proverbs,
for example, "*and liftest up thy voice for understanding; if thou seekest her as silver, and searchest for her
as for hid treasures; then shalt thou understand the
fear of the Lord, and find the knowledge of God.*"
Thirdly, Christ "perceived things truly and adequately.
"For Christ was not so much a prophet as the mouth of
"God" (*os Dei*). Spinoza adds that it could not have
been otherwise, for Christ was sent to the whole human
race, and it was necessary, therefore, that He should have
a mind which should not be "fashioned merely to accord
"with the opinions of the Jews, but rather with the
"universal opinions and ways of thought of the human
"race—that is to say, with common and true ideas."
A few pages before Spinoza had declared that "the
"ordinances of God which lead men to salvation were
"revealed to Christ, not by words or visions, but imme-
"diately"; that "the voice of Christ may be called the
"voice of God like that which Moses heard," and that
"in this sense we may say that the wisdom of God, or
"in other words, the wisdom which is more than human,
"took upon itself human nature in Christ, and that
"Christ became the way of salvation." It naturally
follows that the ceremonial law, taken by itself, was not
a law of absolute piety, and Spinoza believes that the
object of its founders was political.

The next question is that of miracles and their
interpretation. For Spinoza there is no miracle in the
ordinary sense of the word. It is characteristic of him
that he does not appeal to evidence. He denies the
possibility *à priori* of miracle, and he also denies that
if miracle were possible it could teach us anything: it is
only that which we clearly and distinctly understand

which can add to our knowledge of God. If such a
thing as a miracle contrary to the laws of nature could
really be, it would cause us to doubt God's existence, and
not to believe in it. If it is merely an event trans-
cending our knowledge, nothing can be inferred from it.
"Absolutely it is to be concluded" that the will of God
is to be learnt from a knowledge of what is natural.
Spinoza adds also that a miracle, being something
limited and expressing nothing but definite and limited
power, could not prove the existence of a cause possessing a power which is unlimited, but, at most, of a cause
possessing a power sufficient for a particular act. As to
the explanation of the Scripture miracles, Spinoza gives
none, and does not pretend to give any which is complete. He thinks many may be explained by figures
of speech and natural causes, and he points out that it is
very difficult for anybody even to perceive a thing
exactly as it happened. Something of ourselves gets
mixed up both with what we think we see and with
what we report. If the Jews in the time of Joshua had
known that the sun did not go round the earth we might
have had another miracle in the Valley of Ajalon, but
not the one with which we are now familiar. What
seems miraculous to us could not have seemed so
miraculous three thousand years ago, for, notwithstanding constant miraculous displays, the people before
whom they were performed remained impenitent. Spinoza is obliged to admit, as we have said, that many
of the Bible stories resist all rationalising. When he
wrote the time had not come for a proper treatment
of the legendary in history, and he winds up the discussion thus: "Wherefore we conclude absolutely that
"everything which is reported in Scripture to have
"actually taken place, necessarily happened, as every-
"thing happens, in accordance with the laws of Nature:
"and if anything be found which it can be conclusively

" demonstrated is in opposition to the laws of Nature, or
" cannot follow from them, we must consider it as
" settled that it has been added to the sacred books
" by sacrilegious men. For whatever is contrary to
" Nature is contrary to reason, and what is contrary
" to reason is absurd, and therefore to be rejected."

The difficulty before mentioned now recurs. Spinoza
proceeds as follows: " Before, however, I finish this
" chapter, I wish to point out that I have adopted a
" method in dealing with miracles different from that
" which I adopted in dealing with prophecy. For of
" prophecy I have affirmed nothing, excepting that
" which I could conclude from principles revealed in
" the sacred books; but with regard to miracles, I have
" deduced the main part of what I have asserted solely
" from principles within the reach of natural reason:
" this I have done advisedly because, inasmuch as pro-
" phecy surpasses·human comprehension and is merely
" a theological question, I cannot say, except from
" revealed principles, anything about it, nor do I know
" in what it chiefly consists. I was therefore compelled
" to prepare a history of prophecy, and to form from
" this history certain dogmas which should instruct me
" as far as possible as to the nature of prophecy and its
" properties. But with regard to miracles, because the
" subject of our investigations is entirely philosophical—
" that is to say, the possibility of something happening
" in nature which is opposed to its laws or cannot follow
" from them—no such method was required. I therefore
" thought it better to settle this question from principles
" recognised by the natural reason and universally ac-
" cepted." Spinoza adds that he might have proved
from Scripture also that God's laws are unchangeable.
As to the curious reservation with regard to prophecy
we will again postpone consideration of it for the present.

The chapters on the Interpretation of Scripture—the

authorship of the Pentateuch and the revision by Ezra—
do not call for many remarks. They are an anticipation
of modern criticism, but they have now been superseded.

We next come to the New Testament. Spinoza lays
stress on the difference between the apostolic epistles and
the Old Testament; the moral teaching of the latter
is simply mandatory, but the apostles appeal to reason,
and he concludes that the epistles are not what we
should call supernaturally inspired. On the other hand,
he admits a revelation in the apostolic preaching, and he
also admits that the apostles were true prophets—" we
" therefore conclude that the apostles received those
" things only by special revelation which they preached
" *vivâ voce* and at the same time confirmed by signs ;
" but those things which they taught either by writing
" or *vivâ voce* simply, without the help of any signs as
" a witness thereto, these things they spoke or wrote
" from knowledge—that is to say from natural know-
" ledge."

The thirteenth, fourteenth, and fifteenth chapters
Spinoza seems to have considered as important as any
in his book. He begins by observing that the speculative
doctrines in the Bible are few and simple, and that it
requires no knowledge of God, save of His justice and
mercy. He translates El Shaddai in Exodus vi. 2—*God
who suffices;* Jehovah, he asserts, expressing absolute
essence. God therefore revealed so much of Himself
to the patriarchs as sufficed them and no more. He
passes on, and does not at this point explain in what
manner God's revelation of Himself to the patriarchs
took place.

If, therefore, the speculative doctrines of the Bible
are few and simple, ecclesiastical differences are fictitious
and the limits of freedom can be greatly widened. In
order to determine them Spinoza finds it necessary—

(*a*) To define faith as to its essentials.

(*b*) To separate faith from philosophy. This separation he declares to be the main object of his book.

With regard to (*a*) he notes that the purpose of the Bible is to enforce obedience ; that the essential " faith " of Scripture consists in such a knowledge of God as leads to obedience and is summed up in a belief that there is a Supreme Being, just and merciful ; that Him we are to obey if we are to be saved, and that the worship of Him means to do what is just and to love our neighbour. This is " faith," and the " obedience," of which Spinoza makes so much, is submission unhesitatingly to the precepts of justice and love. Enumerating more in detail the articles of the faith, he finds them to be as follows :—

I. "God, or in other words, a Supreme Being, exists, "perfectly just and merciful, that is to say, a "pattern of the true life. For he who does not "know, or does not believe, that God exists, cannot "obey Him or acknowledge Him as judge.

II. "He is one. No one can doubt that this truth is "absolutely required for supreme devotion, love to "God and admiration of Him, since devotion, "admiration, and love spring solely from the ex- "cellence of one above others.

III. "He is omnipresent, or, in other words, all things "are open to Him. For if it were believed that "things were concealed from Him, or if men did "not know that He saw everything, they would "doubt or be unaware of the equity of His justice "by which He directs everything.

IV. "He has supreme right and dominion over every- "thing ; nor does he do anything under compulsion, "but of His absolute good pleasure and singular "favour. For all are absolutely bound to obey Him, "but He is not bound to obey anybody.

V. "The worship of God and obedience to Him

" consist solely in justice and charity, that is to say,
" in love to one's neighbour.

VI. " All who obey God by this mode of life and
" these only are saved; the rest, who live under
" the rule of their lusts, are lost. If men did not
" believe this firmly there would be no reason why
" they should obey God rather than their lusts.

VII. " Finally, God pardons the sins of those who
" repent. For there is no one who does not sin,
" and if, therefore, we did not admit that God
" pardons sin, all would despair of salvation, nor
" would there be any reason for believing God to
" be merciful: if, however, we believe this firmly,
" that is to say, believing that God, from the
" mercy and grace with which He directs all things,
" pardons the sins of men, we therefore burn more
" with love to God; we have in truth known Christ
" according to the spirit, and Christ is in us."

This, according to Spinoza, is the essence *of Scripture*,
and all other dogmas are immaterial. We may believe
the things we believe because they are eternal truths, or
because they are laws ordained by a King, we may
believe even " that the reward of the good and the
" punishment of the wicked are natural or supernatural "
—it is of no consequence if we do but hold fast to the
primal verities enunciated. With regard to (*b*) separation of faith from philosophy, it is absurd to attempt
to subdue reason by the authority of the Bible. Spinoza
cannot sufficiently wonder at those who wish to submit
" reason, the greatest gift, and the divine light to the
" dead letter, which may have been corrupted by human
" wickedness; and that it is thought to be no crime to
" speak unworthily of the mind, the true testament of
" God's Word."

Our difficulty now once more reappears. Reason, says
Spinoza, is unable to demonstrate that we are to be

saved by obedience. Why, then, do we believe that it is so? His answer is, that it is precisely because of the insufficiency of reason that "revelation was most neces-" sary" (*revelationem maxime necessariam fuisse*). The conclusion, in his own words, is as follows: "Before I "go any further, I wish here to assert emphatically "(although it has been said before), that I consider "Holy Scripture, or Revelation, to be of the greatest use "and most necessary. For since we cannot perceive by "natural light that simple obedience is the way of salva-"tion,¹ and revelation alone teaches us that this comes "to pass by the peculiar grace of God, a truth to which "we cannot attain by reason, it follows that Scripture "has brought very great comfort to mortals. For all "can obey completely, and there are but very few, if we "compare their number with that of the whole human "race, who acquire the habit of virtue under the guid-"ance of reason alone. Therefore, unless we had this "witness of Scripture, we should doubt of the salvation "almost of all."

It is now clear that Spinoza thought that a belief in some kind of revelation was necessary; but what his own belief was it is difficult to discover; more particularly when we remember what he has to say about miracles generally. It must be admitted that he is not quite himself in some of his concessions. He becomes passionate when he denounces those who deny the authority of reason; but there are no such burning words for those who refuse to submit to the authority of revelation.

We now pass on to consider more directly the question of freedom of thought and speech. It is this which

---

¹ "That is to say, it is revela-"tion, and not reason, which "can teach us that in order to "obtain salvation, or, in other "words, blessedness, it is suf-"ficient if we embrace the divine "decrees as laws or commands; "nor is it necessary to conceive "of them as eternal truths." (Spinoza.)

Spinoza has had in view during the whole of the *Trac-tatus.* He describes the law and ordinance of nature (*jus et institutum naturæ*), as the law of the nature of each individual by which it acts, right being coextensive with power. Human beings, however, cannot exist solely under this law. They therefore, for the sake of peace and comfort, agree to cede a portion of their rights, and in so doing a state arises and justice and injustice are created. Justice, for example, is the rendering to everybody that which is legally assigned to him, and injustice is the deprivation of it. Spinoza is careful to warn us that the laws which the *amor Dei* imposes are entirely apart. The love of God is not obedience, but it is " a virtue necessarily present in the man who rightly "knows God." Laws when we live under the reign of the love of God cease to be laws. They are eternal truths, and obedience, if we like to call it so, follows necessarily from true knowledge.

But, although we have to give up a portion of our rights, there are some with which we cannot part. We cannot part with our right of thinking, and consequently we cannot absolutely yield the right of expressing our thoughts. It would be fatal to the state if its subjects were to acquire the habit of saying one thing and think-ing another, and if any attempt were made to impose such a habit upon the people the supreme authority would find its enemies, not amongst the wicked and foolish, but amongst the virtuous and wise. Incon-veniences may arise from freedom of speech, but they also arise from every human institution. Besides, supposing free speech to be injurious, we ought to ask ourselves, before attempting to limit it, *whether we can do so.* Spinoza adds a couple of sentences worth atten-tion. " He who seeks to determine everything by law " rather provokes vices than corrects them. Those things "which cannot be suppressed we ought to concede as "a necessity, although as a matter of fact they are "vices."

The line should be drawn at *deeds*, and at words which destroy the agreement upon which the state is founded. If a man, for example, preaches that he owes no allegiance to the supreme power, or that contracts are without obligation, he should be silenced. Beyond this we should not go. It might be objected to Spinoza that pure speculation may do more to dissolve a state than an insurrection, and yet may not be openly directed against the social contract. The answer is that in no department of human existence can a line be drawn, and that the demand for one proceeds from the understanding which has merely a regulative authority. It is really no argument in favour of Socialism that everybody agrees that a community ought to support its own disabled poor. Spinoza thought the boundary line ought to be drawn where he drew it, and it is difficult to find any safer position.

Spinoza, as may be imagined, is utterly opposed to giving ecclesiastics any executive power, and he is not in favour of an ecclesiastical order or caste. In an interesting digression on the Hebrew state he points out its weakness in this respect, a departure, he believes, from its original design and one which contributed to its decline. The separation of the Levites and priests in substitution for the first-born brought with it nothing but evil. It was a continual reproach, reminding the people of their sin with the golden calf, and, not only a reproach, but a burden. When provisions were dear it was but human to murmur at the obligation to keep in idleness a whole tribe connected with the others by no ties of blood, and the rebellion of Korah, Dathan, and Abiram, to whom "all the congregation were holy," if it was not justifiable, can at least be understood or even excused. Moses, observes Spinoza, was not able to appease the rebels by argument. He exterminated them by a miracle. It was natural that a desire for a king should arise : it was a revolt against the priests and Levites, and it is probable that the erection of new shrines where men might worship without consulting the Levites was partly due to their tyranny. The prophets, too, must often have been intolerable even to pious rulers, and must have been a serious hindrance to wise government. Asa, being threatened by Baasha, reminded the King of Syria of the league between him and Judah, and by Syria's help defeated Baasha. Whereupon Hanani, the seer, thought it proper to rebuke Asa for not having relied on the Lord alone, and to accuse him of having done foolishly. Who can wonder that Asa, "whose heart was perfect all " his days," should have put Hanani in prison ? Samuel, no doubt, is a great figure in Hebrew history, but it certainly did not contribute to strengthen authority—just at a time, too, when authority and discipline were most necessary—that a private person, simply because he professed to be the mouthpiece of God, should be able to depose a monarch like Saul for no other reason than that he had once disobeyed Samuel's commands.

So much for the *Tractatus.* As before said, it is not an easy book, excepting in so far as its main purpose is concerned—freedom of thought and expression—and the difficulty lies in a precise determination of what Spinoza meant by revelation and in understanding how he could bring himself to believe in it. At times, indeed, his belief seems to vanish. For example, almost towards the end, notwithstanding all we have been told about the real voice on Sinai, we come upon a passage like this : " All the " decrees of God involve eternal truth and necessity, " and God cannot be conceived as a king or legislator " imposing laws upon men. Therefore divine instruction, " whether revealed by natural or prophetic illumina-

" tion, does not receive the authority of a command
" immediately from God, but necessarily from those,
" or through the mediation of those, who have the right
" to rule and to legislate. Therefore it is only through
" them as a medium that we can conceive God as reign-
" ing over men and directing human affairs according to
" justice and equity."

What we have called the puzzle of the *Tractatus* is,
however, incidental. Its twofold purpose is perfectly
clear, noble, and invaluable. It has been supposed to be
destructive, but it is conservative, for Spinoza did his
best to show that the monstrous mass of the scholastic
theology was not Biblical and that the religion of the
Bible is human. The protest in favour of liberty may
now perhaps seem a little antiquated, but we must
remember the time when it was made and we shall
perhaps find that even now the *Tractatus* in this respect
has something to teach us. There may be no danger of
suppression by despotic power of the right of public
meeting, but the advice to be careful in the manufacture
of legal crimes is not superfluous.

We now come to the *Ethic ;* but before saying anything about it, it is as well to make an admission, which
might have been made earlier. This admission is that
the present writer does not pretend to understand the
whole of it, and, so far as he can make out, nobody has
fully understood it. It is easy to obtain what is called
a " general view " of it ; it is easy to follow a handbook ;
the difficulties begin when we study it patiently for
ourselves. We then find that there is much which
is insoluble, and we have to content ourselves with that
which we can comprehend. The speculative doctrine of
the *Ethic* has been discussed at large in books innumerable. But these books, especially those in German, are
mainly, if one may say so, professional, and if Spinoza
were merely a professional metaphysician, he would not

have been what he was to Goethe, to Shelley, to George Eliot, and to the world at large. I propose, therefore, briefly to set forth the teaching of the *Ethic* in so far as it has been a power amongst men outside the schools.

Before we look at it in detail let us consider what the method is. It is mathematical and deductive, and it has been pointed out with truth that this method ought not to be used, excepting with distinct concepts, such as that of a triangle for example. It is of importance, however, to notice that it is a characteristic of the consecutiveness of Spinoza's thought. Systems and creeds are much decried now, and deservedly ; but everybody must have some sort of theory of life if he is to live as an intelligent human being, and he is bound, moreover, to see that so far as possible it hangs together and makes a whole. Spinoza is a singular, an almost unique example of mental thoroughness. His conclusions, too, have not been imposed on him from without, but have been reached step by step by himself and are so firmly held that he lives by them. His theorems about substance, thought, and extension become very practical for him indeed when he deals with human passion.

Almost at the beginning of the *Ethic* we meet with the idea of God, who is defined as substance consisting of infinite attributes, each one of which expresses eternal and infinite essence. Two of these attributes, thought and extension, are the whole of existence as we perceive it. Thought is not a product of extension, nor is extension a product of thought, and neither is created. They *follow* from God, as it follows from the nature of a triangle that its angles are equal to two right angles; and from the necessity of the Divine Nature infinite things follow. Everything which God could create *is* created. He does not and cannot elect that some things should be and some should not be, and we may say that all possible things *are*, are here to-day, and *were* a hundred millions of years ago. De Tschirnhausen,[1] one of Spinoza's most gifted correspondents, asks how from absolute unity, from mere extension, this varied world arises? Spinoza, in the last letter we have from him, dated the 15th of July, 1676,[2] about nine months before his death, promises to discuss the matter fully, but the promise was never fulfilled. He contents himself with the admission that variety cannot be demonstrated *à priori* from extension. It has been supposed by German critics that De Tschirnhausen has pierced the heart of Spinoza's metaphysics; but the answer is that it was no part of Spinoza's business at the time to explain variety, and, if he could not. it does not follow that what he maintained is untrue, for the fact of variety, if not explicable by it, is not contrary to it. Of one thing he is certain, that " individual things " are nothing but affections or modes of God's attributes, " expressing those attributes in a certain and determinate " manner."

Furthermore the attributes of thought and extension express the same thing. Matter and spirit are identical, but differently manifested. "Substance thinking and " substance extended are one and the same substance. " which is now comprehended under this attribute and " now under that." Spinoza finds something of what he means in a Hebrew saying that "God, the intellect " of God, and the things which are the object of that " intellect are one and the same thing." The idea of the circle and the circle itself are one. Revealed as thought we have the former; revealed as extension we

---

[1] Ehrenfried Walter von Tschirnhausen, of noble family, was born on the 10th of April, 1651, at Kieslingswalde, near Görlitz, and died on the 11th of October, 1708. He is known for his researches in caustics, for his great burning glasses, and for his improvements in glass making. His love of knowledge was entirely pure, and for the sake of science he refused honours and advancement.

[2] Letter 83.

have the latter. There are correspondencies to Spinoza on this point in men who have never read him. Emerson, for example, was not a student of Spinoza, but in the "Essays" we meet with passages like these: "There "seems to be a necessity in Spirit to manifest itself in "material forms"; "Visible Nature must have a "spiritual and moral side"; "Moon, plant, gas, crystal, "are concrete geometry and numbers."

But thought and extension are not the only attributes of the Infinite Being, although they are the only attributes known to us. Just because He is infinite He has infinite attributes. "When things," says the Scholium to the seventh proposition of the second part, "are con-"sidered as modes of thought, we must explain the "order of the whole of nature, or the connection of "causes, by the attribute of thought alone, and when "things are considered as modes of extension, the order "of the whole of nature must be explained through the "attribute of extension alone, *and so with other attri-*"*butes.*¹ Therefore God is, in truth, the cause of things "as they are in themselves, in so far as He consists of "infinite attributes, nor for the present can I explain "the matter more clearly." Tschirnhausen thereupon asks how it is we know no other attributes save thought and extension; whether there are as many worlds as there are attributes, and why the mind perceives that modification only which is expressed through the body. Spinoza replies that each thing is expressed in infinite ways in the infinite intellect of God, but that the infinite ideas constitute different minds. The correspondence was not concluded, and consequently we are left without a complete resolution of Tschirnhausen's difficulty. It is dangerous to attempt to illustrate Spinoza by metaphor. We have to remember his perpetual warning against confusing the intellect and the

¹ Italics translator's.

imagination, but we may perhaps realise the possibility
of the reappearance of the same thing upon different
planes, each plane representing a different attribute,
or we may figure to ourselves an infinite variety in
perceptive capacities, the object perceived remaining
the same.

If matter and spirit are one, it follows that body and
mind are one, and body becomes " the object of the idea
" constituting the human mind," or as Lessing puts it,[1]
" the soul is nothing, but the body thinking itself, and
" the body is nothing, but the soul as extension." What
is in the body formally is in the soul objectively, and
hence " to determine the difference between the human
" mind and other things, and its superiority over them,
" we must first know the nature of its object, that is to
" say, the nature of the human body."[2]   This is really
the basis of the whole of the psychology of the *Ethic*,
and this is Spinoza's mode of escape from the antithesis
of matter and spirit. He is neither materialist nor
spiritualist, for he is both. Mind is just as true as body,
and is " part of the infinite intellect of God," although
its ideas are inadequate, while those of God are adequate. " God has this or that idea, not merely in so far
" as He forms the nature of the human mind, but in so far
" as He has at the same time with the human mind the
" idea also of another thing." Our knowledge, therefore, is imperfect because it is incomplete; we do not
stand in the centre.

The final propositions of the second book of the *Ethic*,
beginning with Prop. 40, are of great practical importance. We first have the sources of knowledge as they
are given in the *Tractatus*,[3] but slightly rearranged,

[1] Letter to Mendelssohn. 17th
of April, 1763.

[2] " The soul is a real substance
" which expresses an idea. Such
" a substance is the manifestation
" of the inner meaning of such
" and such a body."—Aristotle's
Psychology (Wallace's translation), p. 63.

[3] Page xxxi of this Preface.

e

and we are also told that reason perceives things " under " a certain form of eternity "—that is to say, not only as necessary, but as having no relation to time. It is of the nature of reason thus to conceive things.

Furthermore, the knowledge of God attained by the reason is " adequate." In a letter to Boxel [1] there is an explanation of what Spinoza means by this proposition. " To your question," he says to Boxel, " Whether " I have as clear an idea of God as I have of a triangle? " I answer, Yes. But if you ask me whether I have as " clear an image of God as I have of a triangle, I shall " say, No; for we cannot imagine God, but we can " understand Him. Here also, it is to be observed that " I do not say that I altogether know God; but that I " understand some of His attributes; not all, nor the " greatest part, and it is clear that my ignorance of very " many does not prevent my knowledge of certain others. " When I learned the Elements of Euclid, I very soon " understood that the three angles of a triangle are " equal to two right angles, and I clearly perceived this " property of a triangle, although I was ignorant of " many others."

Spinoza's demonstration of the proposition that the mind possesses an adequate knowledge of the eternal and infinite essence of God is instructive. We have this knowledge because we know ourselves and the world. He will have no God who is not to be comprehended because he is inaccessible, or because some special method by which to become acquainted with Him is demanded. To our estimate of Him also the nature of man is to contribute. It is because the human mind perceives itself, as well as external bodies, that it possesses an adequate knowledge of the eternal and infinite essence of God.

Spinoza's creed with regard to freedom of the will

[1] Letter 56.

might be anticipated. His way of dealing with the question, however, is his own. Volition is an affirmation which an idea involves. He makes a remark in passing, that there is no such thing as an absolute faculty of willing. He is a Nominalist in fact, and "will is related to this or that volition as rockiness "is to a particular rock." What he means by the will following the idea is clearly illustrated by an example. A man conceives and understands the idea of a triangle. If he distinctly understands it, the affirmation that its three angles are equal to two right angles follows as a necessary consequence. This affirmation is really a type of all volition. He uses the same illustration in a letter to Blyenbergh,[1] and he adds that a man is never more free than when he asserts this property of the triangle. The will, it is true, extends itself beyond the intellect, if by the intellect we understand only clear and distinct ideas, but it does not extend itself more widely than the faculty of conception.

The advantages of this doctrine are summed up with great force and eloquence at the close of the second book. Blyenbergh objected that, if it were true, men are no better than stones. Spinoza's answer[1] deserves to be given in his own words. "This sufficiently shows "that you most perversely misunderstand me, and that "you confound matters which belong to the intellect "with the imagination. For if you had perceived by "the intellect alone (*puro intellectu*) what it is to depend "on God, you would certainly not think that things, in "so far as they are dependent on God, are dead, corporeal "and imperfect (for who has ever dared to speak so "meanly of the Being absolutely perfect!). On the con-"trary, you would see that, because they are dependent "on God, and, in so far as they are dependent on Him, "they are perfect." If once we could imagine ourselves

[1] Letter 21.

detached, free from the necessity which binds the world, we might well consider ourselves outcast and wretched. It is only in the assurance that he is not independent, that he is not outside God, but that he is a part, and a necessary part of the Divine order, that Spinoza can find rest.

With the third book of the *Ethic* comes in view the main subject of the treatise, and that which, let us never forget, was the object for which it was written. The ontology is subsidiary. What Spinoza was most anxious to do was to teach the true doctrine and treatment of human vice and human virtue; to show that hatred, anger, and envy "have certain causes through which "they are to be understood, and certain properties "which are just as worthy of being known as the "properties of any other thing in the contemplation "alone of which we delight."

The principal results at which he arrives are the following : Between action and passion there is a fundamental distinction. We *act* when we ourselves are the adequate cause of what is done : we *suffer* when anything is done within us, or when anything follows from our nature, of which we are but the partial cause ; but passion may be transformed into action by considering it *adequately*—that is to say, if that which is done by passion is made to proceed from the intellect. Furthermore, there is not a single passion which, so considered, is not a virtue.

We then return to a proposition with which in substance we are already acquainted. "The body cannot "determine the mind to thought, neither can the mind "determine the body to motion nor rest, nor to anything "else, if there be anything else." "The mind and body "are one and the same thing, conceived at one time "under the attribute of thought, and at another under "that of extension. *For this reason the order or con-*

"*catenation of things is one*,[1] whether nature be con-
"ceived under this or that attribute, and, consequently,
"the order of the actions and passions of our body
"is coincident in nature with the order of the actions
"and passions of the mind." The dispute, therefore,
whether the mind controls the body, or the body the
mind, is irrelevant, and in fact meaningless. But
although body and mind are equally real, it is noticeable that in the commentary on this proposition, Spinoza
limits himself to a contradiction of the supremacy of
the mind as a separate entity over the body. His
object at this particular point was controversial, and he
presses generally with much greater stress against the
theologians and spiritists than against the other side.
All his bias and instincts were towards freedom, and the
spiritists and theologians represented persecution. "My
"opponents will say," he exclaims, "that from the laws of
"nature alone, in so far as it is considered to be corporeal
"merely, it cannot be that the causes of architecture,
"painting, and things of this sort, which are the results
"of human art alone, could be deduced, and that the
"human body, unless it were determined and guided by
"the mind, would not be able to build a temple. I have
"already shown, however, that they do not know what
"the body can do, nor what can be deduced from the
"consideration of its nature alone."

Everything "endeavours to persevere in its being,"
and this endeavour (*conatus*) "is the very essence of the
"thing." This is Spinoza's definition of life, and it is
important to note that the life *is* the very thing, and
not something inhabiting or informing the thing. Death
is the victory of external forces over the *conatus* which
builds up an organism. The organism is something
lifted above the level of inorganic nature, and struggles
to maintain itself. The *conatus* is what we call *will*,

---

[1] Italics translator's.

when related to the mind alone, and *appetite* when related both to mind and body ; *desire* being conscious appetite. Hence it follows that we do not desire a thing because we think it good, but we adjudge it good because we desire it.

The mind is capable of stronger or weaker affirmation of existence or of perfection. It is to be remembered that perfection and reality are synonymous. When the mind passes to a higher grade of perfection or reality— that is to say, when it more distinctly exists—the passage upwards is accompanied by what we call *joy ; sorrow* marking a corresponding descent. The three primary affects are joy, sorrow, and desire, and from these Spinoza deduces all the other affects. Love, for example, is joy, and hatred is sorrow, accompanied with the idea of an external cause. Love is therefore not a primary affect ; it is the consequence of attainment of greater perfection through some other person.

Spinoza in the Fourth Part sets forth the power of the affects over man, but before he does so he resumes the consideration of final causes and of what we call perfection and imperfection, a subject with which he had already dealt in the Second Part. We will now take together what he says in both parts. God exists for no end, and as the reason for His action is the same as that for His existence, He works to no end in the sense in which we understand an end. Least of all does He propose to Himself the ends which it is usually imagined He has set before Him. If men would but look with their own eyes, and have the courage to report what they saw, they must confess that these ends are figments. Storms, earthquakes, and diseases overwhelm both the just and the unjust. To escape from what is so obvious, it is affirmed that the judgments of God surpass our comprehension, " and this opinion alone would have been " sufficient to keep the human race in darkness to all

" eternity, if mathematics—which does not deal with
" ends, but with the essences and properties of forms—
" had not placed before us another rule of truth." Spinoza
may have had in view the applied mathematics of
astronomy, in which he took great interest, but, if not,
he probably selected mathematics as representative of
the exact sciences.

With regard to perfection and imperfection, Spinoza
insists that imperfection is mere negation, a less degree
of reality. The words "perfection" and "imperfection"
are inapplicable to Nature as the work of God. We use
them because we have formed certain typal conceptions
of things, and what does not conform to these types
we call imperfect. Nothing, *considered in itself*, and
without reference to another thing, is imperfect. But are
not good and evil, deformity and crime, realities? "All
" this," says Spinoza, "is easily answered. For the
" perfection of things is to be judged by their nature
" and power alone; nor are they more or less perfect
" because they delight or offend the human senses, or
" because they are beneficial or prejudicial to human
" nature. But to those who ask why God has not
" created all men in such a manner that they might be
" controlled by the dictates of reason alone, I give but
" this answer: Because to Him material was not want-
" ing for the creation of everything from the highest
" down to the very lowest grade of perfection; or, to
" speak more properly, because the laws of His nature
" were so ample that they sufficed for the production of
" everything which can be conceived by an infinite
" intellect."

In two letters to Blyenbergh, dated the 5th and 28th
of January, 1665,[1] Spinoza explains himself more fully.
" In order to make the best of the present opportunity,
" I will come a little closer, and answer your question,

[1] Letters 19 and 21.

"which in effect is based on the assumption—that
"it seems clearly to follow, both from the Providence
"of God, which does not differ from His will, and
"from His concurrence and the continuous creation
"of things, either that sin and evil do not exist, or
"that God is the cause of sin and evil. But you do
"not explain what you understand by evil, and if one
"can judge from the example of the determinate will
"of Adam, you appear by evil to understand the
"will itself in so far as it might be conceived as de-
"termined in a certain way, or as opposed to the
"command of God. Therefore you say that it is a
"great absurdity—and I say so too, if the case so
"stands—to admit either one or the other of the two
"alternatives—that is to say, that God Himself does
"things which are contrary to His will, or that anything
"can be good which opposes it. But, as for myself, I
"cannot admit that sin and evil are anything positive,
"and still less can I admit that anything is or happens
"in opposition to God's will. On the contrary, I main-
"tain not only that sin is not anything positive, but
"also affirm that we cannot properly say, except it is
"understood that we speak after the manner of men,
"that we sin against God—as when we use the ex-
"pression that men offend God.

"For, as to the first point, we know that everything
"which exists, considered by itself, without reference to
"any other thing, includes a perfection which is coexten-
"sive with the essence of the thing, for essence is nothing
"else. I take, for example, the design or determinate
"will of Adam to eat of the forbidden fruit. This design,
"or determinate will, considered in itself alone in-
"cludes perfection in exact proportion to the reality
"it expresses. This is evident, because we cannot
"conceive any imperfection, unless we consider other
"things which have more reality. Therefore in the

" resolution of Adam, when we consider it by itself,
" and do not compare it with other resolutions which
" are more perfect, or are evidence of a more perfect
" state, we cannot discover any imperfection. Indeed
" we may compare it with an infinite number of things
" far ¹ less perfect, such as stones, stocks, etc. This,
" indeed, is universally admitted, for that which we
" detest in man and regard with disgust, we admire
" in animals, such as the wars of apes, the jealousy of
" doves, etc.; these things we despise in man, and yet
" consider that animals, by reason of them, are more
" perfect. It therefore follows that sins, since they
" prove nothing but imperfection, cannot exist in any-
" thing—such as the decision of Adam and its execution
" —which expresses reality.

" Moreover, we cannot say that the will of Adam con-
" flicts with the law of God, and that it is evil because
" it displeased God; for not only would it argue great
" imperfection in God, if anything were to happen con-
" trary to His will, and if He were to desire anything
" not within His power, and if His nature were deter-
" mined in such a manner that, like created beings, He
" felt sympathy with some and antipathy towards others;
" but the action contrary to God's will, would altogether
" conflict with it; and because God's will is the same
" as His intellect, it is just as impossible for any-
" thing to happen contrary to His will, as for anything
" to happen contrary to His intellect—that is to say, if
" anything were to happen contrary to His will, it would
" be the same as if it were contradictory to His intellect,
" like a round quadrilateral. Since, therefore, the will
" or decision of Adam, considered in itself, was not evil
" nor, properly speaking, opposed to the will of God, it

¹ " Longe perfectioribus " in all editions. But the sense clearly requires " less perfect," and the Dutch version has " veel onvolmaakter."

" follows that God could be the cause of it, or rather, for
" the reason to which you call attention, must be its cause,
" not, indeed, in so far as it was evil, for the evil in it
" was nothing but the condition of privation incurred by
" Adam through what he did, and it is clear that priva-
" tion is nothing positive, and that it can only be called
" so with reference to our own intellect, but not with re-
" ference to the intellect of God.   The reason why we so
" call it is that we include under one and the same defini-
" tion all individuals of the same genus, all those, for
" example, which have the external shape of men, and
" therefore we consider that all are equally capable of
" the greatest perfection deducible from the definition
" of the same.   When, therefore, we find one which,
" in what it does, contradicts that perfection, we say
" that individual is deprived of perfection and has
" departed from its own nature.   This we should not
" say if we did not refer it to that same definition and
" affix the nature of the definition on the individual.
" But since God does not know abstractions, and does not
" form general definitions of that kind, and since no
" greater reality belongs to things than the Divine intel-
" lect and power has put into them and actually allotted
" to them, it manifestly follows that privation can only
" be asserted with reference to our intellect, and not with
" reference to God. . . . I say therefore, in the first
" place, that privation is not an act of deprivation, but
" that it is nothing but mere and simple absence of
" something, and that this absence of something is in
" itself nothing: it is, in fact, only an entity of the
" reason, or a mode of thought, which we construct
" when we compare things with one another.   We say,
" for example, that a blind man is deprived of sight,
" because we easily imagine him as seeing, our imagina-
" tion being thus excited, either because we compare him
" with others who see, or we compare his present state

"with another in the past when he saw. When we con-
"sider the man in this way—that is to say, by comparing
"his nature with the nature of others, or with himself in
"the past—we affirm that sight belongs to his nature,
"and therefore that he is deprived of it. But, if we con-
"sider the decree of God, and His nature, we can no
"more say of that man than we can of a stone that he is
"deprived of sight, for at that time sight cannot without
"contradiction belong to that man any more than it can
"to the stone, since nothing pertains to him and is his
"beyond what the Divine intellect and will have assigned
"to him. Therefore God is no more the cause of the
"man's not-seeing (τοῦ illius non videre) than of the
"not-seeing of the stone (τοῦ non videre lapidis)—which
"is mere negation. So also, when we consider the
"nature of a man who is led by the appetite of lust, and we
"compare his present appetite with that of virtuous men,
"or with that which he had at another time, we affirm
"him to be deprived of a better appetite, because we then
"adjudge the appetite of virtue to belong to him. But
"we cannot do this, if we consider the nature of the
"Divine decree and intellect, for thus considering, the
"better appetite no more pertains to the nature of that
"man at that time than to the nature of the devil or a
"stone. The better appetite, from this point of view, is
"therefore not privation, but negation. So that privation
"is nothing else than the denial of that which we consider
"pertains to the nature of a thing, and negation is nothing
"else than to deny of a thing something, because it does
"not pertain to the nature of the thing. Hence it is
"clear why the appetite of Adam for earthly objects was
"evil only with reference to our intellect, and not with
"reference to the intellect of God, for although God
"knew the past and present state of Adam, He did not
"therefore understand that Adam was deprived of his
"past state—that is to say, that the past state pertained

" to Adam's nature. For if this had been the case, God
" would have understood something contrary to His will,
" that is to say, contrary to His own proper intellect."
It is strange that Spinoza makes no reference, or scarcely
any, to pain, and it can hardly be admitted that pain
is nothing positive or mere privation.

Amongst the propositions which deal with the affects
and describe their power there are some of special importance. The enunciation of the fourteenth is that
" no affect can be restrained by the true knowledge of
" good and evil in so far as it is true, but only in so far
" as it is considered as an affect." For the proof, which
is at once a proof and an explanation, we are referred
to the first proposition of the fourth book. From the
scholium to that proposition we learn that " imagina-
" tions do not disappear with the presence of the truth,
" in so far as it is true, but because other imaginations
" arise which are stronger and which exclude the present
" existence of the objects we imagine." An ignorant
man might imagine the distance of the sun to be about
200 feet. When he learns the true distance, he is un-
deceived, but the imagination remains. Imagination
consequently is expelled only by imagination. Applied
morally, this scholium becomes the fourteenth proposition
as given above. and put into our own language it means
that a passion is not to be subdued save by a stronger
passion.

Virtue and power are declared to be the same thing—
" that is to say, virtue, in so far as it is related to man,
" is the essence itself or nature of the man in so far as
" it has the power of effecting certain things which can
" be understood through the laws of its nature alone."
Virtue consequently is nothing but action according to
the laws of our own nature, and is the effort to preserve
our being. Hence the more we seek our own profit and
to preserve our being the more virtuous we are ; but " a

"man cannot be absolutely said to act in conformity
"with virtue, in so far as he is determined to any action
"because he has inadequate ideas, but only in so far as
"he is determined because he understands." So we
are led on to see that "the effort to understand is the
"primary and sole foundation of virtue," and that "we
"do not know that anything is certainly good, excepting
"that which actually conduces to understanding, and, on
"the other hand, we do not know that anything is evil
"excepting that which can hinder us from understand-
"ing." In order fully to comprehend Spinoza on this
point, we must remember that to him the office of the
mind is interpretation ; that in fact the mind, as thought,
is the interpretation, or the spiritual side of extension,
and understanding in this sense is consequently the
virtue of the mind. Secondly, although we are liable
to passion through inadequate ideas it is possible to
pass from these inadequate ideas to those which are
adequate. When we do this the passion is no longer a
passion, but something reasonable: we *see* in fact what
we are doing : we do it intellectually, as God Himself
would do it. Thirdly, we must remember Spinoza's account of the connection between the will and the understanding. If a man clearly discerns the nature of a
triangle, he is compelled to admit that its three angles
are equal to two right angles, and volition therefore is
nothing but understanding. Thus in every way virtue
is understanding. We then arrive at the twenty-eighth
proposition, that "the highest good of the mind is the
"knowledge of God, and the highest virtue of the mind
"is to know God." The question here presents itself more
distinctly than ever, whether the only interpretation
which Spinoza intended to be put on a passage like this
is one which, for want of a better word, we may call
natural, or whether by the words "God" and "knowledge of God" he intended something more. There can,

however, be no doubt that Spinoza becomes practically fruitful when we consider what he says as *science*, and dismiss any conception of God which resembles that of the theologian. What is most instructive and significant here is the identification of understanding and virtue; the object of the understanding process being, as he himself says, the infinite attributes of God. Virtue, that is to say mental work or activity, is summed up in a twofold understanding, that of nature and of ourselves, but the *act* is the same in both cases. That which makes me what people call good is the faculty by which I comprehend the laws of gravity. There is no separate department of theology, or even of morals, with its own separate axioms and modes of procedure. There is but one department—there is but one set of axioms and the mode of procedure is one.

Another instance of the ease with which the propositions that contain an apparently theological term can be naturally understood, is the definition of a religious act, "everything which we desire and do, of which we are "the cause, in so far as we possess an idea of God, "or in so far as we know God, I refer to Religion." A religious act is therefore one which is performed from the idea or knowledge of the Highest and it is one which is performed with the fullest exercise of our faculties. It is the act which is done with the most unclouded insight.

A desire which springs from "reason can never "be in excess," for it is a desire which is begotten in us in so far as we act—that is to say, in so far as we do not suffer—and of such a desire there can never be too much. This proposition is one of a few towards the end of the fourth book, which lie rather apart from its main object, but are nevertheless remarkably pregnant and beautiful. The enunciation of the sixty-seventh is " a free man thinks of nothing less than

" of death, and his wisdom is not a meditation upon
" death, but upon life." The formal proof depends upon
a previous proposition that a free man, or, in other words,
a man who lives according to the dictates of reason
alone, is not led by the fear of death but directly desires
the good—that is to say, he actively endeavours to
obtain it. Meditation upon death is more or less a
passion, and, as such, to be avoided. How true this is
everybody can testify from his own experience. Thinking
about death is not thinking: it is merely suffering ourselves to drift. Spinoza therefore avoided reflection on it,
not because it was disagreeable, or because he was afraid
of it, but because, in reflecting on it, he was not active.

In the scholium to the seventy-second proposition is
a remarkable anticipation of Kant. Spinoza supposes
himself asked whether, under any circumstances, breach
of faith is permissible; whether a man might, for
instance, tell a lie to save his life. His answer is that
the true test is the possibility of making the permission
general. This, in substance, is exactly Kant's rule.

The reiterated teaching of the *Ethic*, that passion can
be turned into action by the reason, is pushed to its
furthest extreme in the appendix to the fourth book.
Spinoza selects the most powerful instinct in man, and
maintains that it can and ought to be informed with reason.
" The lust of sexual intercourse, which arises from mere
" external form, and absolutely all love which recognises
" any other cause than the freedom of the mind, easily
" passes into hatred, unless, which is worse, it becomes
" a species of delirium . . . marriage is in accordance
" with reason, if the desire of connection is engendered,
" not merely by external form, but by a love of begetting
" children and wisely educating them; and if, in addi-
" tion, the love, both of the husband and wife, has for
" its cause not external form merely, but chiefly liberty
" of mind."

Another of the miscellaneous observations with which the fourth book closes is that "He who desires to assist "other people . . . in common conversation will avoid "referring to the vices of men, and will take care only "sparingly to speak of human impotence, while he will "talk largely of human virtue or power, and of the way "by which it may be made perfect, so that men, being "moved not by fear or aversion, but solely by the affect "of joy, may endeavour as much as they can to live "under the rule of reason." We can easily understand from such a sentence as this how it was that Spinoza exercised such an influence upon Goethe. Writing to Zelter in 1816 he says that he has been reading Linnæus, and that, "excepting Shakespeare and Spinoza," no human being not then alive ever had such an effect upon him.'

The first part of the fifth and last book explains the power of the mind over the affects. The remedies against them are summed up in the scholium to the twentieth proposition, but they are hardly to be understood, unless we refer to the previous propositions upon which they rest.

The first lies in a knowledge of the affects. If we understand an affect distinctly it is no longer a passion. The mind "passes from the affect to think those things "which it perceives clearly and distinctly and with "which it is entirely satisfied," and it strives also "to separate the affect from the thought of an external "cause and to connect it with true thoughts." "For it "is above everything to be observed," says Spinoza, insisting again on the point on which he has so often insisted before, "the appetite by which a man is said to

---

"It is so much the more our "duty, not like the advocate of "the Evil Spirit, always to keep "our eyes fixed upon the naked-"ness and weaknesses of our "nature, but rather to seek out "all those perfections through "which we can make good our "claims to a likeness to God."— *Wilhelm Meister's Apprenticeship,* part ii., book vi. *Confessions of a Beautiful Soul.*

"act is one and the same appetite as that by which he
"is said to suffer," and consequently "all the appetites
"or desires are passions only in so far as they arise
"from inadequate ideas, and are classed among the
"virtues whenever they are excited or begotten by
"adequate ideas." The second remedy is "the separa-
"tion by the mind of the affects from the thought of
"an external cause, which we imagine confusedly."
The third is the "duration, in which the affects
"which are related to objects we understand surpass
"those related to objects conceived in a mutilated or
"confused manner." A reference to the seventh proposition shows us what is intended. The affects which
spring from reason are more powerful, so far as time is
concerned, than those which are produced by objects
which are temporary and fleeting. The affect which
springs from reason, says the seventh proposition, "is
"necessarily related to the common properties of things,
"which we always contemplate as present (for nothing
"can exist which excludes their present existence), and
"which we always imagine in the same way." Hatred
of a person not actually before me will yield to the
affects of the reason because they are always before me,
and it will yield to the contemplation of the "common
properties of things."

The fourth remedy consists "in the multitude of causes
"by which the affects which are related to the common
"properties of things or to God are nourished." Passion
holds the mind to a single thought and prevents us from
thinking of other things. That is one reason why it is
so injurious. But the "common properties of things"
are everywhere, and each one of them can produce its
own affect. These affects, as they are so varied, are
thus a cure for passion.

The fifth and last remedy lies "in the order in which
"the mind can arrange its affects and connect them one

f

"with the other." Spinoza advises that every man should have certain sure maxims—*dogmata,* he calls them—which should even be committed to memory, so that they may be ready whenever we need them : one of these *dogmata* is never to oppose hatred by hatred. By constant practice, an affect such as hatred will recall its own appropriate maxim. The mind can also "cause all "the affections of the body or the images of things to be "related to the idea of God," which means that we can transport ourselves to the centre and see things by the rule or guidance of this idea.

Such is Spinoza's scheme of salvation. It is noticeable that it is purely intellectual. That it should not be mystical or supernatural we had a right to expect, but it will probably surprise many of his readers to hear nothing of struggle, blind resistance, obligation to an unknown lawgiver or even to a law, the authority for which is concealed. He sums up by insisting again on the power which "clear and distinct knowledge" has over the affects, and concludes as follows : "Moreover, clear and "distinct knowledge begets a love towards an immutable "and eternal object, of which we are really partakers ; "a love therefore which cannot be vitiated by the defects "which are in common love, but which can always "become greater and greater, occupy the largest part of "the mind and thoroughly affect it."

The conclusion of the Fifth Part of the *Ethic* is perhaps the most difficult portion of the whole work, although to some persons the most fascinating. It consists of two sections, the first of which is a group of propositions on what is called the "love of God." As these propositions are not consecutive we had better put them together.

"He who clearly and distinctly understands himself "and his affects loves God, and loves Him better, the "better he understands himself and his affects."

"This love to God, above everything else, ought to "occupy the mind."

"God is free from passions, nor is He affected with "any affect of joy or sorrow." Hence as a corollary, "properly speaking, God loves no one and hates no one."

"No one can hate God," not even if we consider Him as the cause of sorrow; for "in so far as we understand "the causes of sorrow, it ceases to be a passion—that is "to say, it ceases to be sorrow."

"He who loves God cannot strive that God should love "him in return."

"This love to God cannot be defiled, either by the "affect of envy or jealousy, but is the more strengthened "the more people we imagine to be connected with God "by the same bond of love."

"There is no affect directly contrary to this love and "able to destroy it, and so we may conclude that this "love to God is the most constant of all the affects."

"As each person, therefore, becomes stronger in this "(the third) kind of knowledge, the more is he conscious "of himself and of God—that is to say, the more perfect "and happier he is."

"From the third kind of knowledge necessarily springs "the intellectual love of God."

"The intellectual love of God, which arises from the "third kind of knowledge, is eternal."

"God loves Himself with an infinite, intellectual love."

"The intellectual love of the mind towards God is the "very love with which He loves Himself, not in so far as "He is infinite, but in so far as He can be manifested "through the essence of the human mind considered "under the form of eternity—that is to say, the intellec-"tual love of the mind towards God is part of the infinite "love with which God loves Himself."

"God, in so far as He loves Himself, loves men, and "consequently the love of God towards men and the

"intellectual love of the mind towards God are one and
"the same thing."

"Our salvation, or blessedness, or liberty consists in
"a constant and eternal love towards God, or in the
"love of God towards men."

"There is nothing in nature which is contrary to this
"intellectual love, or which can negate it."

Goethe refers to these propositions in his Autobio-
graphy.[1] "The mind," he says, "which worked upon
"me so decisively, and which was destined to affect so
"deeply my whole mode of thinking, was Spinoza. After
"looking through the world in vain to find a means of
"development for my strange nature, I at last fell upon
"the *Ethic* of this man. Of what I read out of the
"work and of what I read into it, I can give no account.
"Enough that here I found a sedative for my passions,
"and that a free, wide view over the material world
"seemed to open before me. But what especially bound
"me to him, was the great disinterestedness which
"shone from every proposition. That wonderful expres-
"sion, 'who loves God truly must not desire God to love
"him in return,' with all the preliminary propositions
"on which it rests, and all the consequences that follow
"from it, filled my whole mind. To be disinterested in
"everything, but the most so in love and friendship, was
"my highest desire, my maxim, my practice, and so
"that audacious saying of mine afterwards, 'If I love
"thee, what is that to thee?' was spoken right out of
"my heart.[2] Moreover, it must not here be denied that
"the most inward unions are those of opposites. The
"all-composing calmness of Spinoza was in striking

---

[1] *Truth and Poetry out of My Life,*
part iii., book 14.

[2] It is curious and suggestive
that this fine saying should be
put by Goethe into the mouth of
Philina, who says to Wilhelm,
when he lies wounded and is un-
comfortable because she waits on
him so assiduously, "Wenn ich
dich lieb habe, was geht's dich
an?" (*Wilhelm's Meister's Apprenticeship,* part i., book 4, chap. 9.)

"contrast with my all-disturbing activity, his mathe-
"matical method was the opposite of my poetic imagi-
"nation and way of writing, and the very precision which
"was thought not adapted to moral subjects made me
"his enthusiastic disciple, his most decided worshipper.
"Mind and heart, understanding and feeling sought each
"other with an eager affinity, binding together the most
"different natures."

What is the meaning in Spinoza of the words "love of
"God," or, as he puts it more precisely, "the intellectual
"love of the mind towards God"?

We ought always to interpret Spinoza by himself.
In the *Short Treatise* we hear of a blessedness which
comes to man through the fourth kind of knowledge,
answering to the third of the *Ethic*. If we become
united with God through knowledge of this order we are
happy. [1] "Hence it follows incontrovertibly that it is
"knowledge which is the cause of love, so that when we
"learn to know God in this way, we must necessarily
"unite ourselves to Him, for He cannot be known, nor
"can He reveal Himself save as that which is supremely
"great and good. In this union alone, as we have
"already said, our happiness consists. I do not say that
"we must know Him adequately; but it is sufficient for
"us, in order to be united with Him, to know Him in
"a measure, for the knowledge we have of the body is
"not of such a kind that we can know it as it is or
"perfectly, and yet what a union! what love!"

We were born when we were united with the body:
our second birth is our union with this spiritual object.
[2] "When we say that God does not love man we are not
"to suppose that God has left him, so to speak, to wander
"alone where he pleases, but we are to understand God's
"love in this way, that, inasmuch as man, together with
"everything which exists, is in God, so that God consists

[1] *Short Treatise*, part ii. chap. 22.   [2] *Short Treatise*, part ii. chap. 24.

"in this whole, there can be no special love in God,
"because everything really subsists in a single thing,
"which is God Himself."

This really corresponds with the account given in the
Ethic, though it is expressed in different language.

If we read carefully, not only the propositions concerning the love of God, but those upon which these
propositions depend, we find that it is caused by a
better understanding of ourselves and our affects, and a
reference to the "idea of God" so that our active power
is increased. This means joy; and joy, accompanied
with the idea of God as a cause, is love to Him. This
is not all, however; there is an intellectual love of God.
It comes through a knowledge of individual objects; it
comes also through understanding individual objects by
the third kind of knowledge—the "intuitive science"
—which "advances from an adequate idea of the formal
"essence of certain attributes of God to the adequate
"knowledge of the essence of things"—that is to say,
a knowledge of things through a complete knowledge of
God's attributes. But the knowledge of the attributes
is only obtainable through a knowledge of things.
Spinoza nowhere says that we know God's attributes in
any other way; in fact, he expressly states the contrary.
As before pointed out, he is not arguing in a circle.
We obtain a law from observation; but after obtaining
it, we unhesitatingly apply it to other cases which may
be new. The intellectual love of God, therefore, is the
discovery of law or attribute, and the inclusion of the
world under it. It is observable that Spinoza gives
the name *mentis acquiescentia* to the condition which
arises from understanding things by the third kind of
knowledge. It is the repose which the mind feels in the
exercise of its true function and in the contemplation
of the order of the universe. We cannot be absolutely
certain that Spinoza intended nothing more than this.

Occasionally, in his description of the intellectual love, it looks as if something more was included ; but that the interpretation here given was at least the largest part of his meaning seems clear. He does not express himself as we should express ourselves now ; but he was a Jew, and those persons who have been trained in a religion never lose its influence, and generally find, however free they may afterwards become, that much of its terminology still suits them, and expresses more exactly than any other what they have to say. Furthermore, Spinoza evidently wished to distinguish the emotion which, for him at least, accompanied mental exercise. It was not dull, dry, mechanical work which Kepler, Copernicus, Galileo, and Huyghens had been doing. It was joy, peace of mind, delight ; the love of God was in it. If not there, they were nowhere to be found.[1]

We now come to the last and greatest difficulty of the *Ethic*—the argument for the eternity of the mind. It is introduced in the middle of the Fifth Part. I cannot promise to make it fully intelligible to my readers, for it is not clearly intelligible to myself. It is not easy to deal with these singular propositions and yet keep perfectly close to their author. The tendency is to

---

[1] " It (the doctrine of the One) "presents itself once more, now "altogether beyond Christian in-"fluence, in the hard and am-"bitious intellectualism of Spi-"noza ; a doctrine of pure repel-"lent substance—substance 'in "vacuo,' to be lost in which, "however, would be the proper "consummation of the transitory "individual life. Spinoza's own "absolutely colourless existence "was a practical comment on it." —*Plato and Platonism*, by Walter Pater, p. 33.

This characterisation of Spinoza seems strange, even after a superficial study of these propositions. The word " colourless," in one sense, may certainly be applied to him ; for sunlight is colourless, for the reason that it includes *all* the rays of the spectrum. The coloured light is that of the priest, the prophet, or the Church. " Repellent " and " in vacuo " are instructive examples of the seductive influence of phrases on an artist in style, and of the danger to which he is continually exposed of lapsing thereby into unintelligibility.

diverge into statements which may have their own value, but are not his. An attempt, however, will be made to throw a little light upon his doctrine, and to ascertain, by reference to and comparison with himself, what some of the principal ascertainable points in it are.

It is certain that Spinoza is no believer in immortality in the ordinary sense of the word. Nobody can be plainer than he in its denial. The mind, he expressly says, cannot imagine, nor can it recollect anything that is past, except while the body lasts, and there is no continuation of the self without memory and imagination. It is noticeable that although in the *Short Treatise* the word "immortality" is used, it is not used in the *Ethic.*

It is also certain, on the other hand, that Spinoza believed in something more than a survival of what we have done. Aristotle was to him a partaker in eternity, not only because he filled the world with ideas which will never die, but in some different sense. If Spinoza believed in nothing but the simple fact of the immortality of achievements, he would not have gone out of his way to express himself in such abstruse language.

The difficulty which lies at the threshold is the phrase "form of eternity." The twenty-second proposition declares that, although imagination and memory depend upon the body, "in God, nevertheless, there necessarily "exists an idea which expresses the essence of this or "that human body under the form of eternity." The eighth axiom of the first book defines eternity as "exist- "ence itself, so far as it is conceived necessarily to follow "from the definition alone of the eternal thing." In a letter to Meyer of the 20th of April, 1663,[1] Spinoza distinguishes between eternity and duration, even if duration be prolonged indefinitely. "Through dura- "tion," he says, "we can explain only the existence of

[1] Letter 12.

" modes ; but through eternity that of substance—that
" is to say, an infinite enjoyment of existence, or rather
" (although the Latin does not lend itself to such a mode
" of expression) of Being (*essendi*)." He goes on to warn
us that eternity is not conceivable by the imagination,
but by the intellect alone.   In the second corollary of
the forty-fourth proposition of the second book we are
told that " it is of the nature of reason to perceive things
" under a certain form of eternity," and the demonstration shows that, when we conceive them under the form
of eternity, we conceive them as necessary, and this necessity is a part of the eternal nature of God.   The same
thing is said in the thirtieth proposition of the fifth
book ; and it is added that things are conceived under
the form of eternity when " through the essence of God
" they involve existence."   To the same purpose, and a
little clearer, is the scholium to the twenty-ninth proposition of the fifth book : " 'Things are conceived by us
" as actual in two ways—either in so far as we conceive
" them to exist with relation to a fixed time and place,
" or in so far as we conceive them to be contained in
" God and to follow from the necessity of the Divine
" nature.   But those things which are conceived in this
" second way as true or real, we conceive under the form
" of eternity, and their ideas involve the eternal and
" infinite essence of God."   Perhaps we shall now be
able to obtain some insight into Spinoza's thought.
We have to dismiss the imagination altogether ; we are
not to use it in any way in our conception of eternity ;
we have to conceive an existence to which time is not
applicable—as, for example, geometrical truths.   We
feel that it is absurd to apply time to the theorem
that the three angles of a triangle are equal to two
right angles, for there was no time when that truth
came into being, nor will it cease to be at any given
time.   Necessary truths, in short, are not subject to the

category of time, and the form of eternity and necessity
correspond.

Notwithstanding there is no memory without the body,
the twenty-second proposition declares that "in God
"nevertheless there necessarily exists an idea which
"expresses the essence of this or that human body under
"the form of eternity." Essence is that "which, being
"given, the thing itself is necessarily posited, and being
"taken away, the thing is necessarily taken; or, in other
"words, that, without which the thing can neither be
"nor be conceived, and which in its turn cannot be nor
"be conceived without the thing." Also "the essence
"of man consists of certain modifications of the attri-
"butes of God," and "the human mind is a part of the
"infinite intellect of God." This definition of essence
and the two following propositions we have already
passed in the second book. Now comes the question—
as the essence of the human body is the mind, does
Spinoza mean that the whole complete idea of the body—
that is to say mind—is eternal? He does not say distinctly in this twenty-second proposition what he means,
but that he does not mean the whole complete idea is
evident from what follows. For example, take the
undermentioned scholia and corollaries.

Schol. Prop. xxiii.: "Our mind, in so far as it involves
"the essence of the body under the form of eternity, is
"eternal."

Schol. Prop. xxxi.: "The mind is eternal, in so far
"as it conceives things under the form of eternity."

Coroll. Prop. xxxiv.: "No love, except intellectual
"love, is eternal."

Schol. Prop. xxxviii.: "It is possible for the human
"mind to be of such a nature that that part of it which
"we have shown perishes with its body, in comparison
"with the part of it which remains is of no conse-
"quence."

Coroll. Prop. xl.: "That part of the mind which "abides, whether great or small, is more perfect than "the other part. For the part of the mind which is "eternal is the intellect, through which alone we are "said to act; but that part which, as we have shown, "perishes is the imagination, through which alone we "are said to suffer."

Lastly, the twenty-third proposition says that "the "human mind cannot be absolutely destroyed with the "body, but something of it remains which is eternal."

We are now another step further, and we note in the next place the scholium to the twenty-third proposition. "Nevertheless we feel and know by experience that we "are eternal. For the mind is no less sensible of those "things which it conceives through intelligence than of "those which it remembers, for demonstrations are the "eyes of the mind by which it sees and observes things." Spinoza here does not refer to vague presentiments of immortality.

The eternal part, therefore, is plainly that which is conversant with demonstrations, or that which is not affected by the duration of the body. This is the knowledge of God, and through this knowledge the mind "knows that it is in God, and is conceived through "Him."

A quotation from the *Short Treatise*[1] may be appended. After saying that the soul dies, in so far as it is united with the body, it is added, "If the soul is united with "some other thing which is and remains unchangeable, "it must on the contrary also remain unchangeable and "permanent."

What then can we conclude for our own purposes from this presentation, which has been made as far as possible in Spinoza's own words. What can we extract from them after putting on one side what we cannot

---

[1] Part ii. chap. 23.

understand? Spinoza believes that the more reasonable
we are the better will it be for us both here and hereafter; for *us* in some sense, although in what sense *us*
is obscure.   There is no heaven for him but this.
Heaven is not a hereafter of reward: it is the here and
hereafter of the intellectual love of God.   In so far as
the mind is capable of intellectual love, it is not only
eternal but a part of God Himself.   Man perceiving
things under the form of eternity is not a thing down
here created by a Being up there, of whom he knows
nothing, save what has been revealed to him, but he is
actually one with the God who has created Arcturus,
Orion, the Pleiades, and the chambers of the south, and
in a sense may be said to have had a share in their
creation.   Spinoza never goes nearer to inspiration than
in the propositions on the relationship between God and
man, and there is an unmistakable heat in them which
shows that they were dear to him.   " God loves Himself
" with an infinite, intellectual love," and "the intel-
" lectual love of the mind towards God is the very love
" with which He loves Himself, not in so far as He is
" infinite, but in so far as He can be manifested through
" the essence of the human mind considered under the
" form of eternity; that is to say, the intellectual love of
" the mind towards God is part of the infinite love with
" which God loves Himself. . . . Hence it follows that
"God, in so far as He loves Himself, loves men, and
" consequently that the love of God towards men, and
" the intellectual love of the mind towards God, are one
" and the same thing." [1]

---

[1] "Further, this creative reason "does not at one time think, at "another time not think [it "thinks eternally]: and when "separated from the body it re-"mains nothing but what it "essentially is: and thus it is "alone immortal and eternal. "Of this unceasing work of "thought, however, we retain " no memory, because this reason "is unaffected by its objects; "whereas the receptive, passive "intellect (which is affected) is

Spinoza could not, however, thus conclude his *Ethic*, and in a few words at the end he reminds us that the advantages of piety and religion and the superiority of reason to passion are not dependent upon any theory of eternity. A man may not believe he is going to live for ever, but that is no reason why he should prefer poisons to food. Morality is not martyrdom, and life is not a continual sacrifice. Blessedness is not a reward for restraint, but we restrain ourselves because we are blessed.

To prevent all misunderstanding it may be as well again to say that I have not attempted in this account of the *Ethic* to do what has been done so completely in Germany, and partially in this country—that is to say, to connect Spinoza with metaphysics before and after. In the first place I have not the necessary knowledge, for the mere titles of Germany's contributions on this subject would fill a couple of pages of small octavo print: in the second place much that is in Spinoza is not completely luminous to me, and lastly, he himself, I believe, would have desired to rest his claim to men's attention mainly upon his *Ethic*, strictly so called. Enough, however, has perhaps been said to explain his influence. It is impossible, after familiar acquaintance with him, to live for a single day as we should have lived without him. He was the first to protest against the ordinary treatment of wrongdoing—the theological treatment we may say—although it is current beyond the limits of theology, and will survive it. It was he who relieved men, or who did his best to relieve them from the trouble and despair consequent upon what is

" perishable, and can really think " nothing without the support of " the creative intellect."—Aristotle's *Psychology* (Wallace's translation), p. 161.

" I believe," said Pantagruel,

" that all intellectual souls are " exempt from the scissors of " Atropos. They are all immor- " tal."—Rabelais, *Pantagruel*, book iv. chap. 27.

really a dual government of the world, and it was he who gave vitality and a practical meaning to the great doctrine of the Unity of God. Lastly, he may be said to have contributed something towards a truly human religion. Religion has been said to consist in that of which we are assured, but it is partly that which we hope or even that which we dream, and perhaps the influence of the hope and the dream is greater than that of the certainty.

PARALLEL PASSAGES FROM GIORDANO BRUNO.

The passages quoted below from Giordano Bruno may serve to show in a measure the correspondence between him and Spinoza. It must however be borne in mind that many of them may be taken to show, not a correspondence between Spinoza and Bruno alone, but between Spinoza and earlier thinkers from whom Bruno derived them :—

The universal intellect is related to the production of natural things as our intellect is related to the congruous production of rational species (*De la Causa*, Dial. 2).

Dicsono. I should like to see you distinguish how you understand it to be external cause and how as internal.

Teofilo. I call it external cause because, as being the efficient cause, it is not a part of the components and the things produced, and I call it internal cause, in so far as it does not operate round about matter, or outside of it (*De la Causa*, Dial. 2).

The aim and final cause which the Efficient Cause sets before himself are the perfection of the universe, which means that in the different parts of matter all forms should have actual existence, in which end the intellect delights so much that it is never weary of exciting all sorts of forms from matter (*De la Causa,* Dial. 2).

_____

If anything whatever of the substances should be destroyed, the world would become a void (*De la Causa,* Dial. 2).[1]

_____

Teofilo. We do not see with one and the same eye the substratum of the arts (ordinary matter) and the substratum of Nature.

Gervasio. You mean to say that we see the former with the sensuous eye and the latter with the eye of the reason.

Teofilo. Exactly so (*De la Causa,* Dial. 3).

_____

Of the existence of this basis of all natural things we can convince ourselves through the reason alone (*De la Causa,* Dial. 3).

_____

The universe is everything which it can be, in a mode which is explicit, dispersed, differentiated (*De la Causa,* Dial. 3).

_____

These things (death, corruption, evil, defects, mis-carriages) are not reality and potence, but unreality and impotence (*De la Causa,* Dial. 3).

_____

Teofilo. The whole (the all), as to substance, is one, as perhaps Parmenides understood?

Dicsono. Do you mean that substance is twofold, the one spiritual, the other corporeal : that both belong to one being, to one root ? (*De la Causa,* Dial. 3).

_____

[1] This is one of the most re-markable coincidences between Bruno and Spinoza. Spinoza says in a letter to Oldenburg (No. 4) (undated), in reply to Oldenburg's letter of Sept. 27, 1661, *si una pars materiæ annihilaretur, simul etiam tota extensio evanesceret.*

Granted then that there are countless individuals, at last is everything one, and the recognition of this unity forms the goal and end of all philosophy and all natural research (*De la Causa*, Dial. 4).

It is not changeable into another form, because it has no external through which it may suffer, or through which it may be affected in any way (*De la Causa*, Dial. 5).

The universe is one, infinite, immovable. . . . It cannot diminish nor increase, since it is infinite, from which, just as nothing can be added to it, so nothing can be taken away, because the infinite has not proportionate parts. . . . There is no proportionate part, nor part at all which differs from the whole. . . . Because, if you wish to say part of the infinite, you must call it infinite; and, if it is infinite, it unites in one being with the whole; therefore the universe is one, infinite indivisible. And, if in the infinite there is no difference, as of a whole and part, or as of one and another, then certainly the infinite is one (*De la Causa*, Dial. 5).

In the One, infinite and immovable, which is substance, which is Being, there is multitude, number, which by being mode and variety of Being that distinguishes thing from thing, does not make that which is Being more than one, but multiform, many-figured. . . . Every production, of whatever kind it may be, is a change, while substance remains always the same. . . . So think the philosophers who say that nothing is produced as to substance, nor is destroyed (*De la Causa*, Dial. 5).

Everything which we apprehend in the Universe, since it has that which is all in all in itself, embraces in its own way the whole world-soul, which is in every part of the same completely, but, as we have said above, not totally (*De la Causa*, Dial. 5).

Why shall we, or can we, think that the Divine efficacy is idle? Why shall we say that the Divine goodness, which can communicate itself to infinite things, and can diffuse itself infinitely, desires to withdraw itself and to contract itself into nothing? since every finite thing, with regard to the infinite, is nothing (*De l'infinito universo*, Dial. 1).

Since the universe is infinite and immovable, there is no need to seek the mover of it. . . . All the worlds are moved by an internal principle . . . and therefore it is vain to seek their external motor (*De l'infinito*, Dial. 1).

As it is immutable, there is no contingency in its operation nor in its efficacy, but from a determined and certain efficacy depends a determined and certain effect immutably; thus it cannot be other than what it is; it cannot be what it is not; it cannot have power to do anything but what it can; it cannot will anything but what it wills; and necessarily it cannot do anything but what it does; since to have power distinct from action belongs solely to mutable things (*De l'infinito*, Dial. 1).

The Divine action is necessary because it proceeds from a will which is most immutable—or rather immutability itself—and yet necessity itself, whence liberty, will, necessity, are entirely the same thing, and so are voluntary action, power and being (*De l'infinito*, Dial. 1).

In number, then, and multitude, there is the infinite movable and infinite moving; but in unity and singularity there is the infinite immovable mover, and the infinite immovable universe; and this infinite number and magnitude, and that infinite unity and simplicity, coincide in one very simple and individual principle, true Being. Thus there is no *primum mobile* to which, in a fixed order, the second succeeds, and so on to the last, or rather *ad infinitum;* but all the movable things are equally near to, and distant from, the first and universal mover. As, speaking logically, all the species have an equal relation to the same genus, all the individuals to the same species, thus from one infinite universal mover in an infinite space there is a universal infinite movement, from which infinite movables and infinite movers depend, each of which is finite in nature and action (*De l'infinito*, Dial. 5).

ETHIC.

---·---

First Part.

OF GOD.

DEFINITIONS.

I. BY cause of itself, I understand that, whose essence involves existence; or that, whose nature cannot be conceived unless existing.

II. That thing is called finite in its own kind (*in suo genere*) which can be limited by another thing of the same nature. For example, a body is called finite, because we always conceive another which is greater. So a thought is limited by another thought; but a body is not limited by a thought, nor a thought by a body.

III. By substance, I understand that which is in itself and is conceived through itself; in other words, that, the conception of which does not need the conception of another thing from which it must be formed.

IV. By attribute, I understand that which the intellect perceives of substance, as if constituting its essence.

V. By mode, I understand the affections of substance, or that which is in another thing through which also it is conceived.

VI. By God, I understand Being absolutely infinite, that is to say, substance consisting of infinite attributes, each one of which expresses eternal and infinite essence.

Explanation.—I say absolutely infinite but not infinite

A

in its own kind (*in suo genere*); for of whatever is infinite only in its own kind (*in suo genere*), we can deny infinite attributes; but to the essence of that which is absolutely infinite pertains whatever expresses essence and involves no negation.

VII. That thing is called free which exists from the necessity of its own nature alone, and is determined to action by itself alone. That thing, on the other hand, is called necessary, or rather compelled, which by another is determined to existence and action in a fixed and prescribed manner.

VIII. By eternity, I understand existence itself, so far as it is conceived necessarily to follow from the definition alone of the eternal thing.

Explanation.—For such existence, like the essence of the thing, is conceived as an eternal truth. It cannot therefore be explained by duration or time, even if the duration be conceived without beginning or end.

AXIOMS.

I. Everything which is, is either in itself or in another.

II. That which cannot be conceived through another must be conceived through itself.

III. From a given determinate cause an effect necessarily follows; and, on the other hand, if no determinate cause be given, it is impossible that an effect can follow.

IV. The knowledge (cognitio) of an effect depends upon and involves the knowledge of the cause.

V. Those things which have nothing mutually in common with one another cannot through one another be mutually understood, that is to say, the conception of the one does not involve the conception of the other.

VI. A true idea must agree with that of which it is the idea (*cum suo ideato*).

VII. The essence of that thing which can be conceived as not existing does not involve existence.

PROP. I.—*Substance is by its nature prior to its affections.*

Demonst.—This is evident from Defs. 3 and 5.

PROP. II.—*Two substances having different attributes have nothing in common with one another.*

Demonst.—This is also evident from Def. 3. For each substance must be in itself and must be conceived through itself, that is to say, the conception of one does not involve the conception of the other.—Q.E.D.

PROP. III.—*If two things have nothing in common with one another, one cannot be the cause of the other.*

Demonst.—If they have nothing mutually in common with one another, they cannot (Ax. 5) through one another be mutually understood, and therefore (Ax. 4) one cannot be the cause of the other.—Q.E.D.

PROP. IV.—*Two or more distinct things are distinguished from one another, either by the difference of the attributes of the substances, or by the difference of their affections.*

Demonst.—Everything which is, is either in itself or in another (Ax. 1), that is to say (Defs. 3 and 5), outside the intellect there is nothing but substances and their affections. There is nothing therefore outside the intellect by which a number of things can be distinguished one from another, but substances or (which is the same thing by Def. 4) their attributes and their affections.—Q.E.D.

PROP. V.—*In nature there cannot be two or more substances of the same nature or attribute.*

Demonst.—If there were two or more distinct substances, they must be distinguished one from the other
by difference of attributes or difference of affections
(Prop. 4). If they are distinguished only by difference
of attributes, it will be granted that there is but one
substance of the same attribute. But if they are distinguished by difference of affections, since substance is
prior by nature to its affections (Prop. 1), the affections
therefore being placed on one side, and the substance
being considered in itself, or, in other words (Def. 3 and
Ax. 6), truly considered, it cannot be conceived as distinguished from another substance, that is to say (Prop. 4),
there cannot be two or more substances, but only one
possessing the same nature or attribute.—Q.E.D.

PROP. VI.—*One substance cannot be produced by another
substance.*

Demonst.—There cannot in nature be two substances
of the same attribute (Prop. 5), that is to say (Prop. 2),
two which have anything in common with one another.
And therefore (Prop. 3) one cannot be the cause of the
other, that is to say, one cannot be produced by the
other.—Q.E.D.

Corol.—Hence it follows that there is nothing by
which substance can be produced, for in nature there is
nothing but substances and their affections (as is evident
from Ax. 1 and Defs. 3 and 5). But substance cannot
be produced by substance (Prop. 6). Therefore absolutely there is nothing by which substance can be produced.—Q.E.D.

Another Demonst.—This corollary is demonstrated
more easily by the *reductio ad absurdum.* For if there
were anything by which substance could be produced,
the knowledge of substance would be dependent upon

the knowledge of its cause (Ax. 4), and therefore (Def. 3) it would not be substance.

PROP. VII.—*It pertains to the nature of substance to exist.*

Demonst.—There is nothing by which substance can be produced (Corol. Prop. 6). It will therefore be the cause of itself, that is to say (Def. 1), its essence necessarily involves existence, or in other words it pertains to its nature to exist.—Q.E.D.

PROP. VIII.—*Every substance is necessarily infinite.*

Demonst.—Substance which has only one attribute cannot exist except as one substance (Prop. 5), and to the nature of this one substance it pertains to exist (Prop. 7). It must therefore from its nature exist as finite or infinite. But it cannot exist as finite substance, for (Def. 2) it must (if finite) be limited by another substance of the same nature, which also must necessarily exist (Prop. 7), and therefore there would be two substances of the same attribute, which is absurd (Prop. 5). It exists therefore as infinite substance.—Q.E.D.

Schol. 1.—Since finiteness is in truth partly negation, and infinitude absolute affirmation of existence of some kind, it follows from Prop. 7 alone that all substance must be infinite.

Schol. 2.—I fully expect that those who judge things confusedly, and who have not been accustomed to cognise things through their first causes, will find it difficult to comprehend the demonstration of the 7th Proposition, since they do not distinguish between the modifications of substances and substances themselves, and are ignorant of the manner in which things are produced. Hence it comes to pass that they erroneously ascribe to substances a beginning like that which they see belongs to natural things; for those who are ignorant of the true causes of things confound everything, and without any mental repugnance represent trees speaking like men, or imagine

that men are made out of stones as well as begotten
from seed, and that all forms can be changed the one
into the other. So also those who confound human nature
with the divine, readily attribute to God human affects,[1]
especially so long as they are ignorant of the manner in
which affects are produced in the mind. But if men
would attend to the nature of substance, they could not
entertain a single doubt of the truth of Proposition 7;
indeed this proposition would be considered by all to be
axiomatic, and reckoned amongst common notions. For
by "substance" would be understood that which is in
itself and is conceived through itself, or, in other words,
that, the knowledge of which does not need the knowledge of another thing. But by "modifications" would be
understood those things which are in another thing—those
things, the conception of which is formed from the conception of the thing in which they are. Hence we can have
true ideas of non-existent modifications, since although
they may not actually exist outside the intellect, their
essence nevertheless is so comprehended in something else,
that they may be conceived through it. But the truth
of substances is not outside the intellect unless in the
substances themselves, because they are conceived through
themselves. If any one, therefore, were to say that he
possessed a clear and distinct, that is to say, a true idea
of substance, and that he nevertheless doubted whether
such a substance exists, he would forsooth be in the same
position as if he were to say that he had a true idea and
nevertheless doubted whether or not it was false (as is
evident to any one who pays a little attention). Similarly
if any one were to affirm that substance is created, he
would affirm at the same time that a false idea had become
true, and this is a greater absurdity than can be conceived.

[1] *Affectus* is translated by "affect" and *affectio* by "affection."
There seems to be no other way in
the English language of marking
the relationship of the two words
and preserving their exact meaning. *Affectus* has sometimes been translated "passion," but Spinoza uses
passio for passion, and means something different from *affectus*. See
Def. III., part 3.

It is therefore necessary to admit that the existence of substance, like its essence, is an eternal truth. Hence a
demonstration (which I have thought worth while to
append) by a different method is possible, showing that
there are not two substances possessing the same nature.
But in order to prove this methodically it is to be noted :
1. That the true definition of any one thing neither
involves nor expresses anything except the nature of the
thing defined. From which it follows, 2. That a definition does not involve or express any certain number of
individuals, since it expresses nothing but the nature of
the thing defined. For example, the definition of a
triangle expresses nothing but the simple nature of
a triangle, and not any certain number of triangles.
3. It is to be observed that of every existing thing
there is some certain cause by reason of which it
exists. 4. Finally, it is to be observed that this cause,
by reason of which a thing exists, must either be contained in the nature itself and definition of the existing
thing (simply because it pertains to the nature of the
thing to exist), or it must exist outside the thing.
This being granted, it follows that if a certain number of individuals exist in nature, there must necessarily be a cause why those individuals, and neither
more nor fewer, exist. If, for example, there are twenty
men in existence (whom, for the sake of greater clearness,
I suppose existing at the same time, and that no others
existed before them), it will not be sufficient, in order
that we may give a reason why twenty men exist, to
give a cause for human nature generally ; but it will be
necessary, in addition, to give a reason why neither more
nor fewer than twenty exist, since, as we have already
observed under the third head, there must necessarily be
a cause why each exists. But this cause (as we have
shown under the second and third heads) cannot be contained in human nature itself, since the true definition of
a man does not involve the number twenty, and therefore

(by the fourth head) the cause why these twenty men
exist, and consequently the cause why each exists, must
necessarily lie outside each one; and therefore we must
conclude generally that whenever it is possible for several
individuals of the same nature to exist, there must necessarily be an external cause for their existence.

Since now it pertains to the nature of substance to
exist (as we have shown in this scholium), its definition
must involve necessary existence, and consequently from
its definition alone its existence must be concluded. But
from its definition (as we have already shown under the
second and third heads) the existence of more substances
than one cannot be deduced. It follows, therefore, from
this definition necessarily that there cannot be two substances possessing the same nature.

PROP. IX.—*The more reality or being a thing possesses, the
more attributes belong to it.*

Demonst.—This is evident from Def. 4.

PROP. X.—*Each attribute of a substance must be conceived
through itself.*

Demonst.—For an attribute is that which the intellect perceives of substance, as if constituting its essence
(Def. 4), and therefore (Def. 3) it must be conceived
through itself.—Q.E.D.

Schol.—From this it is apparent that although two
attributes may be conceived as really distinct—that is to
say, one without the assistance of the other—we cannot
nevertheless thence conclude that they constitute two
beings or two different substances; for this is the nature of
substance, that each of its attributes is conceived through
itself, since all the attributes which substance possesses
were always in it together, nor could one be produced by another; but each expresses the reality or
being of substance. It is very far from being absurd,

therefore, to ascribe to one substance a number of
attributes, since nothing in nature is clearer than that
each being must be conceived under some attribute,
and the more reality or being it has, the more attributes
it possesses expressing necessity or eternity and infinity.
Nothing consequently is clearer than that Being absolutely infinite is necessarily defined, as we have shown
(Def. 6), as Being which consists of infinite attributes,
each one of which expresses a certain essence, eternal
and infinite. But if any one now asks by what sign,
therefore, we may distinguish between substances, let
him read the following propositions, which show that in
nature only one substance exists, and that it is absolutely
infinite. For this reason that sign would be sought for in
vain.

PROP. XI.—*God, or substance consisting of infinite attri-*
butes, each one of which expresses eternal and infinite
essence, necessarily exists.

Demonst.—If this be denied, conceive, if it be possible,
that God does not exist. Then it follows (Ax. 7) that
His essence does not involve existence. But this (Prop.
7) is absurd. Therefore God necessarily exists.—Q.E.D.

Another proof.—For the existence or non-existence of
everything there must be a reason or cause. For example,
if a triangle exists, there must be a reason or cause why
it exists; and if it does not exist, there must be a reason
or cause which hinders its existence or which negates
it. But this reason or cause must either be contained in
the nature of the thing or lie outside it. For example,
the nature of the thing itself shows the reason why a
square circle does not exist, the reason being that a
square circle involves a contradiction. And the reason, on
the other hand, why substance exists follows from its
nature alone, which involves existence (see Prop. 7).
But the reason why a circle or triangle exists or does

not exist is not drawn from their nature, but from the order of corporeal nature generally; for from that it must follow, either that a triangle necessarily exists, or that it is impossible for it to exist. But this is self-evident. Therefore it follows that if there be no cause nor reason which hinders a thing from existing, it exists necessarily. If, therefore, there be no reason nor cause which hinders God from existing, or which negates His existence, we must conclude absolutely that He necessarily exists. But if there be such a reason or cause, it must be either in the nature itself of God or must lie outside it, that is to say, in another substance of another nature. For if the reason lay in a substance of the same nature, the existence of God would be by this very fact admitted. But substance possessing another nature could have nothing in common with God (Prop. 2), and therefore could not give Him existence nor negate it. Since, therefore, the reason or cause which could negate the divine existence cannot be outside the divine nature, it will necessarily, supposing that the divine nature does not exist, be in His nature itself, which would therefore involve a contradiction. But to affirm this of the Being absolutely infinite and consummately perfect is absurd. Therefore neither in God nor outside God is there any cause or reason which can negate His existence, and therefore God necessarily exists.—Q.E.D.

Another proof.—Inability to exist is impotence, and, on the other hand, ability to exist is power, as is self-evident. If, therefore, there is nothing which necessarily exists excepting things finite, it follows that things finite are more powerful than the absolutely infinite Being, and this (as is self-evident) is absurd; therefore either nothing exists or Being absolutely infinite also necessarily exists. But we ourselves exist, either in ourselves or in something else which necessarily exists (Ax. 1 and Prop. 7). Therefore the Being absolutely infinite, that is to say, (Def. 6), God, necessarily exists.—Q.E.D.

Schol.—In this last demonstration I wished to prove the existence of God *a posteriori*, in order that the demonstration might be the more easily understood, and not because the existence of God does not follow *a priori* from the same grounds. For since ability to exist is power, it follows that the more reality belongs to the nature of anything, the greater is the power for existence it derives from itself; and it also follows, therefore, that the Being absolutely infinite, or God, has from Himself an absolutely infinite power of existence, and that He therefore necessarily exists. Many persons, nevertheless, will perhaps not be able easily to see the force of this demonstration, because they have been accustomed to contemplate those things alone which flow from external causes, and they see also that those things which are quickly produced from these causes, that is to say, which easily exist, easily perish, whilst, on the other hand, they adjudge those things to be more difficult to produce, that is to say, not so easy to bring into existence, to which they conceive more properties pertain. In order that these prejudices may be removed, I do not need here to show in what respect this saying, "What is quickly made quickly perishes," is true, nor to inquire whether, looking at the whole of nature, all things are or are not equally easy. But this only it will be sufficient for me to observe, that I do not speak of things which are produced by external causes, but that I speak of substances alone which (Prop. 6) can be produced by no external cause. For whatever perfection or reality those things may have which are produced by external causes, whether they consist of many parts or of few, they owe it all to the virtue of an external cause, and therefore their existence springs from the perfection of an external cause alone and not from their own. On the other hand, whatever perfection substance has is due to no external cause. Therefore its existence must follow from its nature alone, and is therefore nothing else than its essence. Perfection consequently does not prevent the existence of a thing, but establishes it; imperfection, on the other hand, prevents existence, and so of no existence can we be more sure than of the existence of the Being absolutely infinite or perfect, that is to say, God. For since His essence shuts out all imperfection and involves absolute perfection, for this very reason all cause of doubt concerning His existence is taken away, and the highest certainty concerning it is given,—a truth which I trust will be evident to any one who bestows only moderate attention.

PROP. XII.—*No attribute of substance can be truly conceived from which it follows that substance can be divided.*

Demonst.—For the parts into which substance thus conceived would be divided will or will not retain the nature of substance. If they retain it, then (Prop. 8) each part will be infinite, and (Prop. 6) the cause of itself, and will consist of an attribute differing from that of any other part (Prop. 5), so that from one substance more substances could be formed, which (Prop. 6) is absurd. Moreover the parts (Prop. 2) would have nothing in common with their whole, and the whole (Def. 4 and Prop. 10) could be, and could be conceived without its parts, which no one will doubt to be an absurdity. But if the second case be supposed, namely, that the parts will not retain the nature of substance, then, since the whole substance might be divided into equal parts, it would lose the nature of substance and cease to be, which (Prop. 7) is absurd.

PROP. XIII.—*Substance absolutely infinite is indivisible.*

Demonst.—For if it were divisible, the parts into which it would be divided will or will not retain the nature of substance absolutely infinite. If they retain it, there will be a plurality of substances possessing the same nature, which (Prop. 5) is absurd.   If the second case be supposed, then (as above), substance absolutely infinite can cease to be, which (Prop. 11) is also absurd.

Corol.—Hence it follows that no substance, and consequently no bodily substance in so far as it is substance, is divisible.

Schol.—That substance is indivisible is more easily to be understood from this consideration alone, that the nature of substance cannot be conceived unless as infinite, and that by a part of substance nothing else can be understood than finite substance, which (Prop. 8) involves a manifest contradiction.

PROP. XIV.—*Besides God, no substance can be nor can be conceived.*

Demonst.—Since God is Being absolutely infinite, of whom no attribute can be denied which expresses the essence of substance (Def. 6), and since He necessarily exists (Prop. 11), it follows that if there were any substance besides God, it would have to be explained by some attribute of God, and thus two substances would exist possessing the same attribute, which (Prop. 5) is absurd; and therefore there cannot be any substance excepting God, and consequently none other can be conceived.   For if any other could be conceived, it would necessarily be conceived as existing, and this (by the first part of this demonstration) is absurd.   Therefore besides God no substance can be, nor can be conceived.—Q.E.D.

Corol. 1.—Hence it follows with the greatest clearness, firstly, that God is one, that is to say (Def. 6), in nature there is but one substance, and it is absolutely infinite, as (Schol. Prop. 10) we have already intimated.

Corol. 2.—It follows, secondly, that the thing extended *(rem extensam)* and the thing thinking *(rem cogitantem)* are either attributes of God or (Ax. 1) affections of the attributes of God.

Prop. XV.—*Whatever is, is in God, and nothing can either be or be conceived without God.*

Demonst.—Besides God there is no substance, nor can any be conceived (Prop. 14), that is to say (Def. 3), nothing which is in itself and is conceived through itself. But modes (Def. 5) can neither be nor be conceived without substance; therefore in the divine nature only can they be, and through it alone can they be conceived. But besides substances and modes nothing is assumed (Ax. 1). Therefore nothing can be or be conceived without God. —Q.E.D.

Schol.—There are those who imagine God to be like a man, composed of body and soul and subject to passions; but it is clear enough from what has already been demonstrated how far off men who believe this are from the true knowledge of God. But these I dismiss, for all men who have in any way looked into the divine nature deny that God is corporeal. That He cannot be so they conclusively prove by showing that by "body" we understand a certain quantity possessing length, breadth, and depth, limited by some fixed form; and that to attribute these to God, a being absolutely infinite, is the greatest absurdity. But yet at the same time, from other arguments by which they endeavour to confirm their proof, they clearly show that they remove altogether from the divine nature substance itself corporeal or extended, affirming that it was created by God. By what divine power, however, it could have been created they are altogether ignorant, so that it is clear they do not understand what they themselves say. But I have demonstrated, at least in my own opinion, with sufficient clearness (see Corol. Prop. 6 and Schol. 2, Prop. 8), that no substance can be produced or created by another being (*ab alio*). Moreover (Prop. 14), we have shown that besides God no substance can be nor can be conceived; and hence we have concluded that extended substance is one of the infinite attributes of God. But for the sake of a fuller explanation, I will refute my adversaries' arguments, which, taken altogether, come to this. First, that corporeal substance, in so far as it is substance, consists, as they suppose, of parts, and therefore they deny that it can be infinite, and consequently that it can pertain to God. This they illustrate by many examples, one or two of which I will adduce. If corporeal substance, they say, be infinite, let us conceive it to be divided into two parts; each part, therefore, will be either finite or infinite. If each part be finite, then the infinite is composed of two finite parts, which is absurd. If each part be infinite, there is then an infinite twice as great as another infinite, which is also absurd. Again, if infinite quantity be measured by equal parts of a foot each, it must contain an infinite number of such parts, and similarly if it be measured by equal parts of an inch each; and therefore one infinite number will be twelve times greater than another infinite number. Lastly, if from one point of any infinite quantity it be imagined that two lines, AB, AC, which at first are at a certain

and determinate distance from one another, be infinitely extended, it is plain that the distance between B and C will be continually increased, and at length from being determinate will be indeterminable. Since therefore these absurdities follow, as they think, from supposing quantity to be infinite, they conclude that corporeal substance must be finite, and consequently cannot pertain to the essence of God. A second argument is assumed from the absolute perfection of God. For God, they say, since He is a being absolutely perfect, cannot suffer; but corporeal substance, since it is divisible, can suffer: it follows, therefore, that it does not pertain to God's essence. These are the arguments which I find in authors, by which they endeavour to show that corporeal substance is unworthy of the divine nature, and cannot pertain to it. But any one who will properly attend will discover that I have already answered these arguments, since the sole foundation of them is the supposition that bodily substance consists of parts, a supposition which (Prop. 12 and Corol. Prop. 13) I have shown to be absurd. Moreover, if any one will rightly consider the matter, he will see that all these absurdities (supposing that they are all absurdities, a point which I will now take for granted), from which these authors attempt to draw the conclusion that substance extended is finite, do not by any means follow from the supposition that quantity is infinite, but from the supposition that infinite quantity is measurable, and that it is made up of finite parts. Therefore, from the absurdities to which this leads nothing can be concluded, excepting that infinite quantity is not measurable, and that it cannot be composed of finite parts. But this is what we have already demonstrated (Prop. 12, &c.), and the shaft therefore which is aimed at us turns against those who cast it. If, therefore, from these absurdities any one should attempt to conclude that substance extended must be finite, he would, forsooth, be in the position of the man who supposes a circle to have the properties of a square, and then concludes that it has no centre, such that all the lines drawn from it to the circumference are equal. For corporeal substance, which cannot be conceived except as infinite, one and indivisible (Props. 8, 5, and 12), is conceived by those against whom I argue to be composed of finite parts, and to be multiplex and divisible, in order that they may prove it finite. Just in the same way others, after they have imagined a line to consist of points, know how to discover many arguments, by which they show that a line cannot be divided *ad infinitum ;* and indeed it is not less absurd to suppose that corporeal substance is composed of bodies or parts than to suppose that a body is composed of surfaces, surfaces of lines, and that lines, finally, are composed of points. Every one who knows that clear reason is infallible ought to admit this, and especially those who deny that a vacuum can exist. For if corporeal substance could be so divided that its parts could be really distinct, why could not one part be annihilated, the rest remaining, as before, connected with one another ? And why must all be so fitted together that there can be no vacuum ? For of things which are really distinct the one from the other, one can be and remain in its own position without the other. Since, therefore, it is supposed that there is no vacuum in nature (about which I will speak at another time), but that all the parts must be united, so that no vacuum can exist, it follows that they cannot be really separated; that is to say, that corporeal substance, in so far as it is substance, cannot be divided. If, nevertheless, any one should now ask why there is a natural tendency to consider quantity as capable of division, I reply that quantity is conceived by us in two ways : either abstractly or superficially ; that is to say, as we imagine it, or else as substance, in which way it is conceived by the intellect alone. If, therefore, we regard quantity (as we do very often and easily) as it exists in the imagination, we find it to be finite, divisible, and composed of parts; but if we regard it as it exists in the intellect, and conceive it in so far as it is substance, which is very difficult, then, as we have already sufficiently demonstrated, we find it to be infinite, one, and indivisible. This will be plain enough to all who know how to distinguish between the imagination and the intellect, and more especially if we remember that matter is everywhere the same, and that, except in so far as we regard it as affected in different ways, parts are not distinguished in it; that is to say, they are dis-

B

tinguished with regard to mode, but not with regard to
reality. For example, we conceive water as being
divided, in so far as it is water, and that its parts are
separated from one another; but in so far as it is
corporeal substance we cannot thus conceive it, for as
such it is neither separated nor divided. Moreover, water,
in so far as it is water, is originated and destroyed; but
in so far as it is substance, it is neither originated nor
destroyed. By this reasoning I think that I have also
answered the second argument, since that too is based
upon the assumption that matter, considered as substance, is divisible and composed of parts. And even if
what I have urged were not true, I do not know why
matter should be unworthy of the divine nature, since
(Prop. 14) outside God no substance can exist from which
the divine nature could suffer. All things, I say, are in
God, and everything which takes place takes place by the
laws alone of the infinite nature of God, and follows (as I
shall presently show) from the necessity of His essence.
Therefore in no way whatever can it be asserted that
God suffers from anything, or that substance extended,
even if it be supposed divisible, is unworthy of the
divine nature, provided only it be allowed that it is eternal
and infinite. But enough on this point for the present.

PROP. XVI.—*From the necessity of the divine nature
infinite numbers of things in infinite ways (that is
to say, all things which can be conceived by the infinite
intellect) must follow.*

Demonst.—This proposition must be plain to every
one who considers that from the given definition of anything a number of properties necessarily following from
it (that is to say, following from the essence of the thing
itself) are inferred by the intellect, and just in proportion
as the definition of the thing expresses a greater reality,
that is to say, just in proportion as the essence of the

thing defined involves a greater reality, will more properties be inferred. But the divine nature possesses absolutely infinite attributes (Def. 6), each one of which expresses infinite essence in its own kind (*in suo genere*), and therefore, from the necessity of the divine nature, infinite numbers of things in infinite ways (that is to say, all things which can be conceived by the infinite intellect) must necessarily follow.—Q.E.D.

Corol. 1.—Hence it follows that God is the efficient cause of all things which can fall under the infinite intellect.

Corol. 2.—It follows, secondly, that God is cause through Himself, and not through that which is contingent (*per accidens*).

Corol. 3.—It follows, thirdly, that God is absolutely the first cause.

PROP. XVII.—*God acts from the laws of His own nature only, and is compelled by no one.*

Demonst.—We have just shown (Prop. 16) that from the necessity, or (which is the same thing) from the laws only of the divine nature, infinite numbers of things absolutely follow ; and we have demonstrated (Prop. 15) that nothing can be, nor can be conceived, without God, but that all things are in God. Therefore, outside Himself, there can be nothing by which He may be determined or compelled to act ; and therefore He acts from the laws of His own nature only, and is compelled by no one.—Q.E.D.

Corol. 1.—Hence it follows, firstly, that there is no cause, either external to God or within Him, which can excite Him to act except the perfection of His own nature.

Corol. 2.—It follows, secondly, that God alone is a free cause ; for God alone exists from the necessity alone of His own nature (Prop. 11, and Corol. 1, Prop. 14), and acts from the necessity alone of His own nature (Prop. 17). Therefore (Def. 7) He alone is a free cause.—Q.E.D.

Schol.—There are some who think that God is a free cause because He can, as they think, bring about that those things which we have said follow from His nature—that is to say, those things which are in His power—should not be, or should not be produced by Him. But this is simply saying that God could bring about that it should not follow from the nature of a triangle that its three angles should be equal to two right angles, or that from a given cause an effect should not follow, which is absurd. But I shall show farther on, without the help of this proposition, that neither intellect nor will pertain to the nature of God.

I know, indeed, that there are many who think themselves able to demonstrate that intellect of the highest order and freedom of will both pertain to the nature of God, for they say that they know nothing more perfect which they can attribute to Him than that which is the chief perfection in ourselves. But although they conceive God as actually possessing the highest intellect, they nevertheless do not believe that He can bring about that all those things should exist which are actually in His intellect, for they think that by such a supposition they would destroy His power. If He had created, they say, all things which are in His intellect, He could have created nothing more, and this, they believe, does not accord with God's omnipotence; so then they prefer to consider God as indifferent to all things, and creating nothing excepting that which He has decreed to create by a certain absolute will. But I think that I have shown with sufficient clearness (Prop. 16) that from the supreme power of God, or from His infinite nature, infinite things in infinite ways, that is to say, all things, have necessarily flowed, or continually follow by the same necessity, in the same way as it follows from the nature of a triangle, from eternity and to eternity, that its three angles are equal to two right angles. The omnipotence of God has therefore been actual from eternity, and in the same actuality will remain to eternity. In this way the omnipotence of God, in my opinion, is far more firmly established. My adversaries, indeed (if I may be permitted to speak plainly), seem to deny the omnipotence of God, inasmuch as they are forced to admit that He has in His mind an infinite number of things which might be created, but which, nevertheless, He will never be able to create, for if He were to create all things which He has in His mind, He would, according to them, exhaust His omnipotence and make Himself imperfect. Therefore, in order to make a perfect God, they are compelled to make Him incapable of doing all those things to which His power extends, and anything more absurd than this, or more opposed to God's omnipotence, I do not think can be imagined. Moreover—to say a word, too, here about the intellect and will which we commonly attribute to God—if intellect and will pertain to His eternal essence, these attributes cannot be understood in the sense in which men generally use them, for the intellect and will which could constitute His essence would have to differ entirely from our intellect and will, and could resemble ours in nothing except in name. There could be no further likeness than that between the celestial constellation of the Dog and the animal which barks. This I will demonstrate as follows. If intellect pertains to the divine nature, it cannot, like our intellect, follow the things which are its object (as many suppose), nor can it be simultaneous in its nature with them, since God is prior to all things in causality (Corol. 1, Prop. 16) ; but, on the contrary, the truth and formal essence of things is what it is, because as such it exists objectively in God's intellect. Therefore the intellect of God, in so far as it is conceived to constitute His essence, is in truth the cause of things, both of their essence and of their existence,—a truth which seems to have been understood by those who have maintained that God's intellect, will, and power are one and the same thing. Since, therefore, God's intellect is the sole cause of things, both of their essence and of their existence (as we have already shown), it must necessarily differ from them with regard both to its essence and existence; for an effect differs from its cause precisely in that which it has from its cause. For example, one man is the cause of the existence but not of the essence of another, for the essence is an eternal truth; and therefore with regard to essence the two men may exactly resemble one another, but with regard to existence they must differ. Consequently if the existence of one should perish, that of the other will not therefore perish; but if the essence of one could be destroyed and become false, the essence of the other would be likewise destroyed. Therefore a thing which is the cause both of the essence and of the existence of any effect must differ from that effect both with regard to its essence and with regard to its existence. But the intellect of God is the cause both of the essence and existence of our intellect; therefore the intellect of God, so far as it is conceived to constitute the divine essence, differs from our intellect both with regard to its essence and its existence, nor can it coincide with our intellect in anything except the name, which is what we essayed to prove. The same demonstration may be applied to the will, as any one may easily see for himself.

PROP. XVIII.—*God is the immanent, and not the transitive[1] cause of all things.*

Demonst.—All things which are, are in God and must be conceived through Him (Prop. 15), and therefore (Corol. 1, Prop. 16) He is the cause of the things which are in Himself. This is the first thing which was to be proved. Moreover, outside God there can be no sub-

[1] *Transiens*, passing over and into from the outside.

stance (Prop. 14), that is to say (Def. 3), outside Him nothing can exist which is in itself. This was the second thing to be proved. God, therefore, is the immanent, but not the transitive cause of all things.—Q.E.D.

PROP. XIX.—*God is eternal, or, in other words, all His attributes are eternal.*

Demonst.—For God (Def. 6) is substance, which (Prop. 11) necessarily exists, that is to say (Prop. 7), a substance to whose nature it pertains to exist, or (which is the same thing) a substance from the definition of which it follows that it exists, and therefore (Def. 8) He is eternal. Again, by the attributes of God is to be understood that which (Def. 4) expresses the essence of the divine substance, that is to say, that which pertains to substance. It is this, I say, which the attributes themselves must involve. But eternity pertains to the nature of substance (Prop. 7). Therefore each of the attributes must involve eternity, and therefore all are eternal.—Q.E.D.

Schol.—This proposition is as clear as possible, too, from the manner in which (Prop. 11) I have demonstrated the existence of God. From that demonstration I say it is plain that the existence of God, like His essence, is an eternal truth. Moreover (Prop. 19 of the " Principles of the Cartesian Philosophy "), I have demonstrated by another method the eternity of God, and there is no need to repeat the demonstration here.

PROP. XX.—*The existence of God and His essence are one and the same thing.*

God (Prop. 19) and all His attributes are eternal, that is to say (Def. 8), each one of His attributes expresses existence. The same attributes of God, therefore, which (Def. 4) manifest the eternal essence of God, at the same time manifest His eternal existence; that is to say, the very same thing which constitutes the essence of

God constitutes at the same time His existence, and therefore His existence and His essence are one and the same
thing.—Q.E.D.

Corol. 1.—Hence it follows, 1. That the existence of
God, like His essence, is an eternal truth.

Corol. 2.—It follows, 2. That God is immutable, or
(which is the same thing) all His attributes are immutable;
for if they were changed as regards their existence, they
must be changed also as regards their essence (Prop. 20);
that is to say (as is self-evident), from being true, they
would become false, which is absurd.

PROP. XXI.—*All things which follow from the absolute
nature of any attribute of God must for ever exist,
and must be infinite; that is to say, through that same
attribute they are eternal and infinite.*

Demonst.—Conceive, if possible (supposing that the
truth of the proposition is denied), that in some attribute
of God something which is finite and has a determinate
existence or duration follows from the absolute nature of
that attribute; for example, an idea of God in thought.[1]
But thought, since it is admitted to be an attribute of God,
is necessarily (Prop. 11) in its nature infinite. But so far
as it has the idea of God it is by supposition finite. But
(Def. 2) it cannot be conceived as finite unless it be determined by thought itself. But it cannot be determined
by thought itself so far as it constitutes the idea of God,
for so far by supposition it is finite. Therefore it must
be determined by thought so far as it does not constitute
the idea of God, but which, nevertheless (Prop. 11), necessarily exists. Thought, therefore, exists which does not
form the idea of God, and therefore from its nature, in
so far as it is absolute thought, the idea of God does not
necessarily follow (for it is conceived as forming and as

[1] Not the idea which man forms of God, but rather one of God's ideas. The original "idea Dei" admits either interpretation when taken without the context.—TR.

not forming the idea of God), which is contrary to the
hypothesis. Therefore, if an idea of God in thought, or
anything else in any attribute of God, follow from the
necessity of the absolute nature of that attribute (for the
demonstration being universal will apply in every case),
that thing must necessarily be infinite, which was the
first thing to be proved.

Again, that which thus follows from the necessity of
the nature of any attribute cannot have a determinate
duration. For, if the truth of this be denied, let it be
supposed that in some attribute of God a thing exists
which follows from the necessity of the nature of the
attribute—for example, an idea of God in thought—and
let it be supposed that at some time it has either not
existed or will not exist. But since thought is supposed
to be an attribute of God, it must exist both necessarily
and unchangeably (Prop. 11, and Corol. 2, Prop. 20).
Therefore, beyond the limits of the duration of the idea
of God (for it is supposed that at some time it has either
not existed or will not exist), thought must exist without the idea of God; but this is contrary to hypothesis,
for the supposition is that thought being given, the idea
of God necessarily follows. Therefore neither an idea
of God in thought, nor anything else which necessarily
follows from the absolute nature of any attribute of God,
can have a determinate duration, but through the same
attribute is eternal; which was the second thing to be
proved. Observe that what we have affirmed here is true
of everything which in any attribute of God necessarily
follows from the absolute nature of God.

PROP. XXII.—*Whatever follows from any attribute of God,
in so far as it is modified by a modification which
through the same attribute exists necessarily and infinitely, must also exist necessarily and infinitely.*

Demonst.—This proposition is demonstrated in the
same manner as the preceding proposition.

PROP. XXIII.—*Every mode which exists necessarily and infinitely must necessarily follow either from the absolute nature of some attribute of God, or from some attribute modified by a modification which exists necessarily and infinitely.*

Demonst.—Mode is that which is in something else through which it must be conceived (Def. 5), that is to say (Prop. 15), it is in God alone and through God alone can be conceived. If a mode, therefore, be conceived to exist necessarily and to be infinite, its necessary existence and infinitude must be concluded from some attribute of God or perceived through it, in so far as it is conceived to express infinitude and necessity of existence, that is to say (Def. 8), eternity, or, in other words (Def. 6 and Prop. 19), in so far as it is considered absolutely. A mode, therefore, which exists necessarily and infinitely must follow from the absolute nature of some attribute of God, either immediately (Prop. 21), or mediately through some modification following from His absolute nature, that is to say (Prop. 22), a modification which necessarily and infinitely exists.—Q.E.D.

PROP. XXIV.—*The essence of things produced by God does not involve existence.*

This is evident from the first Definition; for that thing whose nature (considered, that is to say, in itself) involves existence, is the cause of itself and exists from the necessity of its own nature alone.

Corol.—Hence it follows that God is not only the cause of the commencement of the existence of things, but also of their continuance in existence, or, in other words (to use scholastic phraseology), God is the *causa essendi rerum.* For if we consider the essence of things, whether existing or non-existing, we discover that it neither involves existence nor duration, and therefore the essence of existing things cannot be the cause of their existence nor of their duration, but God only is the cause, to whose nature alone existence pertains (Corol. 1, Prop. 14).

PROP. XXV.—*God is not only the efficient cause of the existence of things, but also of their essence.*

Demonst.—Suppose that God is not the cause of the essence of things; then (Ax. 4) the essence of things can be conceived without God, which (Prop. 15) is absurd. Therefore God is the cause of the essence of things.—Q.E.D.

Schol.—This proposition more clearly follows from Prop. 16. For from this proposition it follows that, from the existence of the divine nature, both the essence of things and their existence must necessarily be concluded, or, in a word, in the same sense in which God is said to be the cause of Himself He must be called the cause of all things. This will appear still more clearly from the following corollary.

Corol.—Individual things are nothing but affections or modes of God's attributes, expressing those attributes in a certain and determinate manner. This is evident from Prop. 15 and Def. 5.

PROP. XXVI.—*A thing which has been determined to any action was necessarily so determined by God, and that which has not been thus determined by God cannot determine itself to action.*

Demonst.—That by which things are said to be determined to any action is necessarily something positive (as is self-evident); and therefore God, from the necessity of His nature, is the efficient cause both of its essence and of its existence (Props. 25 and 16), which was the first thing to be proved. From this also the second part

of the proposition follows most clearly. For if a thing
which has not been determined by God could determine
itself, the first part of the proposition would be false,
and to suppose this possible is an absurdity, as we have
shown.

PROP. XXVII.—*A thing which has been determined by
God to any action cannot render itself indeterminate.*

Demonst.—This proposition is evident from the third
Axiom.

PROP. XXVIII.—*An individual thing, or a thing which
is finite and which has a determinate existence, cannot
exist nor be determined to action unless it be determined to existence and action by another cause which
is also finite and has a determinate existence; and
again, this cause cannot exist nor be determined to
action unless by another cause which is also finite and
determined to existence and action, and so on* ad
infinitum.

Demonst.—Whatever is determined to existence and
action is thus determined by God (Prop. 26 and Corol.
Prop. 24). But that which is finite and which has a determinate existence could not be produced by the absolute
nature of any attribute of God, for whatever follows from
the absolute nature of any attribute of God is infinite
and eternal (Prop. 21). The finite and determinate
must therefore follow from God, or from some attribute
of God, in so far as the latter is considered to be affected
by some mode, for besides substance and modes nothing
exists (Ax. 1, and Defs. 3 and 5), and modes (Corol.
Prop. 25) are nothing but affections of God's attributes.
But the finite and determinate could not follow from
God, or from any one of His attributes, so far as that
attribute is affected with a modification which is eternal

and infinite (Prop. 22). It must, therefore, follow or be determined to existence and action by God, or by some attribute of God, in so far as the attribute is modified by a modification which is finite, and which has a determinate existence. This was the first thing to be proved. Again, this cause or this mode (by the same reasoning by which we have already demonstrated the first part of this proposition) must be determined by another cause, which is also finite, and which has a determinate existence, and this last cause (by the same reasoning) must, in its turn, be determined by another cause, and so on continually (by the same reasoning) *ad infinitum.*

Schol.—Since certain things must have been immediately produced by God, that is to say, those which necessarily follow from His absolute nature ; these primary products being the mediating cause for those things which, nevertheless, without God can neither be nor can be conceived ; it follows, firstly, that of things immediately produced by God He is the proximate cause absolutely, and not in their own kind (*in suo genere*), as we say ; for effects of God can neither be nor be conceived without their cause (Prop. 15, and Corol. Prop. 24).

It follows, secondly, that God cannot be properly called the remote cause of individual things, unless for the sake of distinguishing them from the things which He has immediately produced, or rather which follow from His absolute nature. For by a remote cause we understand that which is in no way joined to its effect. But all things which are, are in God, and so depend upon Him that without Him they can neither be nor be conceived.

PROP. XXIX.—*In nature there is nothing contingent, but all things are determined from the necessity of the divine nature to exist and act in a certain manner.*

Demonst.—Whatever is, is in God (Prop. 15); but God cannot be called a contingent thing, for (Prop. 11) He exists necessarily and not contingently. Moreover, the modes of the divine nature have followed from it necessarily and not contingently (Prop. 16), and that, too, whether it be considered absolutely (Prop. 21), or as determined to action in a certain manner (Prop. 27). But God is the cause of these modes, not only in so far as they simply exist (Corol. Prop. 24), but also (Prop. 26) in so far as they are considered as determined to any action. And if they are not determined by God (by the same proposition), it is an impossibility and not a contingency that they should determine themselves; and, on the other hand (Prop. 27), if they are determined by God, it is an impossibility and not a contingency that they should render themselves indeterminate. Wherefore all things are determined from a necessity of the divine nature, not only to exist, but to exist and act in a certain manner, and there is nothing contingent.—Q.E.D.

Schol.—Before I go any farther, I wish here to explain, or rather to recall to recollection, what we mean by *natura naturans* and what by *natura naturata.*[1] For, from what has gone before, I think it is plain that by *natura naturans* we are to understand that which is in itself and is conceived through itself, or those attributes of substance which express eternal and infinite essence, that is to say (Corol. 1, Prop. 14, and Corol. 2, Prop. 17), God in so far as He is considered as a free cause. But by *natura naturata* I understand everything which follows from the necessity of the nature of God, or of any one of God's attributes, that is to say, all the modes of God's attributes in so far as they are considered as

---

[1] These are two expressions derived from a scholastic philosophy which strove to signify by the same verb the oneness of God and the world, and yet at the same time to mark by a difference of inflexion that there was not absolute identity. —Tr.

things which are in God, and which without God can neither be nor can be conceived.

Prop. XXX.—*The actual intellect,*[1] *whether finite or infinite, must comprehend the attributes of God and the affections of God, and nothing else.*

Demonst.—A true idea must agree with that of which it is the idea (Ax. 6), that is to say (as is self-evident), that which is objectively contained in the intellect must necessarily exist in nature. But in nature (Corol. 1, Prop. 14) only one substance exists, namely, God, and no affections (Prop. 15) excepting those which are in God, and which (by the same proposition) can neither be nor be conceived without God. Therefore the actual intellect, whether finite or infinite, must comprehend the attributes of God and the affections of God, and nothing else.—Q.E.D.

Prop. XXXI.—*The actual intellect, whether it be finite or infinite, together with the will, desire, love, &c., must be referred to the* natura naturata *and not to the* natura naturans.

Demonst.—For by the intellect (as is self-evident) we do not understand absolute thought, but only a certain mode of thought, which mode differs from other modes, such as desire, love, &c., and therefore (Def. 5) must be conceived through absolute thought, that is to say (Prop. 15 and Def. 6), it must be conceived through some attribute of God which expresses the eternal and infinite essence of thought in such a manner that without that attribute it can neither be nor can be conceived. Therefore (Schol. Prop. 29) the actual intellect, &c., must be referred to the *natura naturata,* and not to the *natura naturans,* in the same manner as all other modes of thought.—Q.E.D.

---

[1] Distinguished from potential intellect, Schol. Prop. 31.—Tr.

Schol.—I do not here speak of the *actual* intellect because I admit that any intellect *potentially* exists, but because I wish, in order that there may be no confusion, to speak of nothing excepting of that which we perceive with the utmost clearness, that is to say, the understanding itself, which we perceive as clearly as we perceive anything. For we can understand nothing through the intellect which does not lead to a more perfect knowledge of the understanding.

PROP. XXXII.—*The will cannot be called a free cause, but can only be called necessary.*

Demonst.—The will is only a certain mode of thought, like the intellect, and therefore (Prop. 28) no volition can exist or be determined to action unless it be determined by another cause, and this again by another, and so on *ad infinitum.* And if the will be supposed infinite, it must be determined to existence and action by God, not in so far as He is substance absolutely infinite, but in so far as He possesses an attribute which expresses the infinite and eternal essence of thought (Prop. 23). In whatever way, therefore, the will be conceived, whether as finite or infinite, it requires a cause by which it may be determined to existence and action, and therefore (Def. 7) it cannot be called a free cause, but only necessary or compelled.—Q.E.D.

Corol. 1.—Hence it follows, firstly, that God does not act from freedom of the will.

Corol. 2.—It follows, secondly, that will and intellect are related to the nature of God as motion and rest, and absolutely as all natural things, which (Prop. 29) must be determined by God to existence and action in a certain manner. For the will, like all other things, needs a cause by which it may be determined to existence and action in a certain manner, and although from a given will or intellect infinite things may follow, God cannot on this account be said to act from freedom of will, any more than He can be said to act from freedom of motion and rest by reason of the things which follow from motion and rest (for from motion and rest infinite numbers of things follow). Therefore, will does not appertain to the nature of God more than other natural things, but is related to it as motion and rest and all other things are related to it; these all following, as we have shown, from the necessity of the divine nature, and being determined to existence and action in a certain manner.

PROP. XXXIII.—*Things could have been produced by God in no other manner and in no other order than that in which they have been produced.*

Demonst.—All things have necessarily followed from the given nature of God (Prop. 16), and from the necessity of His nature have been determined to existence and action in a certain manner (Prop. 29). If, therefore, things could have been of another nature, or could have been determined in another manner to action, so that the order of nature would have been different, the nature of God might then be different to that which it now is, and hence (Prop. 11) that different nature would necessarily exist, and there might consequently be two or more Gods, which (Corol. 1, Prop. 14) is absurd. Therefore, things could be produced by God in no other manner and in no other order than that in which they have been produced.—Q.E.D.

Schol. 1.—Since I have thus shown, with greater clearness than that of noonday light, that in things there is absolutely nothing by virtue of which they can be called contingent, I wish now to explain in a few words what is to be understood by *contingent*, but firstly, what is to be understood by *necessary* and *impossible*. A thing is called necessary either in reference to its essence or its cause. For the existence of a thing necessarily follows

c

either from the essence and definition of the thing itself, or from a given efficient cause. In the same way a thing is said to be impossible either because the essence of the thing itself or its definition involves a contradiction, or because no external cause exists determinate to the production of such a thing. But a thing cannot be called contingent unless with reference to a deficiency in our knowledge. For if we do not know that the essence of a thing involves a contradiction, or if we actually know that it involves no contradiction, and nevertheless we can affirm nothing with certainty about its existence because the order of causes is concealed from us, that thing can never appear to us either as necessary or impossible, and therefore we call it either contingent or possible.

Schol. 2.—From what has gone before it clearly follows that things have been produced by God in the highest degree of perfection, since they have necessarily followed from the existence of a most perfect nature. Nor does this doctrine accuse God of any imperfection, but, on the contrary, His perfection has compelled us to affirm it. Indeed, from its contrary would clearly follow, as I have shown above, that God is not absolutely perfect, since, if things had been produced in any other fashion, another nature would have had to be assigned to Him, different from that which the consideration of the most perfect Being compels us to assign to Him. I do not doubt that many will reject this opinion as ridiculous, nor will they care to apply themselves to its consideration, and this from no other reason than that they have been in the habit of assigning to God another liberty widely different from that absolute will which (Def. 7) we have taught. On the other hand, I do not doubt, if they were willing to study the matter and properly to consider the series of our demonstrations, that they would altogether reject this liberty which they now assign to God, not only as of no value, but as a great obstacle to knowledge. Neither is there any need that i should here repeat those things which are said in the scholium to Prop. 17. But for the sake of those who differ from me, I will here show that although it be granted that will pertains to God's essence, it follows nevertheless from His perfection that things could be created in no other mode or order by Him. This it will be easy to show if we first consider that which my opponents themselves admit, that it depends upon the decree and will of God alone that each thing should be what it is, for otherwise God would not be the cause of all things. It is also admitted that all God's decrees were decreed by God Himself from all eternity, for otherwise imperfection and inconstancy would be proved against Him. But since in eternity there is no *when* nor *before* nor *after*, it follows from the perfection of God alone that He neither can decree nor could ever have decreed anything else than that which He has decreed; that is to say, God has not existed before His decrees, and can never exist without them. But it is said that although it be supposed that God had made the nature of things different from that which it is, or that from eternity He had decreed something else about nature and her order, it would not thence follow that any imperfection exists in God. But if this be said, it must at the same time be allowed that God can change His decrees. For if God had decreed something about nature and her order other than that which He has decreed—that is to say, if He had willed and conceived something else about nature—He would necessarily have had an intellect and a will different from those which He now has. And if it be allowed to assign to God another intellect and another will without any change of His essence and of His perfections, what is the reason why He cannot now change His decrees about creation and nevertheless remain equally perfect? For His intellect and will regarding created things and their order remain the same in relationship to His essence and per-

fection in whatever manner His intellect and will are
conceived. Moreover, all the philosophers whom I have
seen admit that there is no such thing as an intellect
existing potentially in God, but only an intellect existing
actually. But since His intellect and His will are not
distinguishable from His essence, as all admit, it follows
from this also that if God had had another intellect actually and another will, His essence would have been necessarily different, and hence, as I showed at the beginning,
if things had been produced by God in a manner different
from that in which they now exist, God's intellect and
will, that is to say, His essence (as has been granted),
must have been different, which is absurd.

Since, therefore, things could have been produced by
God in no other manner or order, this being a truth which
follows from His absolute perfection, there is no sound
reasoning which can persuade us to believe that God was
unwilling to create all things which are in His intellect
with the same perfection as that in which they exist in His
intellect. But we shall be told that there is no perfection
nor imperfection in things, but that that which is in them
by reason of which they are perfect or imperfect and are
said to be good or evil depends upon the will of God alone,
and therefore if God had willed He could have effected
that that which is now perfection should have been the
extreme of imperfection, and *vice versa*. But what else
would this be than openly to affirm that God, who necessarily understands what He wills, is able by His will to
understand things in a manner different from that in which
He understands them, which, as I have just shown, is a
great absurdity? I can therefore turn the argument on
my opponents in this way. All things depend upon the
power of God. In order that things may be differently
constituted, it would be necessary that God's will should
be differently constituted; but God's will cannot be other
than it is, as we have lately most clearly deduced from
His perfection. Things therefore cannot be differently

constituted. I confess that this opinion, which subjects all things to a certain indifferent God's will, and affirms that all things depend upon God's good pleasure, is at a less distance from the truth than the opinion of those who affirm that God does everything for the sake of the Good. For these seem to place something outside of God which is independent of Him, to which He looks while He is at work as to a model, or at which He aims as if at a certain mark. This is indeed nothing else than to subject God to fate, the most absurd thing which can be affirmed of Him whom we have shown to be the first and only free cause of the essence of all things as well as of their existence. Therefore it is not worth while that I should waste time in refuting this absurdity.

PROP. XXXIV.—*The power of God is His essence itself.*

Demonst.—From the necessity alone of the essence of God it follows that God is the cause of Himself (Prop. 11), and (Prop. 16 and its Corol.) the cause of all things. Therefore the power of God, by which He Himself and all things are and act, is His essence itself. —Q.E.D.

PROP. XXXV.—*Whatever we conceive to be in God's power necessarily exists.*

Demonst.—For whatever is in God's power must (Prop. 34) be so comprehended in His essence that it necessarily follows from it, and consequently exists necessarily.—Q.E.D.

PROP. XXXVI.—*Nothing exists from whose nature an effect does not follow.*

Demonst.—Whatever exists expresses the nature or the essence of God in a certain and determinate manner,

(Corol. Prop. 25); that is to say (Prop. 34), whatever exists expresses the power of God, which is the cause of all things, in a certain and determinate manner, and therefore (Prop. 16) some effect must follow from it.

———

APPENDIX.

I have now explained the nature of God and its properties. I have shown that He necessarily exists; that He is one God; that from the necessity alone of His own nature He is and acts; that He is, and in what way He is, the free cause of all things; that all things are in Him, and so depend upon Him that without Him they can neither be nor can be conceived; and, finally, that all things have been predetermined by Him, not indeed from freedom of will or from absolute good pleasure, but from His absolute nature or infinite power.

Moreover, wherever an opportunity was afforded, I have endeavoured to remove prejudices which might hinder the perception of the truth of what I have demonstrated, but because not a few still remain which have been and are now sufficient to prove a very great hindrance to the comprehension of the connection of things in the manner in which I have explained it, I have thought it worth while to call them up to be examined by reason. But all these prejudices which I here undertake to point out depend upon this solely: that it is commonly supposed that all things in nature, like men, work to some end; and indeed it is thought to be certain that God Himself directs all things to some sure end, for it is said that God has made all things for man, and man that he may worship God. This, therefore, I will first investigate by inquiring, firstly, why so many rest in this prejudice, and why all are so naturally inclined to embrace it? I shall then show its falsity, and, finally, the manner in which there have arisen from it pre-

judices concerning *good* and *evil, merit* and *sin, praise*
and *blame, order* and *disorder, beauty* and *deformity,*
and so forth. This, however, is not the place to deduce these things from the nature of the human mind.
It will be sufficient if I here take as an axiom that which
no one ought to dispute, namely, that man is born ignorant of the causes of things, and that he has a desire,
of which he is conscious, to seek that which is profitable
to him. From this it follows, firstly, that he thinks
himself free because he is conscious of his wishes and
appetites, whilst at the same time he is ignorant of
the causes by which he is led to wish and desire, not
dreaming what they are; and, secondly, it follows that
man does everything for an end, namely, for that which
is profitable to him, which is what he seeks. Hence it
happens that he attempts to discover merely the final
causes of that which has happened; and when he has
heard them he is satisfied, because there is no longer
any cause for further uncertainty. But if he cannot hear
from another what these final causes are, nothing remains
but to turn to himself and reflect upon the ends which
usually determine him to the like actions, and thus by
his own mind he necessarily judges that of another.
Moreover, since he discovers, both within and without
himself, a multitude of means which contribute not a
little to the attainment of what is profitable to himself
—for example, the eyes, which are useful for seeing, the
teeth for mastication, plants and animals for nourishment, the sun for giving light, the sea for feeding fish,
&c.—it comes to pass that all natural objects are considered as means for obtaining what is profitable. These
too being evidently discovered and not created by man,
hence he has a cause for believing that some other person exists, who has prepared them for man's use. For
having considered them as means it was impossible to
believe that they had created themselves, and so he
was obliged to infer from the means which he was in

the habit of providing for himself that some ruler or
rulers of nature exist, endowed with human liberty,
who have taken care of all things for him, and have
made all things for his use. Since he never heard anything about the mind of these rulers, he was compelled
to judge of it from his own, and hence he affirmed
that the gods direct everything for his advantage, in
order that he may be bound to them and hold them in
the highest honour. This is the reason why each man
has devised for himself, out of his own brain, a different
mode of worshipping God, so that God might love him
above others, and direct all nature to the service of his
blind cupidity and insatiable avarice.

Thus has this prejudice been turned into a superstition
and has driven deep roots into the mind—a prejudice
which was the reason why every one has so eagerly tried
to discover and explain the final causes of things. The
attempt, however, to show that nature does nothing in
vain (that is to say, nothing which is not profitable to
man), seems to end in showing that nature, the gods,
and man are alike mad.

Do but see, I pray, to what all this has led. Amidst so
much in nature that is beneficial, not a few things must
have been observed which are injurious, such as storms,
earthquakes, diseases, and it was affirmed that these
things happened either because the gods were angry
because of wrongs which had been inflicted on them by
man, or because of sins committed in the method of worshipping them; and although experience daily contradicted
this, and showed by an infinity of examples that both the
beneficial and the injurious were indiscriminately bestowed
on the pious and the impious, the inveterate prejudices
on this point have not therefore been abandoned. For it
was much easier for a man to place these things aside
with others of the use of which he was ignorant, and thus
retain his present and inborn state of ignorance, than to
destroy the whole superstructure and think out a new

one. Hence it was looked upon as indisputable that the judgments of the gods far surpass our comprehension; and this opinion alone would have been sufficient to keep the human race in darkness to all eternity, if mathematics, which does not deal with ends, but with the essences and properties of forms, had not placed before us another rule of truth. In addition to mathematics, other causes also might be assigned, which it is superfluous here to enumerate, tending to make men reflect upon these universal prejudices, and leading them to a true knowledge of things.

I have thus sufficiently explained what I promised in the first place to explain. There will now be no need of many words to show that nature has set no end before herself, and that all final causes are nothing but human fictions. For I believe that this is sufficiently evident both from the foundations and causes of this prejudice, and from Prop. 16 and Corol. Prop. 32, as well as from all those propositions in which I have shown that all things are begotten by a certain eternal necessity of nature and in absolute perfection. Thus much, nevertheless, I will add, that this doctrine concerning an end altogether overturns nature. For that which is in truth the cause it considers as the effect, and *vice versa*. Again, that which is first in nature it puts last; and, finally, that which is supreme and most perfect it makes the most imperfect. For (passing by the first two assertions as self-evident) it is plain from Props. 21, 22, and 23, that that effect is the most perfect which is immediately produced by God, and in proportion as intermediate causes are necessary for the production of a thing is it imperfect. But if things which are immediately produced by God were made in order that He might obtain the end He had in view, then the last things for the sake of which the first exist, must be the most perfect of all. Again, this doctrine does away with God's perfection. For if God works to obtain an end, He necessarily seeks something

of which he stands in need. And although theologians
and metaphysicians distinguish between the end of want
and the end of assimilation (*finem indigentiæ et finem
assimilationis*), they confess that God has done all things
for His own sake, and not for the sake of the things to
be created, because before the creation they can assign
nothing excepting God for the sake of which God could
do anything; and therefore they are necessarily compelled to admit that God stood in need of and desired
those things for which He determined to prepare means.
This is self-evident. Nor is it here to be overlooked that
the adherents of this doctrine, who have found a pleasure
in displaying their ingenuity in assigning the ends of
things, have introduced a new species of argument, not
the *reductio ad impossibile*, but the *reductio ad ignorantiam*,
to prove their position, which shows that it had no other
method of defence left. For, by way of example, if a
stone has fallen from some roof on somebody's head
and killed him, they will demonstrate in this manner
that the stone has fallen in order to kill the man. For
if it did not fall for that purpose by the will of God,
how could so many circumstances concur through chance
(and a number often simultaneously do concur)? You
will answer, perhaps, that the event happened because
the wind blew and the man was passing that way. But,
they will urge, why did the wind blow at that time, and
why did the man pass that way precisely at the same
moment? If you again reply that the wind rose then
because the sea on the preceding day began to be stormy,
the weather hitherto having been calm, and that the
man had been invited by a friend, they will urge again
—because there is no end of questioning—But why
was the sea agitated? why was the man invited at that
time? And so they will not cease from asking the
causes of causes, until at last you fly to the will of God,
the refuge for ignorance.

So, also, when they behold the structure of the human

body, they are amazed; and because they are ignorant
of the causes of such art, they conclude that the body
was made not by mechanical but by a supernatural or
divine art, and has been formed in such a way so that
the one part may not injure the other. Hence it happens
that the man who endeavours to find out the true causes
of miracles, and who desires as a wise man to understand
nature, and not to gape at it like a fool, is generally considered and proclaimed to be a heretic and impious by
those whom the vulgar worship as the interpreters both
of nature and the gods. For these know that if ignorance
be removed, amazed stupidity, the sole ground on which
they rely in arguing or in defending their authority, is
taken away also. But these things I leave and pass on
to that which I determined to do in the third place.

After man has persuaded himself that all things which
exist are made for him, he must in everything adjudge
that to be of the greatest importance which is most useful to him, and he must esteem that to be of surpass-
ing worth by which he is most beneficially affected. In
this way he is compelled to form those notions by which
he explains nature; such, for instance, as *good, evil,
order, confusion, heat, cold, beauty*, and *deformity*, &c.;
and because he supposes himself to be free, notions like
those of *praise* and *blame, sin* and *merit*, have arisen.
These latter I shall hereafter explain when I have treated
of human nature; the former I will here briefly unfold.

It is to be observed that man has given the name
good to everything which leads to health and the worship of God; on the contrary, everything which does
not lead thereto he calls *evil*. But because those who do
not understand nature affirm nothing about things themselves, but only imagine them, and take the imagination
to be understanding, they therefore, ignorant of things
and their nature, firmly believe an *order* to be in things;
for when things are so placed that, if they are represented to us through the senses, we can easily imagine

them, and consequently easily remember them, we call
them well arranged; but if they are not placed so that we
can imagine and remember them, we call them badly
arranged or *confused*. Moreover, since those things are
more especially pleasing to us which we can easily
imagine, men therefore prefer order to confusion, as if
order were something in nature apart from our own
imagination; and they say that God has created everything in order, and in this manner they ignorantly
attribute imagination to God, unless they mean perhaps
that God, out of consideration for the human imagination, has disposed things in the manner in which they
can most easily be imagined. No hesitation either
seems to be caused by the fact that an infinite number
of things are discovered which far surpass our imagination, and very many which confound it through its weakness. But enough of this. The other notions which I
have mentioned are nothing but modes in which the
imagination is affected in different ways, and nevertheless
they are regarded by the ignorant as being specially
attributes of things, because, as we have remarked, men
consider all things as made for themselves, and call the
nature of a thing good, evil, sound, putrid, or corrupt,
just as they are affected by it. For example, if the
motion by which the nerves are affected by means of
objects represented to the eye conduces to well-being,
the objects by which it is caused are called *beautiful*;
while those exciting a contrary motion are called *de-
formed*. Those things, too, which stimulate the senses
through the nostrils are called sweet-smelling or stink-
ing; those which act through the taste are called sweet
or bitter, full-flavoured or insipid; those which act
through the touch, hard or soft, heavy or light; those,
lastly, which act through the ears are said to make a
noise, sound, or harmony, the last having caused men to
lose their senses to such a degree that they have believed
that God even is delighted with it. Indeed, philosophers

may be found who have persuaded themselves that the celestial motions beget a harmony. All these things sufficiently show that every one judges things by the constitution of his brain, or rather accepts the affections of his imagination in the place of things. It is not, therefore, to be wondered at, as we may observe in passing, that all those controversies which we see have arisen amongst men, so that at last scepticism has been the result. For although human bodies agree in many things, they differ in more, and therefore that which to one person is good will appear to another evil, that which to one is well arranged to another is confused, that which pleases one will displease another, and so on in other cases which I pass by both because we cannot notice them at length here, and because they are within the experience of every one. For every one has heard the expressions: So many heads, so many ways of thinking; Every one is satisfied with his own way of thinking; Differences of brains are not less common than differences of taste ;—all which maxims show that men decide upon matters according to the constitution of their brains, and imagine rather than understand things. If men understood things, they would, as mathematics prove, at least be all alike convinced if they were not all alike attracted. We see, therefore, that all those methods by which the common people are in the habit of explaining nature are only different sorts of imaginations, and do not reveal the nature of anything in itself, but only the constitution of the imagination ; and because they have names as if they were entities existing apart from the imagination, I call them entities not of the reason but of the imagination. All argument, therefore, urged against us based upon such notions can be easily refuted. Many people, for instance, are accustomed to argue thus :—If all things have followed from the necessity of the most perfect nature of God, how is it that so many imperfections have arisen in nature—corruption, for instance, of things till they stink ; deformity, exciting disgust ; confusion, evil, crime, &c. ?   But, as I have just observed, all this is easily answered.   For the perfection of things is to be judged by their nature and power alone ; nor are they more or less perfect because they delight or offend the human senses, or because they are beneficial or prejudicial to human nature.   But to those who ask why God has not created all men in such a manner that they might be controlled by the dictates of reason alone, I give but this answer : Because to Him material was not wanting for the creation of everything, from the highest down to the very lowest grade of perfection ; or, to speak more properly, because the laws of His nature were so ample that they sufficed for the production of everything which can be conceived by an infinite intellect, as I have demonstrated in Prop. 16.

These are the prejudices which I undertook to notice here.   If any others of a similar character remain, they can easily be rectified with a little thought by any one.

END OF THE FIRST PART.

ETHIC.

Second Part.

OF THE NATURE AND ORIGIN OF THE MIND.

I PASS on now to explain those things which must necessarily follow from the essence of God or the Being eternal and infinite ; not indeed to explain all these things, for we have demonstrated (Prop. 16, pt. 1) that an infinitude of things must follow in an infinite number of ways, —but to consider those things only which may conduct us as it were by the hand to a knowledge of the human mind and its highest happiness.

DEFINITIONS.

I. By body, I understand a mode which expresses in a certain and determinate manner the essence of God in so far as He is considered as the thing extended. (See Corol. Prop. 25, pt. 1.)

II. I say that to the essence of anything pertains that, which being given, the thing itself is necessarily posited, and being taken away, the thing is necessarily taken ; or, in other words, that, without which the thing can neither be nor be conceived, and which in its turn cannot be nor be conceived without the thing.

III. By idea, I understand a conception of the mind which the mind forms because it is a thinking thing.

Explanation.—I use the word conception rather than perception because the name perception seems to indicate that the mind is passive in its relation to the object. But the word conception seems to express the action of the mind.

IV. By adequate idea, I understand an idea which, in so far as it is considered in itself, without reference to the object, has all the properties or internal signs (*denominationes intrinsecas*) of a true idea.

Explanation.—I say internal, so as to exclude that which is external, the agreement, namely, of the idea with its object.

V. Duration is the indefinite continuation of existence.

Explanation.—I call it indefinite because it cannot be determined by the nature itself of the existing thing nor by the efficient cause, which necessarily posits the existence of the thing but does not take it away.

VI. By reality and perfection I understand the same thing.

VII. By individual things I understand things which are finite and which have a determinate existence; and if a number of individuals so unite in one action that they are all simultaneously the cause of one effect, I consider them all, so far, as a one individual thing.

AXIOMS.

I. The essence of man does not involve necessary existence; that is to say, the existence as well as the non-existence of this or that man may or may not follow from the order of nature.

II. Man thinks.

III. Modes of thought, such as love, desire, or the affections of the mind, by whatever name they may be called, do not exist, unless in the same individual the idea exist of a thing loved, desired, &c. But the idea may exist although no other mode of thinking exist.

IV. We perceive that a certain body is affected in many ways.

V. No individual things are felt or perceived by us excepting bodies and modes of thought.

The postulates will be found after Proposition 13.

PROP. I.—*Thought is an attribute of God, or God is a thinking thing.*

Demonst. — Individual thoughts, or this and that thought, are modes which express the nature of God in a certain and determinate manner (Corol. Prop. 25, pt. 1). God therefore possesses an attribute (Def. 5, pt. 1), the conception of which is involved in all individual thoughts, and through which they are conceived. Thought, therefore, is one of the infinite attributes of God which expresses the eternal and infinite essence of God (Def. 6, pt. 1), or, in other words, God is a thinking thing.—Q.E.D.

Schol.—This proposition is plain from the fact that we can conceive an infinite thinking Being. For the more things a thinking being can think, the more reality or perfection we conceive it to possess, and therefore the being which can think an infinitude of things in infinite ways is necessarily infinite by his power of thinking. Since, therefore, we can conceive an infinite Being by attending to thought alone, thought is necessarily one of the infinite attributes of God (Defs. 4 and 6, pt. 1), which is the proposition we wished to prove.

PROP. II. — *Extension is an attribute of God, or God is an extended thing.*

Demonst.—The demonstration of this proposition is of the same character as that of the last.

PROP. III.—*In God there necessarily exists the idea of His essence, and of all things which necessarily follow from His essence.*

Demonst.—For God (Prop. 1, pt. 2) can think an infinitude of things in infinite ways, or (which is the same thing, by Prop. 16, pt. 1) can form an idea of His essence and of all the things which necessarily follow from it. But everything which is in the power of God

D

is necessary (Prop. 35, pt. 1), and therefore this idea necessarily exists, and (Prop. 15, pt. 1) it cannot exist unless in God.

Schol.—The common people understand by God's power His free will and right over all existing things, which are therefore commonly looked upon as contingent; for they say that God has the power of destroying everything and reducing it to nothing. They very frequently, too, compare God's power with the power of kings. That there is any similarity between the two we have disproved in the first and second Corollaries of Prop. 32, pt. 1, and in Prop. 16, pt. 1, we have shown that God does everything with that necessity with which He understands Himself; that is to say, as it follows from the necessity of the divine nature that God understands Himself (a truth admitted by all), so by the same necessity it follows that God does an infinitude of things in infinite ways. Moreover, in Prop. 34, pt. 1, we have shown that the power of God is nothing but the active essence of God, and therefore it is as impossible for us to conceive that God does not act as that He does not exist. If it pleased me to go farther, I could show besides that the power which the common people ascribe to God is not only a human power (which shows that they look upon God as a man, or as being like a man), but that it also involves weakness. But I do not care to talk so much upon the same subject. Again and again I ask the reader to consider and reconsider what is said upon this subject in the first part, from Prop. 16 to the end. For it is not possible for any one properly to understand the things which I wish to prove unless he takes great care not to confound the power of God with the human power and right of kings.

PROP. IV.—*The idea of God,*[1] *from which infinite numbers of things follow in infinite ways, can be one only.*

Demonst.—The infinite intellect comprehends nothing

---

[1] Or God's idea (*Idea Dei*), see p. 24.—TR.

but the attributes of God and His affections (Prop. 30,
pt. 1). But God is one (Corol. 1, Prop. 14, pt. 1).
Therefore the idea of God, from which infinite numbers of
things follow in infinite ways, can be one only.—Q.E.D.

PROP. V.—*The formal[1] Being of ideas recognises God for
its cause in so far only as He is considered as a
thinking thing, and not in so far as He is manifested
by any other attribute; that is to say, the ideas both
of God's attributes and of individual things do not
recognise as their efficient cause the objects of the ideas
or the things which are perceived, but God Himself in
so far as He is a thinking thing.*

Demonst.—This is plain, from Prop. 3, pt. 2; for we
there demonstrated that God can form an idea of His
own essence, and of all things which necessarily follow
from it, solely because He is a thinking thing, and not
because He is the object of His idea. Therefore the
formal Being of ideas recognises God as its cause in so
far as He is a thinking thing. But the proposition can
be proved in another way. The formal Being of ideas
is a mode of thought (as is self-evident); that is to say,
(Corol. Prop. 25, pt. 1), a mode which expresses in a
certain manner the nature of God in so far as He is a
thinking thing. It is a mode, therefore (Prop. 10,
pt. 1), that involves the conception of no other attribute
of God, and consequently is the effect (Ax. 4, pt. 1) of
no other attribute except that of thought; therefore the
formal Being of ideas, &c.—Q.E.D.

PROP. VI.—*The modes of any attribute have God for a
cause only in so far as He is considered under that
attribute of which they are modes, and not in so far
as He is considered under any other attribute.*

Demonst.—Each attribute is conceived by itself and
without any other (Prop. 10, pt. 1). Therefore the
modes of any attribute involve the conception of that

[1] "Formal" = "objective," as now understood, but it does not necessarily mean materially objective. The "formal Being of ideas" = the mind.—TR.

attribute and of no other, and therefore (Ax. 4, pt. 1) have God for a cause in so far as He is considered under that attribute of which they are modes, and not so far as He is considered under any other attribute.—Q.E.D.

Corol.—Hence it follows that the formal Being of things which are not modes of thought does not follow from the divine nature because of His prior knowledge of these things, but, as we have shown, just as ideas follow from the attribute of thought, in the same manner and with the same necessity the objects of ideas follow and are concluded from their attributes.

PROP. VII.—*The order and connection of ideas is the same as the order and connection of things.*

This is evident from Ax. 4, pt. 1. For the idea of anything caused depends upon a knowledge of the cause of which the thing caused is the effect.

Corol.—Hence it follows that God's power of thinking is equal to His actual power of acting; that is to say, whatever follows *formally* from the infinite nature of God, follows from the idea of God [idea Dei], in the same order and in the same connection *objectively* in God.

Schol.—Before we go any farther, we must here recall to our memory what we have already demonstrated, that everything which can be perceived by the infinite intellect as constituting the essence of substance pertains entirely to the one sole substance only, and consequently that substance thinking and substance extended are one and the same substance, which is now comprehended under this attribute and now under that. Thus, also, a mode of extension and the idea of that mode are one and the same thing expressed in two different ways—a truth which some of the Hebrews appear to have seen as if through a cloud, since they say that God, the intellect of God, and the things which are the objects of that intellect are one and the same thing. For example, the circle existing in nature and the idea that is in God of an existing circle are one and the same thing, which is manifested through different attributes; and, therefore, whether we think of nature under the attribute of extension, or under the attribute of thought, or under any other attribute whatever, we shall discover one and the same order, or one and the same connection of causes; that is to say, in every case the same sequence of things. Nor have I had any other reason for saying that God is the cause of the idea, for example, of the circle in so far only as He is a thinking thing, and of the circle itself in so far as He is an extended thing, but this, that the formal Being of the idea of a circle can only be perceived through another mode of thought, as its proximate cause, and this again must be perceived through another, and so on *ad infinitum.* So that when things are considered as modes of thought, we must explain the order of the whole of nature or the connection of causes by the attribute of thought alone, and when things are considered as modes of extension, the order of the whole of nature must be explained through the attribute of extension alone, and so with other attributes. Therefore God is in truth the cause of things as they are in themselves in so far as He consists of infinite attributes, nor for the present can I explain the matter more clearly.

PROP. VIII.—*The ideas of non-existent individual things or modes are comprehended in the infinite idea of God, in the same way that the formal essences of individual things or modes are contained in the attributes of God.*

Demonst.—This proposition is evident from the preceding proposition, but is to be understood more clearly from the preceding scholium.

Corol.—Hence it follows that when individual things do not exist unless in so far as they are comprehended in the attributes of God, their objective Being or ideas do not exist unless in so far as the infinite idea of God exists; and when individual things are said to exist, not only in so far as they are included in God's attributes, but in so far as they are said to have duration, their ideas involve the existence through which they are said to have duration.

Schol.—If any one desires an instance in order that what I have said may be more fully understood, I cannot give one which will adequately explain what I have been saying, since an exact parallel does not exist: nevertheless, I will endeavour to give as good an illustration as can be found.

The circle, for example, possesses this property, that the rectangles contained by the segments of all straight lines cutting one another in the same circle are equal; therefore in a circle there is contained an infinite number of rectangles equal to one another, but none of them can be said to exist unless in so far as the circle exists, nor can the idea of any one of these rectangles be said to exist unless in so far as it is comprehended in the idea of the circle. Out of this infinite number of rectangles, let two only, E and D, be conceived to exist.

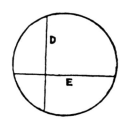 The ideas of these two rectangles do not now exist merely in so far as they are comprehended in the idea of the circle, but because they involve the existence of their rectangles, and it is this which distinguishes them from the other ideas of the other rectangles.

PROP. IX.—*The idea of an individual thing actually existing has God for a cause, not in so far as He is infinite, but in so far as He is considered to be affected by another idea of an individual thing*

actually existing, of which idea also He is the cause in so far as He is affected by a third, and so on ad infinitum.

Demonst.—The idea of any individual thing actually existing is an individual mode of thought, and is distinct from other modes of thought (Corol. and Schol. Prop. 8, pt. 2), and therefore (Prop. 6, pt. 2) has God for a cause in so far only as He is a thinking thing; not indeed as a thinking thing absolutely (Prop. 28, pt. 1), but in so far as He is considered as affected by another mode of thought. Again, He is the cause of this latter mode of thought in so far as He is considered as affected by another, and so on *ad infinitum*. But the order and connection of ideas (Prop. 7, pt. 2) is the same as the order and connection of causes; therefore every individual idea has for its cause another idea, that is to say, God in so far as He is affected by another idea; while of this second idea God is again the cause in the same way, and so on *ad infinitum.*—Q.E.D.

Corol.—A knowledge of everything which happens in the individual object of any idea exists in God in so far only as He possesses the idea of that object.

Demonst.—The idea of everything which happens in the object of any idea exists in God (Prop. 3, pt. 2), not in so far as He is infinite, but in so far as He is considered as affected by another idea of an individual thing (Prop. 9, pt. 2); but (Prop. 7, pt. 2) the order and connection of ideas is the same as the order and connection of things, and therefore the knowledge of that which happens in any individual object will exist in God in so far only as He has the idea of that object.

PROP. X.—*The Being of substance does not pertain to the essence of man, or, in other words, substance does not constitute the form of man.*

Demonst.—The Being of substance involves necessary existence (Prop. 7, pt. 1). If, therefore, the Being of substance pertained to the essence of man, the existence of man would necessarily follow from the existence of substance (Def. 2, pt. 2), and consequently he would necessarily exist, which (Ax. 1, pt. 2) is an absurdity. Therefore the Being of substance does not pertain, &c. —Q.E.D.

Schol.—This proposition may be demonstrated from Prop. 5, pt. 1, which proves that there are not two substances of the same nature. For since it is possible for more men than one to exist, therefore that which constitutes the form of man is not the Being of substance. This proposition is evident also from the other properties of substance; as, for example, that it is by its nature infinite, immutable, indivisible, &c., as any one may easily see.

Corol.—Hence it follows that the essence of man consists of certain modifications of the attributes of God; for the Being of substance does not pertain to the essence of man (Prop. 10, pt. 2). It is therefore something (Prop. 15, pt. 1) which is in God, and which without God can neither be nor be conceived, or (Corol. Prop. 25, pt. 1) an affection or mode which expresses the nature of God in a certain and determinate manner.

Schol.—Every one must admit that without God nothing can be nor be conceived; for every one admits that God is the sole cause both of the essence and of the existence of all things; that is to say, God is not only the cause of things, to use a common expression, *secundum fieri*, but also *secundum esse*. But many people say that that pertains to the essence of a thing without which the thing can neither be nor can be conceived, and they therefore believe either that the nature of God belongs to the essence of created things, or that created things can be or can be conceived without God; or, which is more probable, there is no consistency in their thought. I believe that the cause of this confusion is that they have not observed a proper order of philosophic study. For although the divine nature ought to be studied first, because it is first in the order of knowledge and in the order of things, they think it last; while, on the other hand, those things which are called objects of the senses are believed to stand before everything else. Hence it has come to pass that there was nothing of which men thought less than the divine nature while they have been studying natural objects, and when they afterwards applied themselves to think about God, there was nothing of which they could think less than those prior fictions upon which they had built their knowledge of natural things, for these fictions could in no way help to the knowledge of the divine nature. It is no wonder, therefore, if we find them continually contradicting themselves. But this I pass by. For my only purpose was to give a reason why I did not say that that pertains to the essence of a thing without which the thing can neither be nor can be conceived; and my reason is, that individual things cannot be nor be conceived without God, and yet God does not pertain to their essence. I have rather, therefore, said that the essence of a thing is necessarily that which being given, the thing is posited, and being taken away, the thing is taken away, or that without which the thing can neither be nor be conceived, and which in its turn cannot be nor be conceived without the thing.

PROP. XI.—*The first thing which forms the actual Being of the human mind is nothing else than the idea of an individual thing actually existing.*

Demonst.—The essence of man is formed (Corol. Prop. 10, pt. 2) by certain modes of the attributes of God, that is to say (Ax. 2, pt. 2), modes of thought, the idea of all of them being prior by nature to the modes of thought themselves (Ax. 3, pt. 2); and if this idea exists, other modes (which also have an idea in nature prior to them) must exist in the same individual likewise (Ax. 3, pt. 2). Therefore an idea is the first thing which forms the Being of the human mind. But it is not the idea of a non-existent thing, for then the idea itself (Corol. Prop. 8, pt. 2) could not be said to exist. It will, therefore, be the idea of something actually existing. Neither will it be the idea of an infinite thing, for an infinite thing must always necessarily exist (Props. 21 and 22, pt. 1), and this (Ax. 1, pt. 2) is absurd. Therefore the first thing which forms the actual Being of the human mind is the idea of an individual thing actually existing. —Q.E.D.

Corol.—Hence it follows that the human mind is a part of the infinite intellect of God, and therefore, when we say that the human mind perceives this or that thing, we say nothing else than that God has this or that idea; not indeed in so far as He is infinite, but in so far as He is manifested through the nature of the human mind, or in so far as He forms the essence of the human mind; and when we say that God has this or that idea, not merely in so far as He forms the nature of the human mind, but in so far as He has at the same time with the human mind the idea also of another thing, then we say that the human mind perceives the thing partially or inadequately.

Schol.—At this point many of my readers will no doubt stick fast, and will think of many things which will cause delay; and I therefore beg of them to advance slowly, step by step, with me, and not to pronounce judgment until they shall have read everything which I have to say.

PROP. XII.— *Whatever happens in the object of the idea constituting the human mind must be perceived by the human mind; or, in other words, an idea of that thing will necessarily exist in the human mind. That is to say, if the object of the idea constituting the human mind be a body, nothing can happen in that body which is not perceived by the mind.*

Demonst.—The knowledge of everything which happens in the object of any idea necessarily exists in God (Corol. Prop. 9, pt. 2), in so far as He is considered as affected with the idea of that object; that is to say (Prop 11, pt. 2), in so far as He forms the mind of any being. The knowledge, therefore, necessarily exists in God of everything which happens in the object of the idea constituting the human mind; that is to say, it exists in Him in so far as He forms the nature of the human mind; or, in other words (Corol. Prop. 11, pt. 2), the knowledge of this thing will necessarily be in the mind, or the mind perceives it.—Q.E D.

Schol.—This proposition is plainly deducible and more easily to be understood from Schol. Prop. 7, pt. 2, to which the reader is referred.

PROP. XIII.—*The object of the idea constituting the human mind is a body, or a certain mode of extension actually existing, and nothing else.*

Demonst.—For if the body were not the object of the human mind, the ideas of the affections of the body would not be in God (Corol. Prop. 9, pt. 2) in so far as He has formed our mind, but would be in Him in so far as He has formed the mind of another thing; that is to say (Corol. Prop. 11, pt. 2), the ideas of the affections of the body would not be in our mind. But (Ax. 4, pt. 2) we have ideas of the affections of a body; therefore the object of the idea constituting the human mind is a body, and that too (Prop. 11, pt. 2) actually existing. Again, if there were also any other object of the mind besides a body, since nothing exists from which some effect does not follow (Prop. 36, pt. 1), the idea of some effect produced by this object would necessarily exist in our mind (Prop. 11, pt. 2). But (Ax. 5, pt. 2) there is no such idea, and therefore the object of our mind is a body existing, and nothing else.—Q.E.D.

Corol.—Hence it follows that man is composed of mind and body, and that the human body exists as we perceive it.

Schol.—Hence we see not only that the human mind is united to the body, but also what is to be understood by the union of the mind and body. But no one can understand it adequately or distinctly without knowing adequately beforehand the nature of our body; for those things which we have proved hitherto are altogether general, nor do they refer more to man than to other individuals, all of which are animate, although in different degrees. For of everything there necessarily exists in God an idea of which He is the cause, in the same way as the idea of the human body exists in Him; and therefore everything that we have said of the idea of the human body is necessarily true of the idea of any other thing. We cannot, however, deny that ideas, like objects themselves, differ from one another, and that one is more excellent and contains more reality than another, just as the object of one idea is more excellent and contains more reality than another. Therefore, in order to determine the difference between the human mind and other things and its superiority over them, we must first know, as we have said, the nature of its object, that is to say, the nature of the human body. I am not able to explain it here, nor is such an explanation necessary for what I wish to demonstrate.

Thus much, nevertheless, I will say generally, that in proportion as one body is better adapted than another to do or suffer many things, in the same proportion will the mind at the same time be better adapted to perceive many things, and the more the actions of a body depend upon itself alone, and the less other bodies co-operate with it in action, the better adapted will the mind be for distinctly understanding. We can thus determine the superiority of one mind to another; we can also see the reason why we have only a very confused knowledge of our body, together with many other things which I shall deduce in what follows. For this reason I have thought it worth while more accurately to explain and demonstrate the truths just mentioned, to which end it is necessary for me to say beforehand a few words upon the nature of bodies.

AXIOM 1.—All bodies are either in a state of motion or rest.

AXIOM 2.—Every body moves, sometimes slowly, sometimes quickly.

LEMMA I.—*Bodies are distinguished from one another in respect of motion and rest, quickness and slowness, and not in respect of substance.*

Demonst.—I suppose the first part of this proposition to be self-evident. But it is plain that bodies are not distinguished in respect of substance, both from Prop. 5, pt. 1, and Prop. 8, pt. 1, and still more plainly from what I have said in the scholium to Prop. 15, pt. 1.

LEMMA II.—*All bodies agree in some respects.*

Demonst.—For all bodies agree in this, that they involve the conception of one and the same attribute (Def. 1, pt. 2). They have, moreover, this in common, that they are capable generally of motion and of rest, and of motion at one time quicker and at another slower.

LEMMA III.—*A body in motion or at rest must be determined to motion or rest by another body, which was also determined to motion or rest by another, and that in its turn by another, and so on* ad infinitum.

Demonst.—Bodies (Def. 1, pt. 2) are individual things, which (Lem. 1) are distinguished from one another in respect of motion and rest, and therefore (Prop. 28, pt. 1) each one must necessarily be determined to motion or rest by another individual thing; that is to say (Prop. 6, pt. 1), by another body which (Ax. 1) is also either in motion or at rest. But this body, by the same reasoning, could not be in motion or at rest unless it had been determined to motion or rest by another body, and this again, by the same reasoning, must have been determined by a third, and so on *ad infinitum.*—Q.E.D.

Corol.—Hence it follows that a body in motion will continue in motion until it be determined to a state of rest by another body, and that a body at rest will continue at rest until it be determined to a state of motion by another body. This indeed is self-evident. For if I suppose that a body, A, for example, is at rest, if I pay no regard to other bodies in motion, I can say nothing about the body A except that it is at rest. If it should afterwards happen that the body A should move, its motion could not certainly be a result of its former rest, for from its rest nothing could follow than that the body A should remain at rest. If, on the other hand, A be supposed to be in motion, so long as we regard A alone, the only thing we can affirm about it is that it moves. If it should afterwards happen that A should be at rest, the rest could not certainly be a result of the former motion, for from its motion nothing could follow but that A should move; the rest must therefore be a result of something which was not in A, that is to say, of an external cause by which it was determined to rest.

AXIOM 1.—All the modes by which one body is affected

by another follow from the nature of the body affected, and at the same time from the nature of the affecting body, so that one and the same body may be moved in different ways according to the diversity of the nature of the moving bodies, and, on the other hand, different bodies may be moved in different ways by one and the same body.

AXIOM 2.—When a body in motion strikes against another which is at rest and immovable, it is reflected, in order that it may continue its motion, and the angle of the line of reflected motion with the plane of the body at rest against which it struck will be equal to the angle which the line of the motion of incidence makes with the same plane.

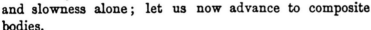

Thus much for simplest bodies which are distinguished from one another by motion and rest, speed and slowness alone; let us now advance to composite bodies.

DEF.—When a number of bodies of the same or of different magnitudes are pressed together by others, so that they lie one upon the other, or if they are in motion with the same or with different degrees of speed, so that they communicate their motion to one another in a certain fixed proportion, these bodies are said to be mutually united, and taken altogether they are said to compose one body or individual, which is distinguished from other bodies by this union of bodies.

AXIOM 3.—Whether it is easy or difficult to force the parts composing an individual to change their situation, and consequently whether it is easy or difficult for the individual to change its shape, depends upon whether the parts of the individual or of the compound body lie with less, or whether they lie with greater surfaces upon one another. Hence bodies whose parts lie upon each other with greater surfaces I will call hard; those soft, whose parts lie on one another with smaller surfaces ; and those fluid, whose parts move amongst each other.

LEMMA IV.—*If a certain number of bodies be separated from the body or individual which is composed of a number of bodies, and if their place be supplied by the same number of other bodies of the same nature, the individual will retain the nature which it had before without any change of form.*

Demonst.—Bodies are not distinguished in respect of substance (Lem. 1) ; but that which makes the form of an individual is the union of bodies (by the preceding definition). This form, however (by hypothesis), is retained, although there may be a continuous change of the bodies. The individual, therefore, will retain its nature, with regard both to substance and to mode, as before.

LEMMA V.—*If the parts composing an individual become greater or less proportionately, so that they preserve towards one another the same kind of motion and rest, the individual will also retain the nature which it had before without any change of form.*

Demonst.—The demonstration is of the same kind as that immediately preceding.

LEMMA VI.—*If any number of bodies composing an individual are compelled to divert into one direction the motion they previously had in another, but are nevertheless able to continue and reciprocally communicate their motions in the same manner as before, the individual will then retain its nature without any change of form.*

Demonst.—This is self-evident, for the individual is supposed to retain everything which, according to the definition, constitutes its form.

LEMMA VII.—*The individual thus composed will, moreover, retain its nature whether it move as a whole or be at rest, or whether it move in this or that direction, provided that each part retain its own motion and communicate it as before to the rest.*

Demonst.—The proof is evident from the definition preceding Lemma 4.

Schol.—We thus see in what manner a composite individual can be affected in many ways and yet retain its nature. Up to this point we have conceived an individual to be composed merely of bodies which are distinguished from one another solely by motion and rest, speed and slowness, that is to say, to be composed of the most simple bodies. If we now consider an individual of another kind, composed of many individuals of diverse natures, we shall discover that it may be affected in many other ways, its nature nevertheless being preserved. For since each of its parts is composed of a number of bodies, each part (by the preceding Lemma), without any change of its nature, can move more slowly or more quickly, and consequently can communicate its motion more quickly or more slowly to the rest. If we now imagine a third kind of individual composed of these of the second kind, we shall discover that it can be affected in many other ways without any change of form. Thus, if we advance *ad infinitum,* we may easily conceive the whole of nature to be one individual, whose parts, that is to say, all bodies, differ in infinite ways without any change of the whole individual. If it had been my object to consider specially the question of a body, I should have had to explain and demonstrate these things more fully. But, as I have already said, I have another end in view, and I have noticed them only because I can easily deduce from them those things which I have proposed to demonstrate.

Postulate 1.—The human body is composed of a

E

number of individuals of diverse nature, each of which is composite to a high degree.

Postulate 2.—Of the individuals of which the human body is composed, some are fluid, some soft, and some hard.

Postulate 3.—The individuals composing the human body, and consequently the human body itself, are affected by external bodies in many ways.

Postulate 4.—The human body needs for its preservation many other bodies by which it is, as it were, continually regenerated.

Postulate 5.—When a fluid part of the human body is determined by an external body, so that it often strikes upon another which is soft, the fluid part changes the plane of the soft part, and leaves upon it, as it were, some traces of the impelling external body.

Postulate 6.—The human body can move and arrange external bodies in many ways.

PROP. XIV.—*The human mind is adapted to the perception of many things, and its aptitude increases in proportion to the number of ways in which its body can be disposed.*

Demonst.—The human body is affected (Post. 3 and 6) in many ways by external bodies, and is so disposed as to affect external bodies in many ways. But the human mind must perceive (Prop. 12, pt. 2) everything which happens in the human body. The human mind is therefore adapted, &c.—Q.E.D.

PROP. XV.—*The idea which constitutes the formal Being of the human mind is not simple, but is composed of a number of ideas.*

Demonst.—The idea which constitutes the formal Being of the human mind is the idea of a body (Prop. 13, pt. 2) which (Post. 1) is composed of a number of individuals composite to a high degree. But an idea of each individual composing the body must necessarily exist in God (Corol. Prop. 8, pt. 2); therefore (Prop. 7, pt. 2) the idea of the human body is composed of these several ideas of the component parts.—Q.E.D.

PROP. XVI.—*The idea of every way in which the human body is affected by external bodies must involve the nature of the human body, and at the same time the nature of the external body.*

Demonst.—All ways in which any body is affected follow at the same time from the nature of the affected body, and from the nature of the affecting body (Ax. 1, following Corol. Lem. 3); therefore the idea of these affections (Ax. 4, pt. 1) necessarily involves the nature of each body, and therefore the idea of each way in which the human body is affected by an external body involves the nature of the human body and of the external body. —Q.E.D.

Corol. 1.—Hence it follows, in the first place, that the human mind perceives the nature of many bodies together with that of its own body.

Corol. 2.—It follows, secondly, that the ideas we have of external bodies indicate the constitution of our own body rather than the nature of external bodies. This I have explained in the Appendix of the First Part by many examples.

PROP. XVII.—*If the human body be affected in a way which involves the nature of any external body, the human mind will contemplate that external body as actually existing or as present, until the human body oe affected by an affect which excludes the existence or presence of the external body.*

Demonst.—This is evident. For so long as the

human body is thus affected, so long will the human mind (Prop. 12, pt. 2) contemplate this affection of the external body, that is to say (Prop. 16, pt. 2), it will have an idea of a mode actually existing which involves the nature of the external body, that is to say, an idea which does not exclude the existence or presence of the nature of the external body, but posits it ; and therefore the mind (Corol. 1, Prop. 16, pt. 2) will contemplate the external body as actually existing, &c.—Q.E.D.

Corol.—The mind is able to contemplate external things by which the human body was once affected as if they were present, although they are not present and do not exist.

Demonst.—When external bodies so determine the fluid parts of the human body that they often strike upon the softer parts, the fluid parts change the plane of the soft parts (Post. 5) ; and thence it happens that the fluid parts are reflected from the new planes in a direction different from that in which they used to be reflected (Ax. 2, following Corol. Lem. 3), and that also afterwards when they strike against these new planes by their own spontaneous motion, they are reflected in the same way as when they were impelled towards those planes by external bodies. Consequently those fluid bodies produce an affection in the human body while they keep up this reflex motion similar to that produced by the presence of an external body. The mind, therefore (Prop. 12, pt. 2), will think as before, that is to say, it will again contemplate the external body as present (Prop. 17, pt. 2). This will happen as often as the fluid parts of the human body strike against those planes by their own spontaneous motion. Therefore, although the external bodies by which the human body was once affected do not exist the mind will perceive them as if they were present so often as this action is repeated in the body.

Schol.—We see, therefore, how it is possible for us to contemplate things which do not exist as if they were actually present. This may indeed be produced by other causes, but I am satisfied with having here shown one cause through which I could explain it, just as if I had explained it through the true cause. I do not think, however, that I am far from the truth, since no postulate which I have assumed contains anything which is not confirmed by an experience that we cannot mistrust after we have proved the existence of the human body as we perceive it (Corol. following Prop. 13, pt. 2). Moreover (Corol. Prop. 17, pt. 2, and Corol. 2, Prop. 16, pt. 2), we clearly see what is the difference between the idea, for example, of Peter, which constitutes the essence of the mind itself of Peter, and the idea of Peter himself which is in another man; for example, in Paul. For the former directly manifests the essence of the body of Peter himself, nor does it involve existence unless so long as Peter exists; the latter, on the other hand, indicates rather the constitution of the body of Paul than the nature of Peter; and therefore so long as Paul's body exists with that constitution, so long will Paul's mind contemplate Peter as present, although he does not exist. But in order that we may retain the customary phraseology, we will give to those affections of the human body, the ideas of which represent to us external bodies as if they were present, the name of *images of things*, although they do not actually reproduce the forms of the things. When the mind contemplates bodies in this way, we will say that it imagines. Here I wish it to be observed, in order that I may begin to show what *error* is, that these imaginations of the mind, regarded by themselves, contain no error, and that the mind is not in error because it imagines, but only in so far as it is considered as wanting in an idea which excludes the existence of those things which it imagines as present. For if the mind, when it imagines non-existent things to be present, could at the same time know that those things did not really exist, it would think its power of imagination to be a virtue of its nature

and not a defect, especially if this faculty of imagining
depended upon its own nature alone, that is to say (Def.
7, pt. 1), if this faculty of the mind were free.

PROP. XVIII.—*If the human body has at any time been
simultaneously affected by two or more bodies, whenever the mind afterwards imagines one of them, it
will also remember the others.*

Demonst.—The mind imagines a body (Corol. Prop.
17, pt. 2) because the human body is affected and disposed by the impressions of an external body, just as
it was affected when certain of its parts received an impulse from the external body itself. But by hypothesis,
the body was at that time disposed in such a manner
that the mind imagined two bodies at once; therefore it
will imagine two at once now, and whenever it imagines
one, it will immediately recollect the other.—Q.E.D.

Schol.—We clearly understand by this what memory
is. It is nothing else than a certain concatenation of
ideas, involving the nature of things which are outside
the human body, a concatenation which corresponds in
the mind to the order and concatenation of the affections of
the human body. I say, firstly, that it is a concatenation
of those ideas only which involve the nature of things
which are outside the human body, and not of those
ideas which explain the nature of those things, for there
are in truth (Prop. 16, pt. 2) ideas of the affections of
the human body, which involve its nature as well as the
nature of external bodies. I say, in the second place, that
this concatenation takes place according to the order
and concatenation of the affections of the human body,
that I may distinguish it from the concatenation of ideas
which takes place according to the order of the intellect,
and enables the mind to perceive things through their
first causes, and is the same in all men. Hence we
can clearly understand how it is that the mind from
the thought of one thing at once turns to the thought

of another thing which is not in any way like the first. For example, from the thought of the word *pomum* a Roman immediately turned to the thought of the fruit, which has no resemblance to the articulate sound *pomum*, nor anything in common with it, excepting this, that the body of that man was often affected by the thing and the sound; that is to say, he often heard the word *pomum* when he saw the fruit. In this manner each person will turn from one thought to another according to the manner in which the habit of each has arranged the images of things in the body. The soldier, for instance, if he sees the footsteps of a horse in the sand, will immediately turn from the thought of a horse to the thought of a horseman, and so to the thought of war. The countryman, on the other hand, from the thought of a horse will turn to the thought of his plough, his field, &c.; and thus each person will turn from one thought to this or that thought, according to the manner in which he has been accustomed to connect and bind together the images of things in his mind.

PROP. XIX.—*The human mind does not know the human body itself, nor does it know that the body exists, except through ideas of affections by which the body is affected.*

Demonst.—The human mind is the idea itself or the knowledge of the human body (Prop. 13, pt. 2). This knowledge (Prop. 9, pt. 2) is in God in so far as He is considered as affected by another idea of an individual thing. But because (Post. 4) the human body needs a number of bodies by which it is, as it were, continually regenerated, and because the order and connection of ideas is the same as the order and connection of causes (Prop. 7, pt. 2), this idea will be in God in so far as He is considered as affected by the ideas of a multitude of individual things.

God, therefore, has the idea of the human body or

knows the human body in so far as He is affected by a multitude of other ideas, and not in so far as He forms the nature of the human mind ; that is to say (Corol. 11, pt. 2), the human mind does not know the human body.   But the ideas of the affections of the body are in God in so far as He forms the nature of the human mind ; that is to say (Prop. 12, pt. 2), the human mind perceives these affections, and consequently (Prop. 16, pt. 2) the human body itself actually existing (Prop. 17, pt. 2).   The human mind, therefore, perceives the human body, &c.—Q.E.D.

PROP. XX.—*There exists in God the idea or knowledge of the human mind, which follows in Him, and is related to Him in the same way as the idea or knowledge of the human body.*

Demonst.—Thought is an attribute of God (Prop. 1, pt. 2), and therefore there must necessarily exist in God an idea of Himself (Prop. 3, pt. 2), together with an idea of all His affections, and consequently (Prop. 11, pt. 2) an idea of the human mind.   Moreover, this idea or knowledge of the mind does not exist in God in so far as He is infinite, but in so far as He is affected by another idea of an individual thing (Prop. 9, pt. 2).   But the order and connection of ideas is the same as the order and connection of causes (Prop. 7, pt. 2).   This idea or knowledge of the mind, therefore, follows in God, and is related to God in the same manner as the idea or knowledge of the body.—Q.E.D.

PROP. XXI.—*This idea of the mind is united to the mind in the same way as the mind itself is united to the body.*

Demonst.—We have shown that the mind is united to the body because the body is the object of the mind (Props. 12 and 13, pt. 2), therefore, by the same reasoning, the idea of the mind must be united with its object, the mind itself, in the same way as the mind itself is united to the body.—Q.E.D.

Schol.—This proposition is to be understood much more clearly from what has been said in the scholium to Prop. 7, pt. 2, for we have there shown that the idea of the body and the body, that is to say (Prop. 13, pt. 2), the mind and the body, are one and the same individual, which at one time is considered under the attribute of thought, and at another under that of extension : the idea of the mind, therefore, and the mind itself are one and the same thing, which is considered under one and the same attribute, that of thought. It follows, I say, that the idea of the mind and the mind itself exist in God from the same necessity and from the same power of thought. For, indeed, the idea of the mind, that is to say, the idea of the idea, is nothing but the form of the idea in so far as this is considered as a mode of thought and without relation to the object, just as a person who knows anything, by that very fact knows that he knows, and knows that he knows that he knows, and so on *ad infinitum.* But more on this subject afterwards.

PROP. XXII.—*The human mind not only perceives the affections of the body, but also the ideas of these affections.*

Demonst.—The ideas of the ideas of affections follow in God and are related to God in the same way as the ideas themselves of affections. This is demonstrated like Prop. 20, pt. 2. But the ideas of the affections of the body are in the human mind (Prop. 12, pt. 2), that is to say, in God (Corol. Prop. 11, pt. 2), in so far as He constitutes the essence of the human mind ; therefore, the ideas of these ideas will be in God in so far as He has the knowledge or idea of the human mind ; that is to say (Prop. 21, pt. 2), they will be in the human mind itself, which, therefore, not only perceives the affections of the body, but also the ideas of these affections.—Q.E.D.

PROP. XXIII.—*The mind does not know itself except in so far as it perceives the ideas of the affections of the body.*

Demonst.—The idea or knowledge of the mind (Prop. 20, pt. 2) follows in God and is related to God in the same way as the idea or knowledge of the body. But since (Prop. 19, pt. 2) the human mind does not know the human body itself, that is to say (Corol. Prop. 11, pt. 2), since the knowledge of the human body is not related to God in so far as He constitutes the nature of the human mind, therefore the knowledge of the mind is not related to God in so far as He constitutes the essence of the human mind; and therefore (Corol. Prop. 11, pt. 2) the human mind so far does not know itself. Moreover, the ideas of the affections by which the body is affected involve the nature of the human body itself (Prop. 16, pt. 2), that is to say (Prop. 13, pt. 2), they agree with the nature of the mind; therefore a knowledge of these ideas will necessarily involve a knowledge of the mind. But (Prop. 22, pt. 2) the knowledge of these ideas is in the human mind itself, and therefore the human mind so far only has a knowledge of itself.—Q.E.D.

PROP. XXIV.—*The human mind does not involve an adequate knowledge of the parts composing the human body.*

Demonst.—The parts composing the human body pertain to the essence of the body itself only in so far as they communicate their motions to one another by some certain method (see Def. following Corol. Lem. 3), and not in so far as they can be considered as individuals without relation to the human body. For the parts of the human body are individuals (Post. 1), composite to a high degree, parts of which (Lem. 4) can be separated from the human body and communicate their motions (Ax. 1, following Lem. 3) to other bodies in another way, although the nature and form of the human body itself is closely preserved. Therefore (Prop. 3, pt. 2) the idea or knowledge of each part will be in God in so far as He is considered as affected (Prop. 9, pt. 2) by another idea of an individual thing, which individual thing is prior to the part itself in the order of nature (Prop. 7, pt. 2). The same thing may be said of each part of the individual itself composing the human body, and therefore the knowledge of each part composing the human body exists in God in so far as He is affected by a number of ideas of things, and not in so far as He has the idea of the human body only; that is to say (Prop. 13, pt. 2), the idea which constitutes the nature of the human mind; and therefore (Corol. Prop. 11, pt. 2) the human mind does not involve an adequate knowledge of the parts composing the human body.— Q.E.D.

PROP. XXV.—*The idea of each affection of the human body does not involve an adequate knowledge of an external body.*

Demonst.—We have shown that the idea of an affection of the human body involves the nature of an external body so far as (Prop. 16, pt. 2) the external body determines the human body in some certain manner. But in so far as the external body is an individual which is not related to the human body, its idea or knowledge is in God (Prop. 9, pt. 2) in so far as He is considered as affected by the idea of another thing, which idea (Prop. 7, pt. 2) is prior by nature to the external body itself. Therefore the adequate knowledge of an external body is not in God in so far as He has the idea of the affection of the human body, or, in other words, the idea of the affection of the human body does not involve an adequate knowledge of an external body.—Q.E.D.

PROP. XXVI.—*The human mind perceives no external body as actually existing, unless through the ideas of the affections of its body.*

Demonst.—If the human body is in no way affected by any external body, then (Prop. 7, pt. 2) the idea of the human body, that is to say (Prop. 13, pt. 2), the human mind, is not affected in any way by the idea of the existence of that body, nor does it in any way perceive the existence of that external body. But in so far as the human body is affected in any way by any external body, so far (Prop. 16, pt. 2, with its Corol.) does it perceive the external body.—Q.E.D.

Corol.—In so far as the human mind imagines an external body, so far it has not an adequate knowledge of it.

Demonst.—When the human mind through the ideas of the affections of its body contemplates external bodies, we say that it then imagines (Schol. Prop. 17, pt. 2), nor can the mind (Prop. 26, pt. 2) in any other way imagine external bodies as actually existing. Therefore (Prop. 25, pt. 2) in so far as the mind imagines external bodies it does not possess an adequate knowledge of them.—Q.E.D.

PROP. XXVII.—*The idea of any affection of the human body does not involve an adequate knowledge of the human body itself.*

Demonst.—Every idea of any affection of the human body involves the nature of the human body in so far as the human body itself is considered as affected in a certain

manner (Prop. 16, pt. 2). But in so far as the human
body is an individual which can be affected in a multitude of other ways, its idea, &c. (See Demonst. Prop.
25, pt. 2.)

PROP. XXVIII.—*The ideas of the affections of the human
body, in so far as they are related only to the human
mind, are not clear and distinct, but confused.*

Demonst.—The ideas of the affections of the human
body involve the nature both of external bodies and
of the human body itself (Prop. 16, pt. 2), and must
involve the nature not only of the human body, but
of its parts, for the affections are ways (Post. 3) in
which the parts of the human body, and consequently
the whole body, is affected. But (Props. 24 and 25, pt.
2) an adequate knowledge of external bodies and of the
parts composing the human body does not exist in God
in so far as He is considered as affected by the human
mind, but in so far as He is affected by other ideas.
These ideas of affections, therefore, in so far as they are
related to the human mind alone, are like conclusions
without premisses, that is to say, as is self-evident, they
are confused ideas.—Q.E.D.

Schol.—The idea which forms the nature of the mind
is demonstrated in the same way not to be clear and
distinct when considered in itself. So also with the
idea of the human mind, and the ideas of the ideas
of the affections of the human body, in so far as they
are related to the mind alone, as every one may easily
see.

PROP. XXIX.—*The idea of the idea of any affection of
the human body does not involve an adequate knowledge of the human mind.*

Demonst.—The idea of an affection of the human body

(Prop. 27, pt. 2) does not involve an adequate knowledge of the body itself, or, in other words, does not adequately express its nature, that is to say (Prop. 13, pt. 2), it does not correspond adequately with the nature of the human mind, and therefore (Ax. 6, pt. 1) the idea of this idea does not adequately express the nature of the human mind, nor involve an adequate knowledge of it.— Q.E.D.

Corol.—From this it is evident that the human mind, when it perceives things in the common order of nature, has no adequate knowledge of itself nor of its own body, nor of external bodies, but only a confused and mutilated knowledge ; for the mind does not know itself unless in so far as it perceives the ideas of the affections of the body (Prop. 23, pt. 2). Moreover (Prop. 19, pt. 2), it does not perceive its body unless through those same ideas of the affections by means of which alone (Prop. 26, pt. 2) it perceives external bodies. Therefore in so far as it possesses these ideas it possesses an adequate knowledge neither of itself (Prop. 29, pt. 2), nor of its body (Prop. 27, pt. 2), nor of external bodies (Prop. 25, pt. 2), but merely (Prop. 28, pt. 2, together with the scholium) a mutilated and confused knowledge.—Q.E.D.

Schol.—I say expressly that the mind has no adequate knowledge of itself, nor of its body, nor of external bodies, but only a confused knowledge, as often as it perceives things in the common order of nature, that is to say, as often as it is determined to the contemplation of this or that *externally*—namely, by a chance coincidence, and not as often as it is determined *internally*—for the reason that it contemplates[1] several things at once, and is determined to understand in what they differ, agree, or oppose one another ; for whenever it is internally disposed in this or in any other way, it then contemplates things clearly and distinctly, as I shall show presently.

[1] In this latter case.—Tr.

PROP. XXX.—*About the duration of our body we can have but a very inadequate knowledge.*

Demonst.—The duration of our body does not depend upon its essence (Ax. 1, pt. 2), nor upon the absolute nature of God (Prop. 21, pt. 1), but (Prop. 28, pt. 1) the body is determined to existence and action by causes which also are determined by others to existence and action in a certain and determinate manner, whilst these, again, are determined by others, and so on *ad infinitum.* The duration, therefore, of our body depends upon the common order of nature and the constitution of things. But an adequate knowledge of the way in which things are constituted, exists in God in so far as He possesses the ideas of all things, and not in so far as He possesses only the idea of the human body (Corol. Prop. 9, pt. 2). Therefore the knowledge of the duration of our body is altogether inadequate in God, in so far as He is only considered as constituting the nature of the human mind, that is to say (Corol. Prop. 11, pt. 2), this knowledge in our mind is altogether inadequate.—Q.E.D.

PROP. XXXI.—*About the duration of individual things which are outside us we can have but a very inadequate knowledge.*

Demonst.—Each individual thing, like the human body, must be determined to existence and action by another individual thing in a certain and determinate manner, and this again by another, and so on *ad infinitum* (Prop. 28, pt. 1). But we have demonstrated in the preceding proposition, from this common property of individual things, that we have but a very inadequate knowledge of the duration of our own body; therefore the same conclusion is to be drawn about the duration of individual things, that is to say, that we can have but a very inadequate knowledge of it.—Q.E.D.

Corol.—Hence it follows that all individual things are contingent and corruptible, for we can have no adequate knowledge concerning their duration (Prop. 31, pt. 2), and this is what is to be understood by us as their contingency and capability of corruption (Schol. 1, Prop. 33, pt. 1); for (Prop. 29, pt. 1) there is no other contingency but this.

PROP. XXXII.—*All ideas, in so far as they are related to God, are true.*

Demonst.—All the ideas which are in God always agree with those things of which they are the ideas (Corol. Prop. 7, pt. 2), and therefore (Ax. 6, pt. 1) they are all true.—Q.E.D.

PROP. XXXIII.—*In ideas there is nothing positive on account of which they are called false.*

Demonst.—If the contrary be asserted, conceive, if it be possible, a positive mode of thought which shall constitute the form or error of falsity. This mode of thought cannot be in God (Prop. 32, pt. 2), but outside God it can neither be nor be conceived (Prop. 15, pt. 1), and therefore in ideas there is nothing positive on account of which they are called false.—Q.E.D.

PROP. XXXIV.—*Every idea which in us is absolute, that is to say, adequate and perfect, is true.*

Demonst.—When we say that an adequate and perfect idea is in us, we say nothing else than (Corol. Prop. 11, pt. 2) that an adequate and perfect idea exists in God in so far as He constitutes the essence of the human mind, and consequently (Prop. 32, pt. 2) we say nothing else than that this idea is true.—Q.E.D.

PROP. XXXV.—*Falsity consists in the privation of know-*

ledge, which inadequate, that is to say, mutilated and confused ideas involve.

Demonst.—There is nothing positive in ideas which can constitute a form of falsity (Prop. 33, pt. 2). But falsity cannot consist in absolute privation (for we say that minds and not bodies err and are mistaken); nor can it consist in absolute ignorance, for to be ignorant and to be in error are different. Falsehood, therefore, consists in the privation of knowledge which is involved by inadequate knowledge of things or by inadequate and confused ideas.—Q.E.D.

Schol.—In the scholium of Prop. 17, pt. 2, I have explained how error consists in the privation of knowledge; but for the sake of fuller explanation, I will give an example. For instance, men are deceived because they think themselves free, and the sole reason for thinking so is that they are conscious of their own actions, and ignorant of the causes by which those actions are determined. Their idea of liberty therefore is this—that they know no cause for their own actions; for as to saying that their actions depend upon their will, these are words to which no idea is attached. What the will is, and in what manner it moves the body, every one is ignorant, for those who pretend otherwise, and devise seats and dwelling-places of the soul, usually excite our laughter or disgust. Just in the same manner, when we look at the sun, we imagine his distance from us to be about 200 feet; the error not consisting solely in the imagination, but arising from our not knowing what the true distance is when we imagine, and what are the causes of our imagination. For although we may afterwards know that the sun is more than 600 diameters of the earth distant from us, we still imagine it near us, since we imagine it to be so near, not because we are ignorant of its true distance, but because an affection of our body involves the essence of the sun, in so far as our body itself is affected by it.

F

PROP. XXXVI.—*Inadequate and confused ideas follow by the same necessity as adequate or clear and distinct ideas.*

Demonst.—All ideas are in God (Prop. 15, pt. 1), and in so far as they are related to God are true (Prop. 32, pt. 2) and (Corol. Prop. 7, pt. 2) adequate. No ideas, therefore, are inadequate or confused unless in so far as they are related to the individual mind of some person (see Props. 24 and 28, pt. 2). All ideas, therefore, both adequate and inadequate, follow by the same necessity (Corol. Prop. 6, pt. 2).

PROP. XXXVII.—*That which is common to everything (see Lemma 2), and which is equally in the part and in the whole, forms the essence of no individual thing.*

Demonst.—For if this be denied, let that which is common be conceived, if possible, to constitute the essence of some individual thing,—the essence, for example, of B. Without B, therefore (Def. 2. pt. 2). that which is common can neither be nor be conceived. But this is contrary to the hypothesis. Therefore that which is common does not pertain to the essence of B, nor does it form the essence of any other individual thing.

PROP. XXXVIII—*Those things which are common to everything, and which are equally in the part and in the whole, can only be adequately conceived.*

Demonst.—Let there be something, A, which is common to all bodies, and which is equally in the part of each body and in the whole. I say that A can only be adequately conceived. For the idea of A (Corol. Prop. 7, pt. 2) will necessarily be adequate in God, both in so far as He has the idea of the human body and in so far as

He has the idea of its affections, which (Props. 16, 25, and 27, pt. 2) involve the nature of the human body, and partly also the nature of external bodies ; that is to say (Props. 12 and 13, pt. 2), this idea will necessarily be adequate in God in so far as He constitutes the human mind, or in so far as He has ideas which are in the human mind. The mind, therefore (Corol. Prop. 11, pt. 2), necessarily perceives A adequately, both in so far as it perceives itself or its own or any external body ; nor can A be conceived in any other manner.—Q.E.D.

Corol.—Hence it follows that some ideas or notions exist which are common to all men, for (Lem. 2) all bodies agree in some things, which (Prop. 38, pt. 2) must be adequately, that is to say, clearly and distinctly, perceived by all.

PROP. XXXIX.—*There will exist in the human mind an adequate idea of that which is common and proper to the human body, and to any external bodies by which the human body is generally affected—of that which equally in the part of each of these external bodies and in the whole is common and proper.*

Demonst.—Let A be something which is common and proper to the human body and certain external bodies ; let it exist equally in the human body and in those external bodies, and let it exist equally in the part of each external body and in the whole. An adequate idea of A itself will exist in God (Corol. Prop. 7, pt. 2), both in so far as He has the idea of the human body and in so far as He has the idea of the given external bodies. Let it be supposed that the human body is affected by an external body through that which it has in common with the external body, that is to say, by A. The idea of this affection will involve the property of A (Prop. 16, pt. 2), and therefore (Corol. Prop. 7, pt. 2) the idea of this affection, in so far as it involves the property of A, will exist adequately in God in so far as He is affected by the idea of the human body, that is to say (Prop. 13, pt. 2), in so far as He constitutes the nature of the human mind. Therefore (Corol. Prop. 11, pt. 2) this idea is also adequate in the human mind.—Q.E.D.

Corol.—Hence it follows that the more things the body has in common with other bodies, the more things will the mind be adapted to perceive.

PROP. XL.—*Those ideas are also adequate which follow in the mind from ideas which are adequate in it.*

Demonst.—This is evident. For when we say that an idea follows in the human mind from ideas which are adequate in it, we do but say (Corol. Prop. 11, pt. 2) that in the divine intellect itself an idea exists of which God is the cause, not in so far as He is infinite, nor in so far as He is affected by the ideas of a multitude of individual things, but in so far only as He constitutes the essence of the human mind.

Schol.—I have thus explained the origin of those notions which are called common, and which are the foundations of our reasoning; but of some axioms or notions other causes exist which it would be advantageous to explain by our method, for we should thus be able to distinguish those notions which are more useful than others, and those which are scarcely of any use; those which are common; those which are clear and distinct only to those persons who do not suffer from prejudice; and, finally, those which are ill-founded. Moreover, it would be manifest whence these notions which are called *second*, and consequently the axioms founded upon them, have taken their origin, and other things, too, would be explained which I have thought about these matters at different times. Since, however, I have set apart this subject for another treatise, and because I do not wish to create disgust with excessive prolixity, I have determined to pass by this matter here. But not to omit anything which is necessary for us to know, I will briefly give the causes from which terms called *Transcendental*, such as *Being, Thing, Something*, have taken their origin. These terms have arisen because the human body, inasmuch as it is limited, can form distinctly in itself a certain number only of images at once. (For the explanation of the word *image*, see Schol. Prop. 17, pt. 2.) If this number be exceeded, the images will become confused; and if the number of images which the body is able to form distinctly be greatly exceeded, they will all run one into another. Since this is so, it is clear (Corol. Prop. 17, and Prop. 18, pt. 2) that in proportion to the number of images which can be formed at the same time in the body will be the number of bodies which the human mind can imagine at the same time. If the images in the body, therefore, are all confused, the mind will confusedly imagine all the bodies without distinguishing the one from the other, and will include them all, as it were, under one attribute, that of being or thing. The same confusion may also be caused by lack of uniform force in the images and from other analogous causes, which there is no need to discuss here, the consideration of one cause being sufficient for the purpose we have in view. For it all comes to this, that these terms signify ideas in the highest degree confused. It is in this way that those notions have arisen which are called *Universal*, such as, *Man, Horse, Dog*, &c.; that is to say, so many images of men, for instance, are formed in the human body at once, that they exceed the power of the imagination, not entirely, but to such a degree that the mind has no power to imagine the determinate number of men and the small differences of each, such as colour and size, &c. It will therefore distinctly imagine that only in which all of them agree in so far as the body is affected by them, for by that the body was chiefly affected, that is to say, by each individual, and this it will express by the name *man*, covering thereby an infinite

number of individuals; to imagine a determinate number
of individuals being out of its power. But we must observe that these notions are not formed by all persons in
the same way, but that they vary in each case according
to the thing by which the body is more frequently affected,
and which the mind more easily imagines or recollects.
For example, those who have more frequently looked
with admiration upon the stature of men, by the name
man will understand an animal of erect stature, while
those who have been in the habit of fixing their thoughts
on something else, will form another common image of
men, describing man, for instance, as an animal capable
of laughter, a biped without feathers, a rational animal,
and so on; each person forming universal images of
things according to the temperament of his own body.
It is not therefore to be wondered at that so many controversies have arisen amongst those philosophers who
have endeavoured to explain natural objects by the images
of things alone.

Schol. 2.—From what has been already said, it clearly
appears that we perceive many things and form universal ideas :

1. From individual things, represented by the senses
to us in a mutilated and confused manner, and without
order to the intellect (Corol. Prop. 29, pt. 2). These
perceptions I have therefore been in the habit of calling
knowledge from vague experience.

2. From signs; as, for example, when we hear or read
certain words, we recollect things and form certain ideas
of them similar to them, through which ideas we imagine
things (Schol. Prop. 18, pt. 2). These two ways of
looking at things I shall hereafter call knowledge of the
first kind, opinion or imagination.

3. From our possessing common notions and adequate
ideas of the properties of things (Corol. Prop. 38, Prop.
39, with Corol. and Prop. 40, pt. 2). This I shall call
reason and knowledge of the second kind.

Besides these two kinds of knowledge, there is a third, as I shall hereafter show, which we shall call intuitive science. This kind of knowing advances from an adequate idea of the formal essence of certain attributes of God to the adequate knowledge of the essence of things. All this I will explain by one example. Let there be three numbers given through which it is required to discover a fourth which shall be to the third as the second is to the first. A merchant does not hesitate to multiply the second and third together and divide the product by the first, either because he has not yet forgotten the things which he heard without any demonstration from his schoolmaster, or because he has seen the truth of the rule with the more simple numbers, or because from the 19th Prop. in the 7th book of Euclid he understands the common property of all proportionals.

But with the simplest numbers there is no need of all this. If the numbers 1, 2, 3, for instance, be given, every one can see that the fourth proportional is 6 much more clearly than by any demonstration, because from the ratio in which we see by one intuition that the first stands to the second we conclude the fourth.

PROP. XLI.—*Knowledge of the first kind alone is the cause of falsity; knowledge of the second and third orders is necessarily true.*

Demonst.—To knowledge of the first kind we have said, in the preceding scholium, that all those ideas belong which are inadequate and confused, and, therefore (Prop. 35, pt. 2), this knowledge alone is the cause of falsity. Moreover, to knowledge of the second and third kind we have said that those ideas belong which are adequate, and therefore this knowledge (Prop. 34, pt. 2) is necessarily true.

PROP. XLII.—*It is the knowledge of the second and third.*

and not that of the first kind, which teaches us to distinguish the true from the false.

Demonst.—This proposition is self-evident. For he who knows how to distinguish between the true and the false must have an adequate idea of the true and the false, that is to say (Schol. 2, Prop. 40, pt. 2), he must know the true and the false by the second or third kind of knowledge.

PROP. XLIII.—*He who has a true idea knows at the same time that he has a true idea, nor can he doubt the truth of the thing.*

Demonst.—A true idea in us is that which in God is adequate, in so far as He is manifested by the nature of the human mind (Corol. Prop. 11, pt. 2). Let us suppose, therefore, that there exists in God, in so far as He is manifested by the nature of the human mind, an adequate idea, A. Of this idea there must necessarily exist in God an idea, which is related to Him in the same way as the idea A (Prop. 20, pt. 2, the demonstration of which is universal). But the idea A is supposed to be related to God in so far as He is manifested by the nature of the human mind. The idea of the idea A must therefore be related to God in the same manner, that is to say (Corol. Prop. 11, pt. 2), this adequate idea of the idea A will exist in the mind itself which has the adequate idea A. He therefore who has an adequate idea, that is to say (Prop. 34, pt. 2), he who knows a thing truly, must at the same time have an adequate idea or a true knowledge of his knowledge, that is to say (as is self-evident) he must be certain.—Q.E.D.

Schol.—In the scholium to Prop. 21, pt. 2, I have explained what is the idea of an idea, but it is to be observed that the preceding proposition is evident by itself. For no one who has a true idea is ignorant that a true idea involves the highest certitude; to have a true idea signifying just this, to know a thing perfectly or as well as possible. No one, in fact, can doubt this, unless he supposes an idea to be something dumb, like a picture on a tablet, instead of being a mode of thought, that is to say, intelligence itself. Moreover, I ask who can know that he understands a thing unless he first of all understands that thing? that is to say, who can know that he is certain of anything unless he is first of all certain of that thing? Then, again, what can be clearer or more certain than a true idea as the standard of truth? Just as light reveals both itself and the darkness, so truth is the standard of itself and of the false. I consider what has been said to be a sufficient answer to the objection that if a true idea is distinguished from a false idea only in so far as it is said to agree with that of which it is the idea, the true idea therefore has no reality nor perfection above the false idea (since they are distinguished by an external sign alone), and consequently the man who has true ideas will have no greater reality or perfection than he who has false ideas only. I consider, too, that I have already replied to those who inquire why men have false ideas, and how a man can certainly know that he has ideas which agree with those things of which they are the ideas. For with regard to the difference between a true and a false idea, it is evident from Prop. 35, pt. 2, that the former is related to the latter as being is to non-being. The causes of falsity, too, I have most clearly shown in Props. 19-35, including the scholium to the last. From what has there been said, the nature of the difference between a man who has true ideas and one who has only false ideas is clear. With regard to the last-mentioned point—how a man can know that he has an idea which agrees with that of which it is the idea—I have shown almost more times than enough that he knows it simply because he has an idea which agrees with that of which it is the idea, that is to say, because truth is its own standard. We must remember, besides, that our mind, in so far as it truly perceives things, is a part of the infinite intellect of God (Corol. Prop. 11, pt. 2), and therefore it must be that the clear and distinct ideas of the mind are as true as those of God.

PROP. XLIV.—*It is not of the nature of reason to consider things as contingent but as necessary.*

Demonst.—It is in the nature of reason to perceive things truly (Prop. 41, pt. 2), that is to say (Ax. 6, pt. 1), as they are in themselves, that is to say (Prop. 29, pt. 1), not as contingent but as necessary.—Q.E.D.

Corol. 1.—Hence it follows that it is through the imagination alone that we look upon things as contingent both with reference to the past and the future.

Schol.—How this happens I will explain in a few words. We have shown above (Prop. 17, pt. 2, with Corol.) that unless causes occur preventing the present existence of things, the mind always imagines them present before it, even if they do not exist. Again (Prop. 18, pt. 2), we have shown that if the human body has once been simultaneously affected by two external bodies, whenever the mind afterwards imagines one it will immediately remember the other; that is to say, it will look upon both as present before it, unless causes occur which prevent the present existence of the things. No one doubts, too, that we imagine time because we imagine some bodies to move with a velocity less, or greater than, or equal to that of others. Let us therefore suppose a boy who yesterday, for the first time, in the morning saw Peter, at midday Paul, in the evening Simeon, and to-day in the morning again sees Peter. It is plain from Prop. 18, pt. 2, that as soon as he sees the morning light he will imagine the sun passing through the same part of the sky as on the day preceding; that is to say, he will imagine the whole day, and at the same time Peter will be connected in his imagination with the morning, Paul with midday, and Simeon with the evening. In the morning, therefore, the existence of Paul and Simeon will be imagined in relation to future time, while in the evening, if the boy should see Simeon, he will refer Peter and Paul to the past, since they will be connected with the past in his imagination. This process will be constant in proportion to the regularity with which he sees Peter, Paul, and Simeon in this order. If it should by some means happen that on some other evening, in the place of Simeon, he should see James, on the following morning he will connect in his imagination with the evening at one time Simeon and at another James, but not both together. For he is supposed to have seen one and then the other in the evening, but not both together. His imagination will therefore fluctuate, and he will connect with a future evening first one and then the other ; that is to say, he will consider neither as certain, but both as a contingency in the future.

This fluctuation of the imagination will take place in the same way if the imagination is dealing with things which we contemplate in the same way with reference to past or present time, and consequently we imagine things related to time past, present, or future as contingent.

Corol. 2.—It is of the nature of reason to perceive things under a certain form of eternity.

Demonst.—It is of the nature of reason to consider things as necessary and not as contingent (Prop. 44, pt. 2). This necessity of things it perceives truly (Prop. 41, pt. 2) ; that is to say (Ax. 6, pt. 1), as it is in itself. But (Prop. 16, pt. 1) this necessity of things is the necessity itself of the eternal nature of God. Therefore it is of the nature of reason to consider things under this form of eternity. Moreover, the foundations of reason are notions which explain those things which are common to all (Prop. 38, pt. 2), and these things explain the essence of no individual thing (Prop. 37, pt. 2), and must therefore be conceived without any relation to time, but under a certain form of eternity.—Q.E.D.

PROP. XLV.—*Every idea of any body or actually existing individual thing necessarily involves the eternal and infinite essence of God.*

Demonst.—The idea of an individual thing actually existing necessarily involves both the essence and existence of the thing itself (Corol. Prop. 8, pt. 2). But individual things (Prop. 15, pt. 1) cannot be conceived without God, and since (Prop. 6, pt. 2) God is their cause in so far as He is considered under that attribute of which they are modes, their ideas (Ax. 4, pt. 1) must necessarily involve the conception of that attribute, or, in other words (Def. 6, pt. 1), must involve the eternal and infinite essence of God.—Q.E.D.

Schol.—By existence is to be understood here not duration, that is, existence considered in the abstract, as if it were a certain kind of quantity, but I speak of the nature itself of the existence which is assigned to individual things, because from the eternal necessity of the nature of God infinite numbers of things follow in infinite ways (Prop. 16, pt. 1). I repeat, that I speak of the existence itself of individual things in so far as they are in God. For although each individual thing is determined by another individual thing to existence in a certain way, the force nevertheless by which each thing perseveres in its existence follows from the eternal necessity of the nature of God (see Corol. Prop. 24, pt. 1).

PROP. XLVI.—*The knowledge of the eternal and infinite essence of God which each idea involves is adequate and perfect.*

Demonst.—The demonstration of the preceding proposition is universal, and whether a thing be considered as a part or as a whole, its idea, whether it be of a part or whole, will involve the eternal and infinite essence of God (Prop. 45, pt. 2). Therefore that which gives a knowledge of the eternal and infinite essence of God is common to all, and is equally in the part and in the whole. This knowledge therefore (Prop. 38, pt. 2) will be adequate.—Q.E.D.

PROP. XLVII.—*The human mind possesses an adequate knowledge of the eternal and infinite essence of God.*

Demonst.—The human mind possesses ideas (Prop. 22, pt. 2) by which (Prop. 23, pt. 2) it perceives itself and its own body (Prop. 19, pt. 2), together with (Corol. 1, Prop. 16, and Prop. 17, pt. 2) external bodies, as actually existing. Therefore (Props. 45 and 46, pt. 2) it possesses an adequate knowledge of the eternal and infinite essence of God.—Q.E.D.

Schol.—Hence we see that the infinite essence and the eternity of God are known to all; and since all things are in God and are conceived through Him, it follows that we can deduce from this knowledge many things which we can know adequately, and that we can thus form that third sort of knowledge mentioned in Schol. 2, Prop. 40, pt. 2, of whose excellence and value the Fifth Part will be the place to speak. The reason why we do not possess a knowledge of God as distinct as that which we have of common notions is, that we cannot imagine God as we can bodies; and because we have attached the name God to the images of things which we are in the habit of seeing, an error we can hardly avoid, inasmuch as we are continually affected by external bodies. Many errors, of a truth, consist merely in the application of the wrong names to things. For if a man says that the lines which are drawn from the centre of the circle to the circumference are not equal, he understands by the circle, at all events for the time, something else than mathematicians understand by it. So when men make errors in calculation, the numbers which are in their minds are not those which are upon the paper. As far as their mind is concerned there is no error, although it seems as if there were, because we think that the numbers in their minds are those which are upon the paper. If we did not think so, we should not believe them to be in error. For example, when I lately heard a man complaining that his court had flown into one of his neighbour's fowls, I understood what he meant, and therefore did not imagine him to be in error. This is the source from which so many controversies arise—that men either do not properly explain their own thoughts, or do not properly interpret those of other people; for, in truth, when they most contradict one another, they either think the same things or something different, so that those things which they suppose to be errors and absurdities in another person are not so.

PROP. XLVIII.—*In the mind there is no absolute or free will, but the mind is determined to this or that volition by a cause, which is also determined by another cause, and this again by another, and so on* ad infinitum.

Demonst.—The mind is a certain and determinate mode of thought (Prop. 11, pt. 2), and therefore (Corol. 2, Prop. 17, pt. 1) it cannot be the free cause of its own actions, or have an absolute faculty of willing or not willing, but must be determined to this or that volition (Prop. 28, pt. 1) by a cause which is also determined by another cause, and this again by another, and so on *ad infinitum.*—Q.E.D.

Schol.—In the same manner it is demonstrated that in the mind there exists no absolute faculty of understanding, desiring, loving, &c. These and the like faculties, therefore, are either altogether fictitious, or else are nothing but metaphysical or universal entities, which we are in the habit of forming from individual cases. The intellect and will, therefore, are related to this or that idea or volition as rockiness is related to this or that rock, or as man is related to Peter or Paul. The reason why men imagine themselves to be free we have explained in the Appendix to the First Part. Before, however, I advance any farther, I must observe that by the will I understand a faculty of affirming or denying, but not a desire; a faculty, I say, by which the mind affirms or denies that which is true or false, and not a desire by which the mind seeks a thing or turns away from it. But now that we have demonstrated that these faculties are universal notions which are not distinguishable from the individual notions from which they are formed, we must now inquire whether the volitions themselves are anything more than the ideas of things. We must inquire, I say, whether in the mind there exists any other affirmation or negation than that which the idea involves in so far as it is an idea. For this purpose see the following proposition, together with Def. 3, pt. 2, so that thought may not fall into pictures. For by ideas I do not understand the images which are formed at the back of the eye, or, if you please, in the middle of the brain, but rather the conceptions of thought.

PROP. XLIX.—*In the mind there is no volition or affirmation and negation excepting that which the idea, in so far as it is an idea, involves.*

Demonst.—In the mind there exists (Prop. 48, pt. 2) no absolute faculty of willing or not willing. Only individual volitions exist, that is to say, this and that affirmation and this and that negation. Let us conceive therefore, any individual volition, that is, any mode of thought, by which the mind affirms that the three angles of a triangle are equal to two right angles. This affirmation involves the conception or idea of the triangle, that is to say, without it the affirmation cannot be conceived. For to say that A must involve the conception B, is the same as saying that A cannot be conceived without B. Moreover, without the idea of the triangle this affirmation (Ax. 3, pt. 2) cannot be, and it can therefore neither be nor be conceived without that idea. But this idea of the triangle must involve this same affirmation that its three angles are equal to two right angles. Therefore also, *vice versa*, this idea of the triangle without this affirmation can neither be nor be conceived. Therefore (Def. 2, pt. 2) this affirmation pertains to the essence of the idea of the triangle, nor is it anything else besides this. Whatever too we have said of this volition (since it has been taken arbitrarily) applies to all other volitions, that is to say, they are nothing but ideas.—Q.E.D.

Corol.—The will and the intellect are one and the same.

Demonst.—The will and the intellect are nothing but the individual volitions and ideas themselves (Prop. 48, pt. 2, and its Schol.) But the individual volition and idea (Prop. 49, pt. 2) are one and the same. Therefore the will and the intellect are one and the same.—Q.E.D.

Schol.—I have thus removed what is commonly thought to be the cause of error. It has been proved above that falsity consists solely in the privation which mutilated and confused ideas involve. A false idea, therefore, in so far as it is false, does not involve certitude. Consequently, when we say that a man assents to what is false and does not doubt it, we do not say that he is certain, but merely that he does not doubt, that is to say, that he assents to what is false, because there are no causes sufficient to make his imagination waver (Schol. Prop. 44, pt. 2) Although, therefore, a man may be supposed to adhere to what is false, we shall never on that account say that he is certain. For by certitude we understand something positive (Prop. 43, pt. 2, with the Schol.), and not the privation of doubt; but by the privation of certitude we understand falsity. If the preceding proposition, however, is to be more clearly comprehended, a word or two must be added; it yet remains also that I should answer the objections which may be brought against our doctrine, and finally, in order to remove all scruples, I have thought it worth while to indicate some of its advantages. I say some, as the principal advantages will be better understood when we come to the Fifth Part. I begin, therefore, with the first, and I warn my readers carefully to distinguish between an idea or conception of the mind and the images of things formed by our imagination. Secondly, it is necessary that we should distinguish between ideas and the words by which things are signified. For it is because these three things, images, words, and ideas, are by many people either altogether confounded or not distinguished with sufficient accuracy and care that such ignorance exists about this doctrine of the will, so necessary to be known both for the purposes of speculation and for the wise government of life. Those who think that ideas consist of images, which are formed in us by meeting with external bodies, persuade themselves that those ideas of things of which we can form no similar image are not ideas, but mere fancies constructed by the free power of the will. They look upon ideas, therefore, as dumb pictures on a tablet, and being prepossessed with this prejudice, they do not see that an idea, in so far as it is an idea, involves affirmation or negation. Again, those who confound words with the idea, or with the affirmation itself which the idea involves, think that they can will contrary to their perception, because they affirm or deny something in words alone contrary to their perception. It will be easy for us, however, to divest ourselves of these prejudices if we attend to the nature of thought, which in no way involves the conception of

G

extension, and by doing this we clearly see that an idea, since it is a mode of thought, is not an image of anything, nor does it consist of words. For the essence of words and images is formed of bodily motions alone, which involve in no way whatever the conception of thought.

Let thus much suffice under this head. I pass on now to the objections to which I have already alluded.

The first is, that it is supposed to be certain that the will extends itself more widely than the intellect, and is therefore different from it. The reason why men suppose that the will extends itself more widely than the intellect is because they say they have discovered that they do not need a larger faculty of assent—that is to say, of affirmation—and denial than that which they now have for the purpose of assenting to an infinite number of other things which we do not perceive, but that they do need a greater faculty for understanding them. The will, therefore, is distinguished from the intellect, the latter being finite, the former infinite. The second objection which can be made is that there is nothing which experience seems to teach more clearly than the possibility of suspending our judgment, so as not to assent to the things we perceive; and we are strengthened in this opinion because no one is said to be deceived in so far as he perceives a thing, but only in so far as he assents to it or dissents from it. For example, a man who imagines a winged horse does not therefore admit the existence of a winged horse; that is to say, he is not necessarily deceived, unless he grants at the same time that a winged horse exists. Experience, therefore, seems to show nothing more plainly than that the will or faculty of assent is free, and different from the faculty of the intellect.

Thirdly, it may be objected that one affirmation does not seem to contain more reality than another; that is to say, it does not appear that we need a greater power for affirming a thing to be true which is true than for

affirming a thing to be true which is false. Nevertheless, we observe that one idea contains more reality or
perfection than another, for as some objects are nobler
than others, in the same proportion are their ideas more
perfect. It appears indisputable, therefore, that there
is a difference between the will and the intellect.

Fourthly, it may be objected that if a man does not act
from freedom of the will, what would he do if he were
in a state of equilibrium, like the ass of Buridanus?
Would he not perish from hunger and thirst? and if
this be granted, do we not seem to conceive him as a
statue of a man or as an ass? If I deny that he would
thus perish, he will consequently determine himself and
possess the power of going where he likes and doing
what he likes.

There may be other objections besides these, but as I
am not bound to discuss what every one may dream, I
shall therefore make it my business to answer as briefly
as possible those only which I have mentioned. In
reply to the first objection, I grant that the will extends
itself more widely than the intellect, if by the intellect
we understand only clear and distinct ideas; but I deny
that the will extends itself more widely than the perceptions or the faculty of conception; nor, indeed, do I see
why the faculty of will should be said to be infinite any
more than the faculty of feeling; for as by the same
faculty of will we can affirm an infinite number of things
(one after the other, for we cannot affirm an infinite
number of things at once), so also by the same faculty
of feeling we can feel or perceive (one after another) an
infinite number of bodies. If it be said that there are
an infinite number of things which we cannot perceive,
I reply that such things as these we can reach by no
thought, and consequently by no faculty of will. But it
is said that if God wished us to perceive those things,
it would be necessary for Him to give us a larger
faculty of perception, but not a larger faculty of will than

ETHIC.

He has already given us, which is the same thing as saying that if God wished us to understand an infinite number of other beings, it would be necessary for Him to give us a greater intellect, but not a more universal idea of being (in order to embrace that infinite number of beings), than He has given us. For we have shown that the will is a Universal, or the idea by which we explain all individual volitions, that is to say, that which is common to them all. It is not to be wondered at, therefore, that those who believe this common or universal idea of all the volitions to be a faculty should say that it extends itself infinitely beyond the limits of the intellect. For the universal is predicated of one or of many, or of an infinite number of individuals.

The second objection I answer by denying that we have free power of suspending judgment. For when we say that a person suspends judgment, we only say in other words that he sees that he does not perceive the thing adequately. The suspension of the judgment, therefore, is in truth a perception and not free will. In order that this may be clearly understood, let us take the case of a boy who imagines a horse and perceives nothing else. Since this imagination involves the existence of the horse (Corol. Prop. 17, pt. 2), and the boy does not perceive anything which negates its existence, he will necessarily contemplate it as present, nor will he be able to doubt its existence although he may not be certain of it. This is a thing which we daily experience in dreams, nor do I believe that there is any one who thinks that he has the free power during dreams of suspending his judgment upon those things which he dreams, and of causing himself not to dream those things which he dreams that he sees; and yet in dreams it nevertheless happens that we suspend our judgment, for we dream that we dream.

I grant, it is true, that no man is deceived in so far as he perceives; that is to say, I grant that mental images considered in themselves involve no error (Schol. Prop. 17, pt. 2); but I deny that a man in so far as he perceives affirms nothing. For what else is it to perceive a winged horse than to affirm of the horse that it has wings? For if the mind perceived nothing else but this winged horse, it would regard it as present, nor would it have any reason for doubting its existence, nor any power of refusing assent to it, unless the image of the winged horse be joined to an idea which negates its existence, or the mind perceives that the idea of the winged horse which it has is inadequate. In either of the two latter cases it will necessarily deny or doubt the existence of the horse.

With regard to the third objection, what has been said will perhaps be a sufficient answer,—namely, that the will is something universal, which is predicated of all ideas, and that it signifies that only which is common to them all, that is to say, affirmation. Its adequate essence, therefore, in so far as it is thus considered in the abstract, must be in every idea, and in this sense only must it be the same in all; but not in so far as it is considered as constituting the essence of an idea, for so far, the individual affirmations differ just as the ideas differ. For example, the affirmation which the idea of a circle involves differs from that which the idea of a triangle involves, just as the idea of a circle differs from the idea of a triangle. Again, I absolutely deny that we need a power of thinking in order to affirm that to be true which is true, equal to that which we need in order to affirm that to be true which is false. For these two affirmations, if we look to the mind, are related to one another as being and non-being, for there is nothing positive in ideas which constitutes a form of falsity (Prop. 35, pt. 2, with its Schol., and Schol. to Prop. 47, pt. 2).

Here therefore particularly is it to be observed how easily we are deceived when we confuse universals with individuals, and the entities of reason and abstractions with realities.

With regard to the fourth objection, I say that I entirely grant that if a man were placed in such a state of equilibrium he would perish of hunger and thirst, supposing he perceived nothing but hunger and thirst, and the food and drink which were equidistant from him. If you ask me whether such a man would not be thought an ass rather than a man, I reply that I do not know; nor do I know what ought to be thought of a man who hangs himself, or of children, fools, and madmen.

It remains for me now to show what service to our own lives a knowledge of this doctrine is. This we shall easily understand from the remarks which follow. Notice—

1. It is of service in so far as it teaches us that we do everything by the will of God alone, and that we are partakers of the divine nature in proportion as our actions become more and more perfect and we more and more understand God. This doctrine, therefore, besides giving repose in every way to the soul, has also this advantage, that it teaches us in what our highest happiness or blessedness consists, namely, in the knowledge of God alone, by which we are drawn to do those things only which love and piety persuade. Hence we clearly see how greatly those stray from the true estimation of virtue who expect to be distinguished by God with the highest rewards for virtue and the noblest actions as if for the completest servitude, just as if virtue itself and the service of God were not happiness itself and the highest liberty.

2. It is of service to us in so far as it teaches us how we ought to behave with regard to the things of fortune, or those which are not in our power, that is to say, which do not follow from our own nature; for it teaches us with equal mind to wait for and bear each form of fortune, because we know that all things follow from

the eternal decree of God, according to that same necessity by which it follows from the essence of a triangle that its three angles are equal to two right angles.

3. This doctrine contributes to the welfare of our social existence, since it teaches us to hate no one, to despise no one, to mock no one, to be angry with no one, and to envy no one. It teaches every one, moreover, to be content with his own, and to be helpful to his neighbour, not from any womanish pity, from partiality, or superstition, but by the guidance of reason alone, according to the demand of time and circumstance, as I shall show in the Third Part.

4. This doctrine contributes not a little to the advantage of common society, in so far as it teaches us by what means citizens are to be governed and led; not in order that they may be slaves, but that they may freely do those things which are best.

Thus I have discharged the obligation laid upon me in this scholium, and with it I make an end of the Second Part, in which I think that I have explained the nature of the human mind and its properties at sufficient length, and, considering the difficulties of the subject, with sufficient clearness. I think, too, that certain truths have been established, from which much that is noble, most useful, and necessary to be known can be deduced, as we shall partly see from what follows.

END OF THE SECOND PART.

ETHIC.

—•—

Third Part.

———

ON THE ORIGIN AND NATURE OF THE AFFECTS.

MOST persons who have written about the affects and man's conduct of life seem to discuss, not the natural things which follow the common laws of nature, but things which are outside her. They seem indeed to consider man in nature as a kingdom within a kingdom. For they believe that man disturbs rather than follows her order; that he has an absolute power over his own actions; and that he is altogether self-determined. They then proceed to attribute the cause of human weakness and changeableness, not to the common power of nature, but to some vice of human nature, which they therefore bewail, laugh at, mock, or, as is more generally the case, detest; whilst he who knows how to revile most eloquently or subtilly the weakness of the mind is looked upon as divine. It is true that very eminent men have not been wanting, to whose labour and industry we confess ourselves much indebted, who have written many excellent things about the right conduct of life, and who have given to mortals counsels full of prudence, but no one so far as I know has determined the nature and strength of the affects, and what the mind is able to do towards controlling them. I remember, indeed, that the celebrated Descartes, although he believed that the mind is absolute master over its own actions, tried nevertheless to explain by their first causes human affects, and at the same time to show the way by which the mind could obtain absolute power over them; but in my opinion he has shown nothing but the acuteness of his great intellect, as I shall make evident in the proper place, for I wish to return to those who prefer to detest and scoff at human affects and actions than understand them. To such as these it will doubtless seem a marvellous thing for me to endeavour to treat by a geometrical method the vices and follies of men, and to desire by a sure method to demonstrate those things which these people cry out against as being opposed to reason, or as being vanities, absurdities, and monstrosities. The following is my reason for so doing. Nothing happens in nature which can be attributed to any vice of nature, for she is always the same and everywhere one. Her virtue is the same, and her power of acting; that is to say, her laws and rules, according to which all things are and are changed from form to form, are everywhere and always the same; so that there must also be one and the same method of understanding the nature of all things whatsoever, that is to say, by the universal laws and rules of nature. The affects, therefore, of hatred, anger, envy, considered in themselves, follow from the same necessity and virtue of nature as other individual things; they have therefore certain causes through which they are to be understood, and certain properties which are just as worthy of being known as the properties of any other thing in the contemplation alone of which we delight. I shall, therefore, pursue the same method in considering the nature and strength of the affects and the power of the mind over them which I pursued in our previous discussion of God and the mind, and I shall consider human actions and appetites just as if I were considering lines, planes, or bodies.

Def. I.—I call that an adequate cause whose effect can be clearly and distinctly perceived by means of the cause. I call that an inadequate or partial cause whose effect cannot be understood by means of the cause alone.

Def. II.—I say that we act when anything is done, either within us or without us, of which we are the adequate cause, that is to say (by the preceding Def.), when from our nature anything follows, either within us or without us, which by that nature alone can be clearly and distinctly understood. On the other hand, I say that we suffer when anything is done within us, or when anything follows from our nature, of which we are not the cause excepting partially.

Def. III.—By affect I understand the affections of the body, by which the power of acting of the body itself is increased, diminished, helped, or hindered, together with the ideas of these affections.

If, therefore, we can be the adequate cause of any of these affections, I understand the affect to be an action, otherwise it is a passion.

Postulate 1.—The human body can be affected in many ways by which its power of acting is increased or diminished, and also in other ways which make its power of acting neither greater nor less.

This postulate or axiom is based upon Post. 1 and Lems. 5 and 7, following Prop. 13, pt. 2.

Postulate 2.—The human body is capable of suffering many changes, and, nevertheless, can retain the impressions or traces of objects (Post 5, pt. 2), and consequently the same images of things. (For the definition of images see Schol. Prop. 17, pt. 2.)

Prop. I.—*Our mind acts at times and at times suffers : in so far as it has adequate ideas, it necessarily acts ; and in so far as it has inadequate ideas, it necessarily suffers.*

Demonst.—In every human mind some ideas are

adequate, and others mutilated and confused (SchoL Prop. 40, pt. 2). But the ideas which in any mind are adequate are adequate in God in so far as He forms the essence of that mind (Corol. Prop. 11, pt. 2), while those again which are inadequate in the mind are also adequate in God (by the same Corol.), not in so far as He contains the essence of that mind only, but in so far as He contains the ideas[1] of other things at the same time in Himself. Again, from any given idea some effect must necessarily follow (Prop. 36, pt. 1), of which God is the adequate cause (Def. 1, pt. 3), not in so far as He is infinite, but in so far as He is considered as affected with the given idea (Prop. 9, pt. 2). But of that effect of which God is the cause, in so far as He is affected by an idea which is adequate in any mind, that same mind is the adequate cause (Corol. Prop. 11, pt. 2). Our mind, therefore (Def. 2, pt. 3), in so far as it has adequate ideas, necessarily at times acts, which is the first thing we had to prove. Again, if there be anything which necessarily follows from an idea which is adequate in God, not in so far as He contains within Himself the mind of one man only, but also, together with this, the ideas[1] of other things, then the mind of that man (Corol. Prop. 11, pt. 2) is not the adequate cause of that thing, but is only its partial cause, and therefore (Def. 2, pt. 3), in so far as the mind has inadequate ideas, it necessarily at times suffers. This was the second thing to be proved. Therefore our mind, &c.—Q.E.D.

Corol.—Hence it follows that the mind is subject to passions in proportion to the number of inadequate ideas which it has, and that it acts in proportion to the number of adequate ideas which it has.

---

[1] "Mentes," both in Paulus, Bruder. and Van Vloten and Land, but obviously a mistake for "ideas," as a reference to Corol. Prop. 11, pt. 2, will show. Kirchmann's translation omits "mentes" in the first passage marked, and renders, "insofern er andere Dinge in sich enthält."

PROP. II.—*The body cannot determine the mind to thought, neither can the mind determine the body to motion nor rest, nor to anything else, if there be anything else.*

Demonst.—All modes of thought have God for a cause in so far as He is a thinking thing, and not in so far as He is manifested by any other attribute (Prop. 6, pt. 2). That which determines the mind to thought, therefore, is a mode of thought and not of extension, that is to say (Def. 1, pt. 2), it is not the body. This is the first thing which was to be proved. Again, the motion and rest of the body must be derived from some other body, which has also been determined to motion or rest by another, and, absolutely, whatever arises in the body must arise from God, in so far as He is considered as affected by some mode of extension, and not in so far as He is considered as affected by any mode of thought (Prop. 6, pt. 2), that is to say, whatever arises in the body cannot arise from the mind, which is a mode of thought (Prop. 11, pt. 2). This is the second thing which was to be proved. Therefore, the body cannot determine, &c.—Q.E.D.

Schol.—This proposition will be better understood from what has been said in the scholium of Prop. 7, pt. 2, that is to say, that the mind and the body are one and the same thing, conceived at one time under the attribute of thought, and at another under that of extension. For this reason, the order or concatenation of things is one, whether nature be conceived under this or under that attribute, and consequently the order of the actions and passions of our body is coincident in nature with the order of the actions and passions of the mind. This is also plain from the manner in which we have demonstrated Prop. 12, pt. 2.

Although these things are so, and no ground for doubting remains, I scarcely believe, nevertheless, that, without a proof derived from experience, men will be induced calmly

to weigh what has been said, so firmly are they persuaded that, solely at the bidding of the mind, the body
moves or rests, and does a number of things which
depend upon the will of the mind alone, and upon the
power of thought. For what the body can do no one has
hitherto determined, that is to say, experience has taught
no one hitherto what the body, without being determined
by the mind, can do and what it cannot do from the laws
of nature alone, in so far as nature is considered merely
as corporeal. For no one as yet has understood the
structure of the body so accurately as to be able to explain
all its functions, not to mention the fact that many things
are observed in brutes which far surpass human sagacity,
and that sleep-walkers in their sleep do very many things
which they dare not do when awake; all this showing
that the body itself can do many things from the laws of
its own nature alone at which the mind belonging to
that body is amazed. Again, nobody knows by what
means or by what method the mind moves the body,
nor how many degrees of motion it can communicate to
the body, nor with what speed it can move the body.
So that it follows that when men say that this or that
action of the body springs from the mind which has command over the body, they do not know what they say,
and they do nothing but confess with pretentious words
that they know nothing about the cause of the action,
and see nothing in it to wonder at. But they will say,
that whether they know or do not know by what means
the mind moves the body, it is nevertheless in their experience that if the mind were not fit for thinking the
body would be inert. They say, again, it is in their experience that the mind alone has power both to speak
and be silent, and to do many other things which they
therefore think to be dependent on a decree of the
mind. But with regard to the first assertion, I ask them
if experience does not also teach that if the body be
sluggish the mind at the same time is not fit for

thinking ? When the body is asleep, the mind slumbers with it, and has not the power to think, as it has when the body is awake. Again, I believe that all have discovered that the mind is not always equally fitted for thinking about the same subject, but in proportion to the fitness of the body for this or that image to be excited in it will the mind be better fitted to contemplate this or that object. But my opponents will say, that from the laws of nature alone, in so far as it is considered to be corporeal merely, it cannot be that the causes of architecture, painting, and things of this sort, which are the results of human art alone, could be deduced, and that the human body, unless it were determined and guided by the mind, would not be able to build a temple. I have already shown, however, that they do not know what the body can do, nor what can be deduced from the consideration of its nature alone, and that they find that many things are done merely by the laws of nature which they would never have believed to be possible without the direction of the mind, as, for example, those things which sleep-walkers do in their sleep, and at which they themselves are astonished when they wake. I adduce also here the structure itself of the human body, which so greatly surpasses in workmanship all those things which are constructed by human art, not to mention what I have already proved, that an infinitude of things follows from nature under whatever attribute it may be considered.

With regard to the second point, I should say that human affairs would be much more happily conducted if it were equally in the power of men to be silent and to speak; but experience shows over and over again that there is nothing which men have less power over than the tongue, and that there is nothing which they are less able to do than to govern their appetites, so that many persons believe that we do those things only with freedom which we seek indifferently; as the desire for such things can easily be lessened by the recollection of another thing which we frequently call to mind; it being impossible, on the other hand, to do those things with freedom which we seek with such ardour that the recollection of another thing is unable to mitigate it. But if, however, we had not found out that we do many things which we afterwards repent, and that when agitated by conflicting affects we see that which is better and follow that which is worse, nothing would hinder us from believing that we do everything with freedom. Thus the infant believes that it is by free will that it seeks the breast; the angry boy believes that by free will he wishes vengeance; the timid man thinks it is with free will he seeks flight; the drunkard believes that by a free command of his mind he speaks the things which when sober he wishes he had left unsaid. Thus the madman, the chatterer, the boy, and others of the same kind, all believe that they speak by a free command of the mind, whilst, in truth, they have no power to restrain the impulse which they have to speak, so that experience itself, no less than reason, clearly teaches that men believe themselves to be free simply because they are conscious of their own actions, knowing nothing of the causes by which they are determined: it teaches, too, that the decrees of the mind are nothing but the appetites themselves, which differ, therefore, according to the different temper of the body. For every man determines all things from his affect; those who are agitated by contrary affects do not know what they want, whilst those who are agitated by no affect are easily driven hither and thither. All this plainly shows that the decree of the mind, the appetite, and determination of the body are coincident in nature, or rather that they are one and the same thing, which, when it is considered under the attribute of thought and manifested by that, is called a decree, and when it is considered under the attribute of extension and is deduced from the laws of motion and rest, is called a determination. This, however, will be better understood as we go on, for there is another thing which I wish to be observed here—that we cannot by a mental decree do a thing unless we recollect it. We cannot speak a word, for instance, unless we recollect it. But it is not in the free power of the mind either to recollect a thing or to forget it. It is believed, therefore, that the power of the mind extends only thus far—that from a mental decree we can speak or be silent about a thing only when we recollect it. But when we dream that we speak, we believe that we do so from a free decree of the mind; and yet we do not speak, or, if we do, it is the result of a spontaneous motion of the body. We dream, again, that we are concealing things, and that we do this by virtue of a decree of the mind like that by which, when awake, we are silent about things we know. We dream, again, that, from a decree of the mind, we do some things which we should not dare to do when awake. And I should like to know, therefore, whether there are two kinds of decrees in the mind—one belonging to dreams and the other free. If this be too great nonsense, we must necessarily grant that this decree of the mind, which is believed to be free, is not distinguishable from the imagination or memory, and is nothing but the affirmation which the idea necessarily involves in so far as it is an idea (Prop. 49, pt. 2). These decrees of the mind, therefore, arise in the mind by the same necessity as the ideas of things actually existing. Consequently, those who believe that they speak, or are silent, or do anything else from a free decree of the mind, dream with their eyes open.

PROP. III.—*The actions of the mind arise from adequate ideas alone, but the passions depend upon those alone which are inadequate.*

Demonst.—The first thing which constitutes the essence

of the mind is nothing but the idea of an actually existing body (Props. 11 and 13, pt. 2). This idea is composed of a number of others (Prop. 15, pt. 2), some of which are adequate and others inadequate (Corol. Prop. 38, pt. 2, and Corol. Prop. 29, pt. 2). Everything, therefore, of which the mind is the proximate cause, and which follows from the nature of the mind, through which it must be understood, must necessarily follow from an adequate or from an inadequate idea. But in so far as the mind (Prop. 1, pt. 3) has inadequate ideas, so far it necessarily suffers; therefore the actions of the mind follow from adequate ideas alone, and the mind therefore suffers only because it has inadequate ideas.

Schol.—We see, therefore, that the passions are not related to the mind, unless in so far as it possesses something which involves negation; in other words, unless in so far as it is considered as a part of nature, which by itself and without the other parts cannot be clearly and distinctly perceived. In the same way I could show that passions are related to individual things, just as they are related to the mind, and that they cannot be perceived in any other way; but my purpose is to treat of the human mind alone.

PROP. IV.—*A thing cannot be destroyed except by an external cause.*

Demonst. — This proposition is self-evident, for the definition of any given thing affirms and does not deny the existence of the thing; that is to say, it posits the essence of the thing and does not negate it. So long, therefore, as we attend only to the thing itself, and not to external causes, we shall discover nothing in it which can destroy it.—Q.E.D.

PROP. V.—*In so far as one thing is able to destroy another*

H

are they of contrary natures ; that is to say, they cannot exist in the same subject.

Demonst.—If it were possible for them to come together, or to coexist in the same subject, there would then be something in that subject able to destroy it, which (Prop. 4, pt. 3) is absurd. Therefore, in so far, &c.—Q.E.D.

PROP. VI.—*Each thing, in so far as it is in itself, endeavours to persevere in its being.*

Demonst.—Individual things are modes by which the attributes of God are expressed in a certain and determinate manner (Corol. Prop. 25, pt. 1) ; that is to say (Prop. 34, pt. 1), they are things which express in a certain and determinate manner the power of God, by which He is and acts. A thing, too, has nothing in itself through which it can be destroyed, or which can negate its existence (Prop. 4, pt. 3), but, on the contrary, it is opposed to everything which could negate its existence (Prop. 5, pt. 3). Therefore, in so far as it can and is in itself, it endeavours to persevere in its own being. —Q.E.D.

PROP. VII.—*The effort by which each thing endeavours to persevere in its own being is nothing but the actual essence of the thing itself.*

Demonst.—From the given essence of anything certain things necessarily follow (Prop. 36, pt. 1); nor are things able to do anything else than what necessarily follows from their determinate nature (Prop. 29, pt. 1). Therefore, the power of a thing, or the effort by means of which it does or endeavours to do anything, either by itself or with others—that is to say (Prop. 6, pt. 3), the power or effort by which it endeavours to persevere in its being—is nothing but the given or actual essence of the thing itself.—Q.E.D.

PROP. VIII.—*The effort by which each thing endeavours to persevere in its own being does not involve finite but indefinite time.*

Demonst.—If it involved a limited time, which would determine the duration of the thing, then from that power alone by which the thing exists it would follow that, after that limited time, it could not exist but must be destroyed. But this (Prop. 4, pt. 3) is absurd. The effort, therefore, by which a thing exists does not involve definite time, but, on the contrary (Prop. 4, pt. 3), if the thing be destroyed by no external cause, by the same power by which it now exists it will always continue to exist, and this effort, therefore, by which it endeavours to persevere, &c.—Q.E.D.

PROP. IX.—*The mind, both in so far as it has clear and distinct ideas, and in so far as it has confused ideas, endeavours to persevere in its being for an indefinite time, and is conscious of this effort.*

Demonst.—The essence of the mind is composed of adequate and inadequate ideas (as we have shown in Prop. 3, pt. 3), and therefore (Prop. 7, pt. 3), both in so far as it has the former and in so far as it has the latter, it endeavours to persevere in its being, and endeavours to persevere in it for an indefinite time (Prop. 8, pt. 3). But since the mind (Prop. 23, pt. 2), through the ideas of the affections of the body, is necessarily conscious of itself, it is therefore conscious (Prop. 7, pt. 3) of its effort.

Schol.—This effort, when it is related to the mind alone, is called *will*, but when it is related at the same time both to the mind and the body, is called *appetite*, which is therefore nothing but the very essence of man, from the nature of which necessarily follow those things which promote his preservation, and thus he is determined to do those things. Hence there is no difference between appetite and desire, unless in this particular, that desire is generally related to men in so far as they are conscious of their appetites, and it may therefore be defined as appetite of which we are conscious. From what has been said it is plain, therefore, that we neither strive for, wish, seek, nor desire anything because we think it to be good, but, on the contrary, we adjudge a thing to be good because we strive for, wish, seek, or desire it.

PROP. X.—*There can be no idea in the mind which excludes the existence of the body, for such an idea is contrary to the mind.*

Demonst.—There can be nothing in our body which is able to destroy it (Prop. 5, pt. 3), and there cannot be, therefore, in God an idea of any such thing in so far as He has the idea of the body (Corol. Prop. 9, pt. 2); that is to say (Props. 11 and 13, pt. 2), no idea of any such thing can exist in our mind, but, on the contrary, since (Props. 11 and 13, pt. 2) the first thing which constitutes the essence of the mind is the idea of a body actually existing, the first and chief thing belonging to our mind is the effort (Prop. 7, pt. 3) to affirm the existence of our body, and therefore the idea which denies the existence of our body is contrary to our mind.—Q.E.D.

PROP. XI.—*If anything increases, diminishes, helps, or limits our body's power of action, the idea of that thing increases, diminishes, helps, or limits our mind's power of thought.*

Demonst.—This proposition is evident from Prop. 7, pt. 2, and also from Prop. 14, pt. 2.

Schol.—We thus see that the mind can suffer great changes, and can pass now to a greater and now to a lesser perfection; these passions explaining to us the affects of joy and sorrow. By *joy*, therefore, in what follows, I shall understand the passion by which the mind passes to a greater perfection; by *sorrow*, on the other hand, the passion by which it passes to a less perfection. The affect of joy, related at the same time both to the mind and the body, I call *pleasurable excitement* (*titillatio*) or *cheerfulness*; that of sorrow I call *pain* or *melancholy*. It is, however, to be observed that pleasurable excitement and pain are related to a man when one of his parts is affected more than the others; cheerfulness and melancholy, on the other hand, when all parts are equally affected. What the nature of desire is I have explained in the scholium of Prop. 9, pt. 3; and besides these three—joy, sorrow, and desire—I know of no other primary affect, the others springing from these, as I shall show in what follows. But before I advance any farther, I should like to explain more fully Prop. 10, pt. 3, so that we may more clearly understand in what manner one idea is contrary to another.

In the scholium of Prop. 17, pt. 2, we have shown that the idea which forms the essence of the mind involves the existence of the body so long as the body exists. Again, from Corol. Prop. 8, pt. 2, and its scholium, it follows that the present existence of our mind depends solely upon this—that the mind involves the actual existence of the body. Finally, we have shown that the power of the mind by which it imagines and remembers things also depends upon this—that it involves the actual existence of the body (Props. 17 and 18, pt. 2, with the Schol.) From these things it follows, that the present existence of the mind and its power of imagination are negated as soon as the mind ceases to affirm the present existence of the body. But the cause by which the mind ceases to affirm this existence of the body cannot be the mind itself (Prop. 4, pt. 2), nor can it be the body's ceasing to be; for (Prop. 6, pt. 2) the mind does not affirm the existence of the body because the body began to exist, and therefore, by the same reasoning, it does not cease to affirm the existence of the body because the body ceases to be, but (Prop. 17, pt. 2) because of another idea excluding the present existence of our body, and consequently of our mind, and contrary, therefore, to the idea which forms the essence of our mind.

PROP. XII.—*The mind endeavours as much as possible to imagine those things which increase or assist the body's power of acting.*

Demonst.—The human mind will contemplate any external body as present so long as the human body is affected in a way which involves the nature of that external body (Prop. 17, pt. 2), and consequently (Prop. 7, pt. 2) as long as the human mind contemplates any external body as present, that is to say (Schol. Prop. 17, pt. 2), imagines it, so long is the human body affected in a way which involves the nature of that external body. Consequently as long as the mind imagines those things which increase or assist our body's power of action, so long is the body affected in a way which increases or assists that power (Post. 1, pt. 3), and consequently (Prop. 11, pt. 3) so long the mind's power of thought is increased or assisted ; therefore (Props. 6 and 9, pt. 3) the mind endeavours as much as possible to imagine those things.—Q.E.D.

PROP. XIII.—*Whenever the mind imagines those things which lessen or limit the body's power of action, it endeavours as much as possible to recollect what ex- cludes the existence of these things.*

Demonst.—So long as the mind imagines anything of this sort, the power of the body and of the mind is lessened or limited (as we have shown in the preced- ing proposition). Nevertheless the mind will continue to imagine these things until it imagines some other thing which will exclude their present existence (Prop.

17, pt. 2); that is to say, as we have just shown, the power of the mind and of the body is diminished or limited until the mind imagines something which excludes the existence of these things. This, therefore (Prop. 9, pt. 3), the mind will endeavour to imagine or recollect as much as possible.—Q.E.D.

Corol.—Hence it follows that the mind is averse to imagine those things which lessen or hinder its power and that of the body.

Schol.—From what has been said we can clearly see what love is and what hatred is. *Love* is nothing but joy accompanied with the idea of an external cause, and *hatred* is nothing but sorrow with the accompanying idea of an external cause. We see too that he who loves a thing necessarily endeavours to keep it before him and to preserve it, and, on the other hand, he who hates a thing necessarily endeavours to remove and destroy it. But we shall speak at greater length upon these points in what follows.

PROP. XIV.—*If the mind at any time has been simultaneously affected by two affects, whenever it is afterwards affected by one of them, it will also be affected by the other.*

Demonst.—If the human body has at any time been simultaneously affected by two bodies, whenever the mind afterwards imagines one of them, it will immediately remember the other (Prop. 18, pt. 2). But the imaginations of the mind indicate rather the affects of our body than the nature of external bodies (Corol. 2, Prop. 16, pt. 2), and therefore if the body, and consequently the mind (Def. 3, pt. 3), has been at any time, &c.—Q.E.D.

PROP. XV.—*Anything may be accidentally the cause of joy, sorrow, or desire.*

Demonst.—Let the mind be supposed to be affected

at the same time by two affects, its power of action not being increased or diminished by one, while it is increased or diminished by the other (Post. 1, pt. 3). From the preceding proposition it is plain that when the mind is afterwards affected by the first affect through its true cause, which (by hypothesis) of itself neither increases nor diminishes the mind's power of thinking, it will at the same time be affected by the other affect, which does increase or diminish that power, that is to say (Schol. Prop. 11, pt. 3), it will be affected with joy or sorrow ; and thus the thing itself will be the cause of joy or of sorrow, not of itself, but accidentally. In the same way it can easily be shown that the same thing may accidentally be the cause of desire.—Q.E.D.

Corol.—The fact that we have contemplated a thing with an affect of joy or sorrow, of which it is not the efficient cause, is a sufficient reason for being able to love or hate it.

Demonst.—For this fact alone is a sufficient reason (Prop. 14, pt. 3) for its coming to pass that the mind in imagining the thing afterwards is affected with the affect of joy or sorrow, that is to say (Prop. 11, pt. 3), that the power of the mind and of the body is increased or diminished, &c., and, consequently (Prop. 12, pt. 3), that the mind desires to imagine the thing or (Corol. Prop. 13, pt. 3) is averse to doing so, that is to say (Schol. Prop. 13, pt. 3), that the mind loves the thing or hates it.

Schol.—We now understand why we love or hate certain things from no cause which is known to us, but merely from sympathy or antipathy, as they say. To this class, too, as we shall show in the following propositions, are to be referred those objects which affect us with joy or sorrow solely because they are somewhat like objects which usually affect us with those affects. I know indeed that the writers who first introduced the words "Sympathy" and "Antipathy" desired thereby to signify certain hidden qualities of things, but nevertheless I believe that we shall be permitted to understand by those names qualities which are plain and well known.

PROP. XVI.—*If we imagine a certain thing to possess something which resembles an object which usually affects the mind with joy or sorrow, although the quality in which the thing resembles the object is not the efficient cause of these affects, we shall nevertheless, by virtue of the resemblance alone, love or hate the thing.*

Demonst.—The quality in which the thing resembles the object we have contemplated in the object itself (by hypothesis) with the affect of joy or sorrow, and since (Prop. 14, pt. 3), whenever the mind is affected by the image of this quality, it is also affected by the former or latter affect, the thing which is perceived by us to possess this quality will be (Prop. 15, pt. 3) accidentally the cause of joy or sorrow. Therefore (by the preceding Corol.), although the quality in which the thing resembles the object is not the efficient cause of these affects, we shall nevertheless love the thing or hate it.

PROP. XVII.—*If we imagine that a thing that usually affects us with the affect of sorrow has any resemblance to an object which usually affects us equally with a great affect of joy, we shall at the same time hate the thing and love it.*

Demonst.—This thing (by hypothesis) is of itself the cause of sorrow, and (Schol. Prop. 13, pt. 3) in so far as we imagine it with this affect we hate it; but in so far as we imagine it to resemble an object which usually affects us equally with a great affect of joy do we love it with an equally great effort of joy (Prop. 16, pt. 3), and so we shall both hate it and love it at the same time.—Q.E.D.

Schol.—This state of mind, which arises from two contrary affects, is called *vacillation of the mind.* It is related to affect as doubt is related to the imagination

(Schol. Prop. 44, pt. 2). Nor do vacillation and doubt differ from one another except as greater and less. It is to be observed that in the preceding proposition I have deduced these vacillations of the mind from causes which occasion the one affect directly and the other contingently. This I have done because the affects could thus be more easily deduced from what preceded, and not because I deny that these vacillations often originate from the object itself which is the efficient cause of both affects. For the human body (Post. 1, pt. 2) is composed of a number of individuals of different natures, and therefore (Ax. 1, after Lem. 3, following Prop. 13, pt. 2) it can be affected by one and the same body in very many and in different ways. On the other hand, the same object can be affected in a number of different ways, and consequently can affect the same part of the body in different ways. It is easy, therefore, to see how one and the same object may be the cause of many and contrary affects.

PROP. XVIII.—*A man is affected by the image of a past or future thing with the same affect of joy or sorrow as that with which he is affected by the image of a present thing.*

Demonst.—As long as a man is affected by the image of anything, he will contemplate the thing as present although it does not exist (Prop. 17, pt. 2, with Corol.), nor does he imagine it as past or future, unless in so far as its image is connected with that of past or future time (Schol. Prop. 44, pt. 2). Therefore the image of the thing considered in itself alone is the same whether it be related to future, past, or present time; that is to say (Corol. 2, Prop. 16, pt. 2), the state of the body or the affect is the same whether the image be that of a past, present, or future thing. The affect, therefore, of joy and sorrow is the same whether the image be that of a past, present, or future thing.—Q.E.D.

Schol. 1.—I call a thing here past or future in so far as we have been or shall be affected by it; for example, in so far as we have seen a thing or are about to see it, in so far as it has strengthened us or will strengthen us; has injured or will injure us. For in so far as we thus imagine it do we affirm its existence; that is to say, the body is affected by no affect which excludes the existence of the thing, and therefore (Prop. 17, pt. 2) the body is affected by the image of the thing in the same way as if the thing itself were present. But because it generally happens that those who possess much experience hesitate when they think of a thing as past or future, and doubt greatly concerning its issue (Schol. Prop. 44, pt. 2), therefore the affects which spring from such images of things are not so constant, but are generally disturbed by the images of other things, until men become more sure of the issue.

Schol. 2.—From what has now been said we understand the nature of Hope, Fear, Confidence, Despair, Gladness, Remorse. *Hope* is nothing but unsteady joy, arising from the image of a future or past thing about whose issue we are in doubt. *Fear*, on the other hand, is an unsteady sorrow, arising from the image of a doubtful thing. If the doubt be removed from these affects, then hope and fear become *Confidence* and *Despair*, that is to say, joy or sorrow, arising from the image of a thing for which we have hoped or which we have feared. *Gladness*, again, is joy arising from the image of a past thing whose issues we have doubted. *Remorse*[1] is the sorrow which is opposed to gladness.

PROP. XIX.—*He who imagines that what he loves is destroyed will sorrow, but if he imagines that it is preserved he will rejoice.*

Demonst.—The mind endeavours as much as it can to imagine those things which increase or assist the body's

---

[1] *Conscientiæ morsus.* So also on pp. 165 and 219 (*Gewissensbiss,* Auerbach). But remorse is something more than is given in this definition, and is more nearly akin to *poenitentia,* repentance, as defined on p. 167.

power of action (Prop. 12, pt. 3), that is to say (Schol. Prop. 13, pt. 3), to imagine those things which it loves. But the imagination is assisted by those things which posit the existence of the object and is restrained by those which exclude its existence (Prop. 17, pt. 2). Therefore the images of things which posit the existence of the beloved object assist the mind's effort to imagine it, that is to say (Schol. Prop. 11, pt. 3), they affect the mind with joy; whilst those, on the other hand, which exclude the existence of the beloved object restrain that same effort of the mind, that is to say (Schol. Prop. 11, pt. 3), they affect the mind with sorrow. He, therefore, who imagines that what he loves is destroyed, &c.— Q.E.D.

PROP. XX.—*He who imagines that what he hates is destroyed will rejoice.*

Demonst.—The mind (Prop. 13, pt. 3) endeavours to imagine those things which exclude the existence of whatever lessens or limits the body's power of action; that is to say (Schol. Prop. 13, pt. 3), it endeavours to imagine those things which exclude the existence of what it hates, and therefore the image of the thing which excludes the existence of what the mind hates assists this endeavour of the mind, that is to say (Schol. Prop. 11, pt. 3), affects the mind with joy. He, therefore, who imagines that what he hates is destroyed will re- joice.—Q.E.D.

PROP. XXI.—*He who imagines that what he loves is affected with joy or sorrow will also be affected with joy or sorrow, and these affects will be greater or less in the lover as they are greater or less in the thing loved.*

Demonst.—The images of things (Prop. 19, pt. 3) which

posit the existence of the beloved object assist the effort
of the mind to imagine it; but joy posits the existence of
the thing which rejoices, and the greater the joy the
more is existence posited, for (Schol. Prop. 11, pt. 3) joy
is the transition to a greater perfection. The image, therefore, in the lover of the joy of the beloved object assists
the effort of his mind to imagine the object, that is to
say (Schol. Prop. 11, pt. 3), affects the lover with joy
proportionate to the joy of the object he loves. This
was the first thing to be proved. Again, in so far as
anything is affected with sorrow, so far is it destroyed,
and the destruction is greater as the sorrow with which
it is affected is greater (Schol. Prop. 11, pt. 3). Therefore
(Prop. 19, pt. 3) he who imagines that what he loves is
affected with sorrow will also be affected with sorrow,
and it will be greater as this affect shall have been
greater in the object beloved.

PROP. XXII.—*If we imagine that a person affects with
joy a thing which we love, we shall be affected with
love towards him. If, on the contrary, we imagine
that he affects it with sorrow, we shall also be affected
with hatred towards him.*

Demonst.—He who affects with joy or sorrow the
thing we love affects us also with joy or sorrow whenever we imagine the beloved object so affected (Prop. 21,
pt. 3). But this joy or sorrow is supposed to exist in
us accompanied with the idea of an external cause;
therefore (Schol. Prop. 13, pt. 3) if we imagine that a
person affects with joy or sorrow a thing which we love,
we shall be affected with love or hatred towards him.—
Q.E.D.

Schol.—Prop. 21 explains to us what *commiseration*
is, which we may define as sorrow which springs from
another's loss. By what name the joy is to be called
which springs from another's good I do not know. Love

toward the person who has done good to another we shall call *favour* (*favor*), whilst hatred towards him who has done evil to another we shall call *indignation* (*indignatio*). It is to be observed, too, that we not only feel pity for the object which we have loved, as we showed in Prop. 21, but also for that to which we have been attached by no affect; provided only we adjudge it to be like ourselves (as I shall show hereafter), and so we shall regard with favour him who has done any good to the object which is like us, and, on the contrary, be indignant with him who has done it any harm.

PROP. XXIII.—*He who imagines that what he hates is affected with sorrow will rejoice; if, on the other hand, he imagines it to be affected with joy he will be sad; and these affects will be greater or less in him in proportion as their contraries are greater or less in the object he hates.*

Demonst.—In so far as the hated thing is affected with sorrow is it destroyed, and the destruction is greater as the sorrow is greater (Schol. Prop. 11, pt. 3). He, therefore (Prop. 20, pt. 3), who imagines that the thing which he hates is affected with sorrow will on the contrary be affected with joy, and the joy will be the greater in proportion as he imagines the hated thing to be affected with a greater sorrow. This was the first thing to be proved. Again, joy posits the existence of the thing which rejoices (Schol. Prop. 11, pt. 3), and it does so the more in proportion as the joy is conceived to be greater. If a person, therefore, imagines that he whom he hates is affected with joy, this idea (Prop. 13, pt. 3) will restrain the effort of the mind of him who hates, that is to say (Schol. Prop. 11, pt. 3), he will be affected with sorrow.—Q.E.D.

Schol.—This joy can hardly be solid and free from any mental conflict. For, as I shall show directly in Prop

27, in so far as we imagine that what is like ourselves is affected with sorrow, we must be sad ; and, on the contrary, if we imagine it to be affected with joy, we rejoice. Here, however, we are considering merely hatred.

PROP. XXIV.—*If we imagine that a person affects with joy a thing which we hate, we are therefore affected with hatred towards him. On the other hand, if we imagine that he affects it with sorrow, we are therefore affected with love towards him.*

Demonst.—This proposition is proved in the same manner as Prop. 22, pt. 3, which see.

Schol.—These and the like affects of hatred are related to *envy,* which is therefore nothing but hatred in so far as it is considered to dispose a man so that he rejoices over the evil and is saddened by the good which befals another.

PROP. XXV.—*We endeavour to affirm everything, both concerning ourselves and concerning the beloved object which we imagine will affect us or the object with joy, and, on the contrary, we endeavour to deny everything that will affect either it or ourselves with sorrow.*

Demonst.—Everything which we imagine as affecting the beloved object with joy or sorrow affects us also with joy or sorrow (Prop. 21, pt. 3). But the mind (Prop. 12, pt. 3) endeavours as much as it can to imagine those things which affect us with joy, that is to say (Prop. 17, pt. 2 and its Corol.), it endeavours to consider them as present. On the contrary (Prop. 13, pt. 3), it endeavours to exclude the existence of what affects us with sorrow : therefore we endeavour to affirm everything both concerning ourselves and concerning the beloved object which we imagine will affect us or it with joy, &c.—Q.E.D.

PROP. XXVI.—*If we hate a thing, we endeavour to affirm concerning it everything which we imagine will affect it with sorrow, and, on the other hand, to deny everything concerning it which we imagine will affect it with joy.*

Demonst.—This proposition follows from Prop. 23, as the preceding proposition follows from Prop. 21.

Schol.—We see from this how easily it may happen, that a man should think too much of himself or of the beloved object, and, on the contrary, should think too little of what he hates. When a man thinks too much of himself, this imagination is called *pride,* and is a kind of delirium, because he dreams with his eyes open, that he is able to do all those things to which he attains in imagination alone, regarding them therefore as realities, and rejoicing in them so long as he cannot imagine anything to exclude their existence and limit his power of action. Pride, therefore, is that joy which arises from a man's thinking too much of himself. The joy which arises from thinking too much of another is called overestimation, and that which arises from thinking too little of another is called contempt.

PROP. XXVII.—*Although we may not have been moved towards a thing by any affect, yet if it is like ourselves, whenever we imagine it to be affected by any affect we are therefore affected by the same.*

Demonst.—The images of things are affections of the human body, and the ideas of these affections represent to us external bodies as if they were present (Schol. Prop. 17, pt. 2), that is to say (Prop. 16, pt. 2), these ideas involve both the nature of our own body and at the same time the present nature of the external body. If, therefore, the nature of the external body be like that of our body, then the idea of the external body which we imagine will involve an affection of our body like that of the external body. Therefore, if we imagine any one who is like ourselves to be affected with any affect, this imagination will express an affection of our body like that affect, and therefore we shall be affected with a similar affect ourselves, because we imagine something like us to be affected with the same. If, on the other hand, we hate a thing which is like ourselves, we shall so far (Prop. 23, pt. 3) be affected with an affect contrary and not similar to that with which it is affected.—Q.E.D.

Schol.—This imitation of affects, when it is connected with sorrow, is called *commiseration* (see Schol. Prop. 22, pt. 3), and where it is connected with desire is called *emulation*, which is nothing else than the desire which is engendered in us for anything, because we imagine that other persons, who are like ourselves, possess the same desire.

Corol. 1.—If we imagine that a person to whom we have been moved by no affect, affects with joy a thing which is like us, we shall therefore be affected with love towards him. If, on the other hand, we imagine that he affects it with sorrow, we shall be affected with hatred towards him.

Demonst.—This Corol. follows from the preceding proposition, just as Prop. 22, pt. 3, follows from Prop. 21, pt. 3.

Corol. 2.—If we pity a thing, the fact that its misery affects us with sorrow will not make us hate it.

Demonst.—If we could hate the thing for this reason, we should then (Prop. 23, pt. 3) rejoice over its sorrow, which is contrary to the hypothesis.

Corol. 3.—If we pity a thing, we shall endeavour as much as possible to free it from its misery.

Demonst.—That which affects with sorrow the thing that we pity, affects us likewise with the same sorrow (Prop. 27, pt. 3), and we shall, therefore, endeavour to devise every means by which we may take away or destroy

I

the existence of the cause of the sorrow (Prop. 1 3, pt. 3); that is to say (SchoL Prop. 9, pt. 3), we shall seek to destroy it, or shall be determined thereto, and therefore we shall endeavour to free from its misery the thing we pity.

Schol.—This will or desire of doing good, arising from our pity for the object which we want to benefit, is called *benevolence,* which is, therefore, simply the desire which arises from commiseration. With regard to the love or hatred towards the person who has done good or evil to the thing we imagine to be like ourselves, see SchoL Prop. 22, pt. 3.

PROP. XXVIII.— *We endeavour to bring into existence everything which we imagine conduces to joy, and to remove or destroy everything opposed to it, or which we imagine conduces to sorrow.*

Demonst.—We endeavour to imagine as much as possible all those things which we think conduce to joy (Prop. 12, pt. 3), that is to say (Prop. 17, pt. 2), we strive as much as possible to perceive them as present or actually existing. But the mind's effort or power in thinking is equal to and correspondent with the body's effort or power in acting, as clearly follows from Corol. Prop. 7, pt. 2, and Corol. Prop. 11, pt. 2, and therefore absolutely whatever conduces to joy we endeavour to make exist, that is to say (Schol. Prop. 9, pt. 3), we seek after it and aim at it. This is the first thing which was to be proved. Again, if we imagine that a thing which we believe causes us sorrow, that is to say (SchoL Prop. 1 3, pt. 3), which we hate is destroyed, we shall rejoice (Prop. 20, pt. 3), and therefore (by the first part of this demonstration) we shall endeavour to destroy it, or (Prop. 1 3, pt. 3) to remove it from us, so that we may not perceive it as present. This is the second thing which was to be proved. We endeavour, therefore, to bring into existence, &c.—Q.E.D.

PROP. XXIX.—*We shall endeavour to do everything which we imagine men*[1] *will look upon with joy, and, on the contrary, we shall be averse to doing anything to which we imagine men are averse.*

Demonst.—If we imagine men to love or hate a thing, we shall therefore love or hate it (Prop. 27, pt. 3); that is to say (Schol. Prop. 13, pt. 3), we shall therefore rejoice or be sad at the presence of the thing, and therefore (Prop. 28, pt. 3) everything which we imagine that men love or look upon with joy, we shall endeavour to do, &c. —Q.E.D.

Schol. — This effort to do some things and omit doing others, solely because we wish to please men, is called *ambition*, especially if our desire to please the common people is so strong that our actions or omissions to act are accompanied with injury to ourselves or to others. Otherwise this endeavour is usually called *humanity*. Again, the joy with which we imagine another person's action, the purpose of which is to delight us, I call *praise*, and the sorrow with which we turn away from an action of a contrary kind I call *blame*.

PROP. XXX.—*If a person has done anything which he imagines will affect others with joy, he also will be affected with joy, accompanied with an idea of himself as its cause ; that is to say, he will look upon himself with joy. If, on the other hand, he has done anything which he imagines will affect others with sorrow, he will look upon himself with sorrow.*

Demonst.—He who imagines that he affects others with joy or sorrow will necessarily be affected with joy or sorrow (Prop. 27, pt. 3). But since man is conscious

[1] Both here and in what follows I understand by the word *men,* men to whom we are moved by no affect (Sp.)

of himself (Props. 19 and 23, pt. 2) by means of the affections by which he is determined to act; therefore he who has done anything which he imagines will affect others with joy will be affected with joy accompanied with a consciousness of himself as its cause; that is to say, he will look upon himself with joy, and, on the other hand, &c.——Q.E.D.

Schol.——Since love (Schol. Prop. 13, pt. 3) is joy attended with the idea of an external cause, and hatred is sorrow attended with the idea of an external cause, the joy and sorrow spoken of in this proposition will be a kind of love and hatred. But because love and hatred are related to external objects, we will therefore give a different name to the affects which are the subject of this proposition, and we will call this kind of joy which is attended with the idea of an external cause *self-exaltation,* and the sorrow opposed to it we will call *shame.* The reader is to understand that this is the case in which joy or sorrow arises because the man believes that he is praised or blamed, otherwise I shall call this joy accompanied with the idea of an external cause *contentment with one's-self,* and the sorrow opposed to it *repentance.* Again, since (Corol. Prop. 17, pt. 2) it may happen that the joy with which a person imagines that he affects other people is only imaginary, and since (Prop. 25, pt. 3) every one endeavours to imagine concerning himself what he supposes will affect himself with joy, it may easily happen that the self-exalted man becomes proud, and imagines that he is pleasing everybody when he is offensive to everybody.

PROP. XXXI.——*If we imagine that a person loves, desires, or hates a thing which we ourselves love, desire, or hate, we shall on that account love, desire, or hate the thing more steadily. If, on the other hand, we imagine that he is averse to the thing we love or loves the thing to which we are averse, we shall then suffer vacillation of mind.*

Demonst.—If we imagine that another person loves a thing, on that very account we shall love it (Prop. 27, pt. 3). But we are supposed to love it independently of this, and a new cause for our love is therefore added, by which it is strengthened, and consequently the object we love will be loved by us on this account the more steadily. Again, if we imagine that a person is averse to a thing, on that very account we shall be averse to it (Prop. 27, pt. 3); but if we suppose that we at the same time love it, we shall both love the thing and be averse to it, that is to say (Schol. Prop. 17, pt. 3), we shall suffer vacillation of mind.—Q.E.D.

Corol.—It follows from this proposition and from Prop. 28, pt. 3, that every one endeavours as much as possible to make others love what he loves, and to hate what he hates. Hence the poet says—

> " Speremus pariter, pariter metuamus amantes;
>   Ferreus est, si quis, quod sinit alter, amat." [1]

This effort to make every one approve what we love or hate is in truth ambition (Schol. Prop. 29, pt. 3), and so we see that each person by nature desires that other persons should live according to his way of thinking; but if every one does this, then all are a hindrance to one another, and if every one wishes to be praised or beloved by the rest, then they all hate one another.

PROP. XXXII.—*If we imagine that a person enjoys a thing which only one can possess, we do all we can to prevent his possessing it.*

Demonst.—If we imagine that a person enjoys a thing, that will be a sufficient reason (Prop. 27, pt. 3, with Corol. 1) for making us love the thing and desiring

---

[1] Ovid, Amor. ii. 19 : Spinoza has, however, transposed the lines.—TR.

to enjoy it. But (by hypothesis) we imagine that his enjoyment of the thing is an obstacle to our joy, and therefore (Prop. 28, pt. 3) we endeavour to prevent his possessing it.—Q.E.D.

Schol.—We see, therefore, that the nature of man is generally constituted so as to pity those who are in adversity and envy those who are in prosperity, and (Prop. 32, pt. 3) he envies with a hatred which is the greater in proportion as he loves what he imagines another possesses. We see also that from the same property of human nature from which it follows that men pity one another it also follows that they are envious and ambitious. If we will consult experience, we shall find that she teaches the same doctrine, especially if we consider the first years of our life. For we find that children, because their body is, as it were, continually in equilibrium, laugh and cry merely because they see others do the same; whatever else they see others do they immediately wish to imitate; everything which they think is pleasing to other people they want. And the reason is, as we have said, that the images of things are the affections themselves of the human body, or the ways in which it is affected by external causes and disposed to this or that action.

PROP. XXXIII.—*If we love a thing which is like ourselves, we endeavour as much as possible to make it love us in return.*

Demonst.—We endeavour as much as possible to imagine before everything else the thing we love (Prop. 12, pt. 3). If, therefore, it be like ourselves, we shall endeavour to affect it with joy before everything else (Prop. 29, pt. 3); that is to say, we shall endeavour as much as possible to cause the beloved object to be affected with joy attended with the idea of ourselves, or, in other words (Schol. Prop. 13, pt. 3), we try to make it love us in return.—Q.E.D.

PROP. XXXIV.—*The greater the affect with which we imagine that a beloved object is affected towards us, the greater will be our self-exaltation.*

Demonst.—We endeavour as much as possible to make a beloved object love us in return (Prop. 33, pt. 3), that is to say (Schol. Prop. 13, pt. 3), to cause it to be affected with joy attended with the idea of ourselves. In proportion, therefore, as we imagine the beloved object to be affected with a joy of which we are the cause, will our endeavour be assisted, that is to say (Prop. 11, pt. 3 with Schol.), will be the greatness of the joy with which we are affected. But since we rejoice because we have affected with joy another person like ourselves, we shall look upon ourselves with joy (Prop. 30, pt. 3); and therefore the greater the affect with which we imagine that the beloved object is affected towards us, the greater will be the joy with which we shall look upon ourselves, that is to say (Schol. Prop. 30, pt. 3), the greater will be our self-exaltation.—Q.E.D.

PROP. XXXV.—*If I imagine that an object beloved by me is united to another person by the same, or by a closer bond of friendship than that by which I myself alone held the object, I shall be affected with hatred towards the beloved object itself, and shall envy that other person.*

Demonst.—The greater the love with which a person imagines a beloved object to be affected towards him, the greater will be his self-exaltation (Prop. 34, pt. 3), that is to say (Schol. Prop. 30, pt. 3), the more will he rejoice. Therefore (Prop. 28, pt. 3) he will endeavour as much as he can to imagine the beloved object united to him as closely as possible, and this effort or desire is strengthened if he imagines that another person desires for himself the same object (Prop. 31, pt. 3). But this effort or desire is supposed to be checked by the image of the beloved object itself attended by the image of the person whom it connects with itself. Therefore (Schol. Prop. 11, pt. 3) the lover on this account will be affected with sorrow attended with the idea of the beloved object as its cause together with the image of another person; that is to say (Schol. Prop. 13, pt. 3), he will be affected with hatred towards the beloved object and at the same time towards this other person (Corol. Prop. 15, pt. 3), whom he will envy (Prop. 23, pt. 3) as being delighted with it.—Q.E.D.

Schol.—This hatred towards a beloved object when joined with envy is called Jealousy, which is therefore nothing but a vacillation of the mind springing from the love and hatred both felt together, and attended with the idea of another person whom we envy. Moreover, this hatred towards the beloved object will be greater in proportion to the joy with which the jealous man has been usually affected from the mutual affection between him and his beloved, and also in proportion to the affect with which he had been affected towards the person who is imagined to unite to himself the beloved object. For if he has hated him, he will for that very reason hate the beloved object (Prop. 24, pt. 3), because he imagines it to affect with joy that which he hates, and also (Corol. Prop. 15, pt. 3) because he is compelled to connect the image of the beloved object with the image of him whom he hates. This feeling is generally excited when the love is love towards a woman. The man who imagines that the woman he loves prostitutes herself to another is not merely troubled because his appetite is restrained, but he turns away from her because he is obliged to connect the image of a beloved object with the privy parts and with what is excremental in another man; and in addition to this, the jealous person is not received with the same favour which the beloved object formerly bestowed on him,—a new cause of sorrow to the lover, as I shall show.

PROP. XXXVI.——*He who recollects a thing with which he has once been delighted, desires to possess it with every condition which existed when he was first delighted with it.*

Demonst.——Whatever a man has seen together with an object which has delighted him will be (Prop. 15, pt. 3) contingently a cause of joy, and therefore (Prop. 28, pt. 3) he will desire to possess it all, together with the object which has delighted him, that is to say, he will desire to possess the object with every condition which existed when he was first delighted with it.——Q.E.D.

Corol.——If, therefore, the lover discovers that one of these conditions be wanting, he will be sad.

Demonst.——For in so far as he discovers that any one condition is wanting does he imagine something which excludes the existence of the object. But since (Prop. 36, pt. 3) he desires the object or condition from love, he will therefore be sad (Prop. 19, pt. 3) in so far as he imagines that condition to be wanting.——Q.E.D.

Schol.——This sorrow, in so far as it is related to the absence of what we love, is called *longing*.

PROP. XXXVII.——*The desire which springs from sorrow or joy, from hatred or love, is greater in proportion as the affect is greater.*

Demonst.——Sorrow lessens or limits a man's power of action (Schol. Prop. 11, pt. 3), that is to say (Prop. 7, pt. 3), it lessens or limits the effort by which a man endeavours to persevere in his own being, and therefore (Prop. 5, pt. 3) it is opposed to this effort; consequently, if a man be affected with sorrow, the first thing he attempts is to remove that sorrow; but (by the definition of sorrow) the greater it is, the greater is the human power of action to which it must be opposed, and so much the greater, therefore, will be the power of action with which the man will endeavour to remove it; that is to say (SchoL Prop. 9, pt. 3), with the greater eagerness or desire will he struggle to remove it. Again, since joy (SchoL Prop. 11, pt. 3) increases or assists a man's power of action, it is easily demonstrated, by the same method, that there is nothing which a man who is affected with joy desires more than to preserve it, and his desire is in proportion to his joy. Again, since hatred and love are themselves affects either of joy or sorrow, it follows in the same manner that the effort, desire, or eagerness which arises from hatred or love will be greater in proportion to the hatred or love.—Q.E.D.

PROP. XXXVIII.—*If a man has begun to hate a beloved thing, so that his love to it is altogether destroyed, he will for this very reason hate it more than he would have done if he had never loved it, and his hatred will be in greater proportion to his previous love.*

Demonst.—If a man begins to hate a thing which he loves, a constraint is put upon more appetites than if he had never loved it. For love is joy (Schol. Prop. 13, pt. 3), which a man endeavours to preserve as much as possible (Prop. 28, pt. 3), both by looking on the beloved object as present (Schol. Prop. 13, pt. 3), and by affecting it with joy as much as possible (Prop. 21, pt. 3); this effort (Prop. 37, pt. 3) to preserve the joy of love being the greater in proportion as his love is greater, and so also is the effort to bring the beloved object to love him in return (Prop. 33, pt. 3). But these efforts are restrained by the hatred towards the beloved object (Corol. Prop. 13, and Prop. 23, pt. 3); therefore the lover (Schol. Prop. 11, pt. 3) for this reason also will be affected with sorrow, and that the more as the love had been greater; that is to say, in addition to the sorrow which was the cause of the hatred there is another produced by his having loved the object, and consequently he will contemplate with a greater affect of sorrow the beloved object; that is to say (Schol. Prop. 13, pt. 3), he will hate it more than he would have done if he had not loved it, and his hatred will be in proportion to his previous love.—Q.E.D.

PROP. XXXIX.—*If a man hates another, he will endeavour to do him evil, unless he fears a greater evil will therefrom arise to himself; and, on the other hand, he who loves another will endeavour to do him good by the same rule.*

Demonst.—To hate a person (Schol. Prop. 13, pt. 3) is to imagine him as a cause of sorrow, and therefore (Prop. 28, pt. 3) he who hates another will endeavour to remove or destroy him. But if he fears lest a greater grief, or, which is the same thing, a greater evil, should fall upon himself, and one which he thinks he can avoid by refraining from inflicting the evil he meditated, he will desire not to do it (Prop. 28, pt. 3); and this desire will be stronger than the former with which he was possessed of inflicting the evil, and will prevail over it (Prop. 37, pt. 3). This is the first part of the proposition. The second is demonstrated in the same way. Therefore if a man hates another, &c. —Q.E.D.

Schol.—By *good*, I understand here every kind of joy and everything that conduces to it; chiefly, however, anything that satisfies longing, whatever that thing may be. By *evil*, I understand every kind of sorrow, and chiefly whatever thwarts longing. For we have shown above (Schol. Prop. 9, pt. 3) that we do not desire a thing because we adjudge it to be good, but, on the contrary, we call it good because we desire it, and conse-

quently everything to which we are averse we call evil.
Each person, therefore, according to his affect judges or
estimates what is good and what is evil, what is better
and what is worse, and what is the best and what is the
worst.   Thus the covetous man thinks plenty of money
to be the best thing and poverty the worst.   The ambitious
man desires nothing like glory, and on the other hand
dreads nothing like shame.   To the envious person, again,
nothing is more pleasant than the misfortune of another,
and nothing more disagreeable than the prosperity of
another.   And so each person according to his affect
judges a thing to be good or evil, useful or useless.   We
notice, moreover, that this affect, by which a man is so
disposed as not to will the thing he wills, and to will
that which he does not will, is called *fear,* which may
therefore be defined as that *apprehension* which leads a
man to avoid an evil in the future by incurring a lesser
evil (Prop. 28, pt. 3).   If the evil feared is shame, then
the fear is called *modesty.*   If the desire of avoiding
the future is restrained by the fear of another evil,
so that the man does not know what he most wishes,
then this apprehension is called *consternation,* especially
if both the evils feared are very great.

PROP. XL.—*If we imagine that we are hated by another
without having given him any cause for it, we shall
hate him in return.*

Demonst.—If we imagine that another person is
affected with hatred, on that account we shall also be
affected with it (Prop. 27, pt. 3) ; that is to say, we
shall be affected with sorrow (Schol. Prop. 13, pt. 3),
accompanied with the idea of an external cause.   But (by
hypothesis) we imagine no cause for this sorrow excepting
the person himself who hates us, and therefore, because we
imagine ourselves hated by another, we shall be affected
with sorrow accompanied with the idea of him who hates

us ; that is to say (Schol. Prop. 13, pt. 3), we shall hate him.—Q.E.D.

Schol.—If we imagine that we have given just cause for the hatred, we shall then (Prop. 30, pt. 3, with its Schol.) be affected with shame. This, however (Prop. 25, pt. 3), rarely happens.

This reciprocity of hatred may also arise from the fact that hatred is followed by an attempt to bring evil upon him who is hated (Prop. 39, pt. 3). If, therefore, we imagine that we are hated by any one else, we shall imagine him as the cause of some evil or sorrow, and thus we shall be affected with sorrow or apprehension accompanied with the idea of the person who hates us as a cause ; that is to say, we shall hate him in return, as we have said above.

Corol. 1.—If we imagine that the person we love is affected with hatred towards us, we shall be agitated at the same time both with love and hatred. For in so far as we imagine that we are hated are we determined (Prop. 40, pt. 3) to hate him in return. But (by hypothesis) we love him notwithstanding, and therefore we shall be agitated both by love and hatred.

Corol. 2.—If we imagine that an evil has been brought upon us through the hatred of some person towards whom we have hitherto been moved by no affect, we shall immediately endeavour to return that evil upon him.

Demonst.—If we imagine that another person is affected with hatred towards us, we shall hate him in return (Prop. 40, pt. 3), and (Prop. 26, pt. 3) we shall endeavour to devise and (Prop. 39, pt. 3) bring upon him everything which can affect him with sorrow. But (by hypothesis) the first thing of this kind we imagine is the evil brought upon ourselves, and therefore we shall immediately endeavour to bring that upon him.—Q.E.D.

Schol.—The attempt to bring evil on those we hate is called *anger*, and the attempt to return the evil inflicted on ourselves is called *vengeance*.

PROP. XLL—*If we imagine that we are beloved by a person without having given any cause for the love (which may be the case by Corol. Prop. 15, pt. 3, and by Prop. 16, pt. 3), we shall love him in return.*

Demonst.—This proposition is demonstrated in the same way as the preceding, to the scholium of which the reader is also referred.

Schol.—If we imagine that we have given just cause for love, we shall pride ourselves upon it (Prop. 30, pt. 3, with its Schol.) This frequently occurs (Prop. 25, pt. 3), and we have said that the contrary takes place when we believe that we are hated by another person (Schol. Prop. 40, pt. 3). This reciprocal love, and consequently (Prop. 39, pt. 3) this attempt to do good to the person who loves us, and who (by the same Prop. 39, pt. 3) endeavours to do good to us, is called *thankfulness* or *gratitude*, and from this we can see how much readier men are to revenge themselves than to return a benefit.

Corol.—If we imagine that we are loved by a person we hate, we shall at the same time be agitated both by love and hatred. This is demonstrated in the same way as the preceding proposition.

Schol.—If the hatred prevail, we shall endeavour to bring evil upon the person by whom we are loved. This affect is called Cruelty, especially if it is believed that the person who loves has not given any ordinary reason for hatred.

PROP. XLII.—*If, moved by love or hope of self-exaltation, we have conferred a favour upon another person, we shall be sad if we see that the favour is received with ingratitude.*

Demonst.—If we love a thing which is of the same nature as ourselves, we endeavour as much as possible to cause it to love us in return (Prop. 33, pt. 3). If we confer a favour, therefore, upon any one because of our love towards him, we do it with a desire by which we are possessed that we may be loved in return; that is to say (Prop. 34, pt. 3), from the hope of self-exaltation, or (Schol. Prop. 30, pt. 3) of joy, and we shall consequently (Prop. 12, pt. 3) endeavour as much as possible to imagine this cause of self-exaltation, or to contemplate it as actually existing. But (by hypothesis) we imagine something else which excludes the existence of that cause, and, therefore (Prop. 19, pt. 3), this will make us sad.—Q.E.D.

PROP. XLIII.—*Hatred is increased through return of hatred, but may be destroyed by love.*

Demonst.—If we imagine that the person we hate is affected with hatred towards us, a new hatred is thereby produced (Prop. 40, pt. 3), the old hatred still remaining (by hypothesis). If, on the other hand, we imagine him to be affected with love towards us, in so far as we imagine it (Prop. 30, pt. 3) shall we look upon ourselves with joy, and endeavour (Prop. 29, pt. 3) to please him; that is to say (Prop. 41, pt. 3), in so far shall we endeavour not to hate him nor to affect him with sorrow. This effort (Prop. 37, pt. 3) will be greater or less as the affect from which it arises is greater or less, and, therefore, should it be greater than that which springs from hatred, and by which (Prop. 26, pt. 3) we endeavour to affect with sorrow the object we hate, then it will prevail and banish hatred from the mind.—Q.E.D.

PROP. XLIV.—*Hatred which is altogether overcome by love passes into love, and the love is therefore greater than if hatred had not preceded it.*

Demonst.—The demonstration is of the same kind as

that of Prop. 38, pt. 3. For if we begin to love a thing which we hated, or upon which we were in the habit of looking with sorrow, we shall rejoice for the very reason that we love, and to this joy which love involves (see its definition in the Schol. of Prop. 13, pt. 3) a new joy is added, which springs from the fact that the effort to remove the sorrow which hatred involves (Prop. 37, pt. 3) is so much assisted, there being also present before us as the cause of our joy the idea of the person whom we hated.

Schol.—Notwithstanding the truth of this proposition, no one will try to hate a thing or will wish to be affected with sorrow in order that he may rejoice the more; that is to say, no one will desire to inflict loss on himself in the hope of recovering the loss, or to become ill in the hope of getting well, inasmuch as every one will always try to preserve his being and to remove sorrow from himself as much as possible. Moreover, if it can be imagined that it is possible for us to desire to hate a person in order that we may love him afterwards the more, we must always desire to continue the hatred. For the love will be the greater as the hatred has been greater, and therefore we shall always desire the hatred to be more and more increased. Upon the same principle we shall desire that our sickness may continue and increase in order that we may afterwards enjoy the greater pleasure when we get well, and therefore we shall always desire sickness, which (Prop. 6, pt. 3) is absurd.

PROP. XLV.—*If we imagine that any one like ourselves is affected with hatred towards an object like ourselves which we love, we shall hate him.*

Demonst.—The beloved object hates him who hates it (Prop. 40, pt. 3), and therefore we who love it, who imagine that any one hates it, imagine also that it is affected with hatred; that is to say, with sorrow (Schol. Prop. 13, pt. 3), and consequently (Prop. 21, pt. 3) we are sad, our sadness being accompanied with the idea of the person, as the cause thereof, who hates the beloved object; that is to say (Schol. Prop. 13, pt. 3), we shall hate him. —Q.E.D.

PROP. XLVI.—*If we have been affected with joy or sorrow by any one who belongs to a class or nation different from our own, and if our joy or sorrow is accompanied with the idea of this person as its cause, under the common name of his class or nation, we shall not love or hate him merely, but the whole of the class or nation to which he belongs.*

Demonst.—This proposition is demonstrated in the same way as Prop. 16, pt. 3.

PROP. XLVII.—*The joy which arises from our imagining that what we hate has been destroyed or has been injured is not unaccompanied with some sorrow.*

Demonst.—This is evident from Prop. 27, pt. 3; for in so far as we imagine an object like ourselves affected with sorrow shall we be sad.

Schol.—This proposition may also be demonstrated from Corol. Prop. 17, pt. 2. For as often as we recollect the object, although it does not actually exist, we contemplate it as present, and the body is affected in the same way as if it were present. Therefore, so long as the memory of the object remains, we are so determined as to contemplate it with sorrow, and this determination, while the image of the object abides, is restrained by the recollection of those things which exclude the existence of the object, but is not altogether removed. Therefore we rejoice only so far as the determination is restrained, and hence it happens that the joy which springs from the misfortune of the object we hate is renewed as often as we recollect the object. For, as we

K

have already shown, whenever its image is excited, inasmuch as this involves the existence of the object, we are so determined as to contemplate it with the same sorrow with which we were accustomed to contemplate it when it really existed. But because we have connected with this image other images which exclude its existence, the determination to sorrow is immediately restrained, and we rejoice anew; and this happens as often as this repetition takes place. This is the reason why we rejoice as often as we call to mind any evil that is past, and why we like to tell tales about the dangers we have escaped, since whenever we imagine any danger, we contemplate it as if it were about to be, and are so determined as to fear it—a determination which is again restrained by the idea of freedom, which we connected with the idea of the danger when we were freed from it, and this idea of freedom again makes us fearless, so that we again rejoice.

PROP. XLVIII.—*Love and hatred towards any object, for example, towards Peter, are destroyed if the joy and the sorrow which they respectively involve be joined to the idea of another cause; and they are respectively diminished in proportion as we imagine that Peter has not been their sole cause.*

Demonst.—This is plain from the very definition of love and hatred (see Schol. Prop. 13, pt. 3), joy being called love to Peter and sorrow being called hatred to him, solely because he is considered to be the cause of this or that affect. Whenever, therefore, we can no longer consider him either partially or entirely its cause, the affect towards him ceases or is diminished.—Q.E.D.

PROP. XLIX.—*For the same reason, love or hatred towards an object we imagine to be free must be greater than towards an object which is under necessity.*

Demonst.—An object which we imagine to be free must

(Def. 7, pt. 1) be perceived through itself and without others. If, therefore, we imagine it to be the cause of joy or sorrow, we shall for that reason alone love or hate it (Schol. Prop. 13, pt. 3), and that too with the greatest love or the greatest hatred which can spring from the given affect (Prop. 48, pt. 3). But if we imagine that the object which is the cause of that affect is necessary, then (by the same Def. 7, pt. 1) we shall imagine it as the cause of that affect, not alone, but together with other causes, and so (Prop. 48, pt. 3) our love or hatred towards it will be less.—Q.E.D.

Schol.—Hence it follows that our hatred or love towards one another is greater than towards other things, because we think we are free. We must take into account also the imitation of affects which we have discussed in Props. 27, 34, 40, and 43, pt. 3.

PROP. L.—*Anything may be accidentally the cause either of hope or fear.*

This proposition is demonstrated in the same way as Prop. 15, pt. 3, which see, together with Schol. 2, Prop. 18, pt. 3.

Schol.—Things which are accidentally the causes either of hope or fear are called good or evil omens. In so far as the omens are the cause of hope and fear (by the Def. of hope and fear in Schol. 2, Prop. 18, pt. 3) are they the cause of joy or of sorrow, and consequently (Corol. Prop. 15, pt. 3) so far do we love them or hate them, and (Prop. 28, pt. 3) endeavour to use them as means to obtain those things for which we hope, or to remove them as obstacles or causes of fear. It follows, too, from Prop. 25, pt. 3, that our natural constitution is such that we easily believe the things we hope for, and believe with difficulty those we fear, and that we think too much of the former and too little of the latter. Thus have superstitions arisen, by which men are everywhere disquieted. I do not consider it worth while to go any farther, and to explain here all those vacillations of mind which arise from hope and fear, since it follows from the definition alone of these affects that hope cannot exist without fear, nor fear without hope (as we shall explain more at length in the proper place). Besides, in so far as we hope for a thing or fear it, we love it or hate it, and therefore everything which has been said about hatred and love can easily be applied to hope and fear.

PROP. LI.—*Different men may be affected by one and the same object in different ways, and the same man may be affected by one and the same object in different ways at different times.*

Demonst.—The human body (Post. 3, pt. 2) is affected by external bodies in a number of ways. Two men, therefore, may be affected in different ways at the same time, and, therefore (Ax. 1, after Lemma 3, following Prop. 13, pt. 2), they can be affected by one and the same object in different ways. Again (Post. 3, pt. 2), the human body may be affected now in this and now in that way, and consequently (by the axiom just quoted) it may be affected by one and the same object in different ways at different times.—Q.E.D.

Schol.—We thus see that it is possible for one man to love a thing and for another man to hate it; for this man to fear what this man does not fear, and for the same man to love what before he hated, and to dare to do what before he feared. Again, since each judges according to his own affect what is good and what is evil, what is better and what is worse (Schol. Prop. 39, pt. 3), it follows that men may change in their judgment as they do in their affects,[1] and hence it comes to pass that when we compare men, we distinguish them solely by

[1] That this may be the case, although the human mind is part of the divine intellect, we have shown in Corol. Prop. 11, pt. 2 (Sp.).

the difference in their affects, calling some brave, others timid, and others by other names. For example, I shall call a man *brave* who despises an evil which I usually fear, and if, besides this, I consider the fact that his desire of doing evil to a person whom he hates or doing good to one whom he loves is not restrained by that fear of evil by which I am usually restrained, I call him *audacious.* On the other hand, the man who fears an evil which I usually despise will appear *timid,* and if, besides this, I consider that his desire is restrained by the fear of an evil which has no power to restrain me, I call him *pusillanimous;* and in this way everybody will pass judgment. Finally, from this nature of man and the inconstancy of his judgment, in consequence of which he often judges things from mere affect, and the things which he believes contribute to his joy or his sorrow, and which, therefore, he endeavours to bring to pass or remove (Prop. 28, pt. 3), are often only imaginary—to say nothing about what we have demonstrated in the Second Part of this book about the uncertainty of things—it is easy to see that a man may often be himself the cause of his sorrow or his joy, or of being affected with sorrow or joy accompanied with the idea of himself as its cause, so that we can easily understand what repentance and what self-approval are. Repentance is sorrow accompanied with the idea of one's self as the cause, and self-approval is joy accompanied with the idea of one's self as the cause; and these affects are very intense because men believe themselves free (Prop. 49, pt. 3).

PROP. LII.—*An object which we have seen before together with other objects, or which we imagine possesses nothing which is not common to it with many other objects, we shall not contemplate so long as that which we imagine possesses something peculiar.*

Demonst.—Whenever we imagine an object which we

have seen with others, we immediately call these to mind (Prop. 18, pt. 2, with Schol.), and thus from the contemplation of one object we immediately fall to contemplating another. This also is our way with an object which we imagine to possess nothing except what is common to a number of other objects. For this is the same thing as supposing that we contemplate nothing in it which we have not seen before with other objects. On the other hand, if we suppose ourselves to imagine in an object something peculiar which we have never seen before, it is the. same as saying that the mind, while it contemplates that object, holds nothing else in itself to the contemplation of which it can pass, turning away from the contemplation of the object, and therefore it is determined to the contemplation solely of the object. Therefore an object, &c.—Q.E.D.

Schol.—This affection of the mind or imagination of a particular thing, in so far as it alone occupies the mind, is called *astonishment*, and if it is excited by an object we dread, we call it *consternation*, because astonishment at the evil so fixes us in the contemplation of itself, that we cannot think of anything else by which we might avoid the evil. On the other hand, if the objects at which we are astonished are human wisdom, industry, or anything of this kind, inasmuch as we consider that their possessor is by so much superior to ourselves, the astonishment goes by the name of *veneration;* whilst, if the objects are human anger, envy, or anything of this sort, it goes by the name of *horror*. Again, if we are astonished at the wisdom or industry of a man we love, then our love on that account (Prop. 12, pt. 3) will be greater, and this love, united to astonishment or veneration, we call *devotion*. In the same manner it is possible to conceive of hatred, hope, confidence, and other affects being joined to astonishment, so that more affects may be deduced than are indicated by the words in common use. From this we see that names have been invented for affects from common usage, rather than from accurate knowledge of them.

To astonishment is opposed contempt, which is usually caused, nevertheless, by our being determined to astonishment, love, or fear towards an object either because we see that another person is astonished at, loves or fears this same object, or because at first sight it appears like other objects, at which we are astonished or which we love or fear (Prop. 15, with Corol. pt. 3, and Prop. 27, pt. 3). But if the presence of the object or a more careful contemplation of it should compel us to deny that there exists in it any cause for astonishment, love, fear, &c., then from its presence itself, the mind remains determined to think rather of those things which are not in it than of those which are in it, although from the presence of an object the mind is accustomed to think chiefly about what is in the object. We may also observe that as devotion springs from astonishment at a thing we love, so *derision* springs from the contempt of a thing we hate or fear, whilst *scorn* arises from the contempt of folly, as veneration arises from astonishment at wisdom. We may also conceive of love, hope, glory, and other affects being joined to contempt, and thus deduce other affects which also we are not in the habit of distinguishing by separate words.

PROP. LIII.—*When the mind contemplates itself and its own power of acting, it rejoices, and it rejoices in proportion to the distinctness with which it imagines itself and its power of action.*

Demonst.—Man has no knowledge of himself except through the affections of his own body and their ideas (Props. 19 and 23, pt. 2); whenever, therefore, it happens that the mind is able to contemplate itself, it is thereby supposed to pass to a greater perfection, that is to say (Schol. Prop. 11, pt. 3), it is supposed to be affected with joy, and the joy is greater in proportion to the distinctness with which it imagines itself and its power of action.—Q.E.D.

Corol.—The more a man imagines that he is praised by other men, the more is this joy strengthened; for the more a man imagines that he is praised by others, the more does he imagine that he affects others with joy accompanied by the idea of himself as a cause (Schol. Prop. 29, pt. 3), and therefore (Prop. 27, pt. 3) he is affected with greater joy accompanied with the idea of himself.—Q.E.D.

PROP. LIV.—*The mind endeavours to imagine those things only which posit its power of acting.*

Demonst.—The effort or power of the mind is the essence of the mind itself (Prop. 7, pt. 3), but the essence of the mind, as is self-evident, affirms only that which the mind is and is able to do, and does not affirm that which the mind is not and cannot do, and therefore the mind endeavours to imagine those things only which affirm or posit its power of acting.—Q.E.D.

PROP. LV.—*When the mind imagines its own weakness it necessarily sorrows.*

Demonst.—The essence of the mind affirms only that which the mind is and is able to do, or, in other words, it is the nature of the mind to imagine those things only which posit its power of acting (Prop. 54, pt. 3). If we say, therefore, that the mind, while it contemplates itself, imagines its own weakness, we are merely saying in other words that the effort of the mind to imagine something which posits its power of acting is restrained, that is to say (Schol. Prop. 11, pt. 3), the mind is sad.—Q.E.D.

Corol.—This sorrow is strengthened in proportion as the mind imagines that it is blamed by others. This is demonstrated in the same way as Corol. Prop. 53, pt. 3.

Schol.—This sorrow, accompanied with the idea of our own weakness, is called *humility*, and the joy which arises from contemplating ourselves is called *self-love* or *self-approval*. Inasmuch as this joy recurs as often as a man contemplates his own virtues or his own power of acting, it comes to pass that every one loves to tell of his own deeds, and to display the powers both of his body and mind ; and that for this reason men become an annoyance to one another. It also follows that men are naturally envious (Schol. Prop. 24, and Schol. Prop. 32, pt. 3), that is to say, they rejoice over the weaknesses of their equals and sorrow over their strength. For whenever a person imagines his own actions he is affected with joy (Prop. 53, pt. 3), and his joy is the greater in proportion as he imagines that his actions express more perfection, and he imagines them more distinctly ; that is to say (by what has been said in Schol. 1, Prop. 40, pt. 2), in proportion as he is able to distinguish them from others, and to contemplate them as individual objects. A man's joy in contemplating himself will therefore be greatest when he contemplates something in himself which he denies of other people. For if he refers that which he affirms of himself to the universal idea of man or of animal nature, he will not so much rejoice; on the other hand, he will be sad if he imagines that his own actions when compared with those of other people are weaker than theirs, and this sorrow he will endeavour to remove (Prop. 28, pt. 3), either by misinterpreting the actions of his equals, or giving as great a lustre as possible to his own. It appears, therefore, that men are by nature inclined to hatred and envy, and we must add that their education assists them in this propensity, for parents are accustomed to excite their children to follow virtue by the stimulus of honour and envy alone. But an objection perhaps may be raised that we not unfrequently venerate men and admire their virtues. In order to remove this objection I will add the following corollary.

Corol.—No one envies the virtue of a person who is not his equal.

Demonst.—Envy is nothing but hatred (Schol. Prop. 24, pt. 3), that is to say (Schol. Prop. 13, pt. 3), sorrow, or, in other words (Schol. Prop. 11, pt. 3), an affection by which the effort of a man or his power of action is restrained. But (Schol. Prop. 9, pt. 3) a man neither endeavours to do nor desires anything excepting what can follow from his given nature, therefore a man will not desire to affirm of himself any power of action, or, which is the same thing, any virtue which is peculiar to another nature and foreign to his own. His desire, therefore, cannot be restrained, that is to say (Schol. Prop. 11, pt. 3), he cannot feel any sorrow because he contemplates a virtue in another person altogether unlike himself, and consequently he cannot envy that person, but will only envy one who is his own equal, and who is supposed to possess the same nature.

Schol.—Since, therefore, we have said in Schol. Prop. 52, pt. 3, that we venerate a man because we are astonished at his wisdom and bravery, &c., this happens because (as is evident from the proposition itself) we imagine that he specially possesses these virtues, and that they are not common to our nature. We therefore envy them no more than we envy trees their height or lions their bravery.

PROP. LVI.—*Of joy, sorrow, and desire, and consequently of every affect which either, like vacillation of mind, is compounded of these, or, like love, hatred, hope, and fear, is derived from them, there are just as many kinds as there are kinds of objects by which we are affected.*

Demonst.—Joy and sorrow, and consequently the affects which are compounded of these or derived from them, are passions (Schol. Prop. 11, pt. 3). But (Prop. 1, pt.

3) we necessarily suffer in so far as we have inadequate ideas, and (Prop. 3, pt. 3) only in so far as we have them; that is to say (see Schol. Prop. 40, pt. 2), we necessarily suffer only in so far as we imagine, or (see Prop. 17, pt. 2, with its Schol.) in so far as we are affected with an affect which involves the nature of our body and that of an external body. The nature, therefore, of each passion must necessarily be explained in such a manner, that the nature of the object by which we are affected is expressed. The joy, for example, which springs from an object A. involves the nature of that object A., and the joy which springs from B. involves the nature of that object B., and therefore these two affects of joy are of a different nature, because they arise from causes of a different nature. In like manner the affect of sorrow which arises from one object is of a different kind from that which arises from another cause, and the same thing is to be understood of love, hatred, hope, fear, vacillation of mind, &c.; so that there are necessarily just as many kinds of joy, sorrow, love, hatred, &c., as there are kinds of objects by which we are affected. But desire is the essence itself or nature of a person in so far as this nature is conceived from its given constitution as determined towards any action (Schol. Prop. 9, pt. 3), and therefore as a person is affected by external causes with this or that kind of joy, sorrow, love, hatred, &c., that is to say, as his nature is constituted in this or that way, so must his desire vary and the nature of one desire differ from that of another, just as the affects from which each desire arises differ. There are as many kinds of desires, therefore, as there are kinds of joy, sorrow, love, &c., and, consequently (as we have just shown), as there are kinds of objects by which we are affected.—Q.E.D.

Schol.—Amongst the different kinds of affects, which (by the preceding Prop.) must be very great in number, the most remarkable are *voluptuousness, drunkenness, lust, avarice,* and *ambition,* which are nothing but notions of love or desire, which explain the nature of this or that affect through the objects to which they are related. For by *voluptuousness, drunkenness, lust, avarice,* and *ambition* we understand nothing but an immoderate love or desire for good living, for drinking, for women, for riches, and for glory. It is to be observed that these affects, in so far as we distinguish them by the object alone to which they are related, have no contraries. For *temperance, sobriety,* and *chastity,* which we are in the habit of opposing to voluptuousness, drunkenness, and lust, are not affects nor passions: but merely indicate the power of the mind which restrains these affects.

The remaining kinds of affects I cannot explain here (for they are as numerous as are the varieties of objects), nor, if I could explain them, is it necessary to do so. For it is sufficient for the purpose we have in view, the determination, namely, of the strength of the affects and the mind's power over them, to have a general definition of each kind of affect. It is sufficient for us, I say, to understand the common properties of the mind and the affects, so that we may determine what and how great is the power of the mind to govern and constrain the affects. Although, therefore, there is a great difference between this or that affect of love, of hatred, or of desire— for example, between the love towards children and the love towards a wife—it is not worth while for us to take cognisance of these differences, or to investigate the nature and origin of the affects any further.

PROP. LVII.—*The affect of one person differs from the corresponding affect of another as much as the essence of the one person differs from that of the other.*

Demonst.—This proposition is evident from Ax. 1 following Lem. 3, after Schol. Prop. 13, pt. 2. Nevertheless, we will demonstrate it from the definitions of the three primitive affects. All affects are related to desire, joy, or sorrow, as the definitions show which we have given of those affects. But desire is the very nature or essence of a person (Schol. Prop. 9, pt. 3), and therefore the desire of one person differs from the desire of another as much as the nature or essence of the one differs from that of the other. Again, joy and sorrow are passions by which the power of a person or his effort to persevere in his own being is increased or diminished, helped, or limited (Prop. 11, pt. 3, with its Schol.) But by the effort to persevere in his own being, in so far as it is related at the same time to the mind and the body, we understand appetite and desire (Schol. Prop. 9, pt. 3), and therefore joy and sorrow are desire or appetite in so far as the latter is increased, diminished, helped, or limited by external causes; that is to say (Schol. Prop. 9, pt. 3), they are the nature itself of each person.

The joy or sorrow of one person therefore differs from the joy or sorrow of another as much as the nature or essence of one person differs from that of the other, and consequently the affect of one person differs from the corresponding affect of another, &c.—Q.E.D.

Schol.—Hence it follows that the affects of animals which are called irrational (for after we have learnt the origin of the mind we can in no way doubt that brutes feel) differ from human affects as much as the nature of a brute differs from that of a man. Both the man and the horse, for example, are swayed by the lust to propagate, but the horse is swayed by equine lust and the man by that which is human. The lusts and appetites of insects, fishes, and birds must vary in the same way; and so, although each individual lives contented with its own nature and delights in it, nevertheless the life with which it is contented and its joy are nothing but the idea or soul of that individual, and so the joy of one differs in character from the joy of the other as much as the essence of the one differs from the essence of the other. Finally, it follows from the preceding proposition that the joy by which the drunkard is enslaved is altogether different from the joy which is the portion of the philosopher,—a thing I wished just to hint in passing. So much, therefore, for the affects which are related to man in so far as he suffers. It remains that I should say a few words about those things which are related to him in so far as he acts.

PROP. LVIII.—*Besides the joys and sorrows which are passions, there are other affects of joy and sorrow which are related to us in so far as we act.*

Demonst.—When the mind conceives itself and its own power of acting, it is rejoiced (Prop. 53, pt. 3). But the mind necessarily contemplates itself whenever it conceives a true or adequate idea (Prop. 43, pt. 2); and as (Schol. 2, Prop. 40, pt. 2) it does conceive some adequate ideas, it is rejoiced in so far as it conceives them, or, in other words (Prop. 1, pt. 3), in so far as it acts. Again, the mind, both in so far as it has clear and distinct ideas and in so far as it has confused ideas, endeavours to persevere in its own being (Prop. 9, pt. 3). But by this effort we understand desire (Schol. Prop. 9, pt. 3), and therefore desire also is related to us in so far as we think; that is to say (Prop. 1, pt. 3), in so far as we act.—Q.E.D.

PROP. LIX.—*Amongst all the affects which are related to the mind in so far as it acts, there are none which are not related to joy or desire.*

Demonst.—All the affects are related to desire, joy, or sorrow, as the definitions we have given of them show. By sorrow, however, we understand that the mind's power of acting is lessened or limited (Prop. 11, pt. 3, and its Schol.), and therefore, in so far as the mind suffers sorrow is its power of thinking, that is to say (Prop. 1, pt. 3), its power of acting, lessened or limited. Therefore no affects of sorrow can be related to the mind in so far as it acts, but only affects of joy and desire, which (by the preceding Prop.) are also so far related to the mind.—Q.E.D.

Schol.—All the actions which follow from the affects which are related to the mind in so far as it thinks I ascribe to *fortitude*, which I divide into *strength of mind* (*animositas*) and *generosity*. By *strength of mind*, I mean the desire by which each person endeavours from the dictates of reason alone to preserve his own being. By *generosity*, I mean the desire by which from the dictates of reason alone each person endeavours to help other people and to join them to him in friendship. Those actions, therefore, which have for their aim the advantage only of the doer I ascribe to strength of mind, whilst those which aim at the advantage of others I ascribe to generosity. Temperance, therefore, sobriety, and presence of mind in danger, are a species of strength of mind, while moderation and mercy are a species of generosity.

I have now, I think, explained the principal affects and vacillations of the mind which are compounded of the three primary affects, desire, joy, and sorrow, and have set them forth through their first causes. From what has been said it is plain that we are disturbed by external causes in a number of ways, and that, like the waves of the sea agitated by contrary winds, we fluctuate in our ignorance of our future and destiny. I have said, however, that I have only explained the prin-cipal mental complications, and not all which may exist. For by the same method which we have pursued above it would be easy to show that love unites itself to re-pentance, scorn, shame, &c.; but I think it has already been made clear to all that the affects can be combined in so many ways, and that so many variations can arise, that no limits can be assigned to their number. It is sufficient for my purpose to have enumerated only those which are of consequence; the rest, of which I have taken no notice, being more curious than important. There is one constantly recurring characteristic of love which I have yet to notice, and that is, that while we are enjoying the thing which we desired, the body acquires from that fruition a new disposition by which it is otherwise determined, and the images of other things are excited in it, and the mind begins to imagine and to desire other things. For example, when we imagine anything which usually delights our taste, we desire to enjoy it by eating it. But whilst we enjoy it the stomach becomes full, and the constitution of the body becomes altered. If, therefore, the body being now otherwise disposed, the image of the food, in consequence of its being present, and therefore also the effort or desire to eat it, become more intense, then this new disposition of the body will oppose this effort or desire, and consequently the presence of the food which we desired will become hateful to us, and this hatefulness is what we call loathing or disgust. As for the external affections of the body which are observed in the affects, such as trembling, paleness, sobbing, laughter, and the like, I have neglected to notice them, because they belong to the body alone without any relationship to the mind. A few things remain to be said about the definitions of the affects, and I will therefore here repeat the definitions in order, appending to them what is necessary to be observed in each.

THE AFFECTS.—DEF. I.—*Desire* is the essence itself of man in so far as it is conceived as determined to any action by any one of his affections.

Explanation.—We have said above, in the Schol. of Prop. 9, pt. 3, that desire is appetite which is self-conscious, and that appetite is the essence itself of man in so far as it is determined to such acts as contribute to his preservation. But in the same scholium I have taken care to remark that in truth I cannot recognise any difference between human appetite and desire. For whether a man be conscious of his appetite or not, it remains one and the same appetite, and so, lest I might appear to be guilty of tautology, I have not explained desire by appetite, but have tried to give such a definition of desire as would include all the efforts of human nature to which we give the name of appetite, desire, will, or impulse. For I might have said that desire is the essence itself of man in so far as it is considered as determined to any action; but from this definition it would not follow (Prop. 23, pt. 2) that the mind could be conscious of its desire or appetite, and therefore, in order that I might include the cause of this consciousness, it was necessary (by the same proposition) to add the words, *in so far as it is conceived as determined to any action by any one of his affections.* For by an affection of the human essence we understand any constitution of that essence, whether it be innate, whether it be conceived through the attribute of thought alone or of extension alone, or whether it be related to both. By the word "desire," therefore, I understand all the efforts, impulses, appetites, and volitions of a man, which vary according to his changing disposition, and not unfrequently are so opposed to one another that he is drawn hither and thither, and knows not whither he ought to turn.

II. *Joy* is man's passage from a less to a greater perfection.

III. *Sorrow* is man's passage from a greater to a less perfection.

Explanation.—I say passage, for joy is not perfection itself. If a man were born with the perfection to which he passes, he would possess it without the affect of joy; a truth which will appear the more clearly from the affect of sorrow, which is the opposite to joy. For that sorrow consists in the passage to a less perfection, but not in the less perfection itself, no one can deny, since in so far as a man shares any perfection he cannot be sad. Nor can we say that sorrow consists in the privation of a greater perfection, for privation is nothing. But the

L

affect of sorrow is a reality, and it therefore must be the reality of the passage to a lesser perfection, or the reality by which man's power of acting is diminished or limited (Schol. Prop. 11, pt. 3). As for the definitions of cheerfulness, pleasurable excitement, melancholy, and grief, I pass these by, because they are related rather to the body than to the mind, and are merely different kinds of joy or of sorrow.

IV. *Astonishment* is the imagination of an object in which the mind remains fixed because this particular imagination has no connection with others.

Explanation.—In the Schol. of Prop. 18, pt. 2, we have shown that that which causes the mind from the contemplation of one thing immediately to pass to the thought of another is that the images of these things are connected one with the other, and are so arranged that the one follows the other; a process which cannot be conceived when the image of the thing is new, for the mind will be held in the contemplation of the same object until other causes determine it to think of other things. The imagination, therefore, considered in itself, of a new object is of the same character as other imaginations; and for this reason I do not class astonishment among the affects, nor do I see any reason why I should do it, since this abstraction of the mind arises from no positive cause by which it is abstracted from other things, but merely from the absence of any cause by which from the contemplation of one thing the mind is determined to think other things. I acknowledge, therefore (as I have shown in Schol. Prop. 11, pt. 3), only three primitive or primary affects, those of joy, sorrow, and desire; and the only reason which has induced me to speak of astonishment is, that it has been the custom to give other names to certain affects derived from the three primitives whenever these affects are related to objects at which we are astonished. This same reason also induces me to add the definition of contempt.

V. *Contempt* is the imagination of an object which so little touches the mind that the mind is moved by the presence of the object to imagine those qualities which are not in it rather than those which are in it. (See Schol. Prop. 52, pt. 3.)

The definitions of veneration and scorn I pass by here, because they give a name, so far as I know, to none of the affects.

VI. *Love* is joy with the accompanying idea of an external cause.

Explanation.—This definition explains with sufficient clearness the essence of love; that which is given by some authors, who define love to be the will of the lover to unite himself to the beloved object, expressing not the essence of love but one of its properties, and in as much as these authors have not seen with sufficient clearness what is the essence of love, they could not have a distinct conception of its properties, and consequently their definition has by everybody been thought very obscure. I must observe, however, when I say that it is a property in a lover to will a union with the beloved object, that I do not understand by will a consent or deliberation or a free decree of the mind (for that this is a fiction we have demonstrated in Prop. 48, pt. 2), nor even a desire of the lover to unite himself with the beloved object when it is absent, nor a desire to continue in its presence when it is present, for love can be conceived without either one or the other of these desires; but by will I understand the satisfaction that the beloved object produces in the lover by its presence, by virtue of which the joy of the lover is strengthened, or at any rate supported.

VII. *Hatred* is sorrow with the accompanying idea of an external cause.

Explanation.—What is to be observed here will easily be seen from what has been said in the explanation of the preceding definition. (See, moreover, Schol. Prop. 13, pt. 3.)

VIII. *Inclination* (*propensio*) is joy with the accompanying idea of some object as being accidentally the cause of the joy.

IX. *Aversion* is sorrow with the accompanying idea of some object which is accidentally the cause of the sorrow. (See Schol. Prop. 15, pt. 3.)

X. *Devotion* is love towards an object which astonishes us.

Explanation. — That astonishment arises from the novelty of the object we have shown in Prop. 52, pt. 3. If, therefore, it should happen that we often imagine the object at which we are astonished, we shall cease to be astonished at it, and hence we see that the affect of devotion easily degenerates into simple love.

XI. *Derision* is joy arising from the imagination that something we despise is present in an object we hate.

Explanation.—In so far as we despise a thing we hate do we deny its existence (Schol. Prop. 52, pt. 3), and so far (Prop. 20, pt. 3) do we rejoice. But inasmuch as we suppose that a man hates what he ridicules, it follows that this joy is not solid. (See Schol. Prop. 47, pt. 3.)

XII. *Hope* is a joy not constant, arising from the idea of something future or past, about the issue of which we sometimes doubt.

XIII. *Fear* is a sorrow not constant, arising from the idea of something future or past, about the issue of which we sometimes doubt. (See Schol. 2, Prop. 18, pt. 3.)

Explanation.—From these definitions it follows that there is no hope without fear nor fear without hope, for the person who wavers in hope and doubts concerning the issue of anything is supposed to imagine something which may exclude its existence, and so far, therefore, to be sad (Prop. 19, pt. 3), and consequently while he wavers in hope, to fear lest his wishes should not be accomplished. So also the person who fears, that is to say, who doubts whether what he hates will not come to pass, imagines something which excludes the existence of what he hates, and therefore (Prop. 20, pt. 3) is rejoiced, and consequently so far hopes that it will not happen.

XIV. *Confidence* is joy arising from the idea of a past or future object from which cause for doubting is removed.

XV. *Despair* is sorrow arising from the idea of a past or future object from which cause for doubting is removed.

Explanation.—Confidence, therefore, springs from hope and despair from fear, whenever the reason for doubting the issue is taken away; a case which occurs either because we imagine a thing past or future to be present and contemplate it as present, or because we imagine other things which exclude the existence of those which made us to doubt.

For although we can never be sure about the issue of individual objects (Corol. Prop. 31, pt. 2), it may nevertheless happen that we do not doubt it. For elsewhere we have shown (Schol. Prop. 49, pt. 2) that it is one thing not to doubt and another to possess certitude, and so it may happen that from the image of an object either past or future we are affected with the same affect of joy or sorrow as that by which we should be affected from the image of an object present, as we have demonstrated in Prop. 18, pt. 3, to which, together with the scholium, the reader is referred.

XVI. *Gladness (gaudium)* is joy with the accompanying idea of something past, which, unhoped for, has happened.

XVII. *Remorse*[1] is sorrow with the accompanying idea of something past, which, unhoped for, has happened.

XVIII. *Commiseration* is sorrow with the accompanying idea of evil which has happened to some one whom we imagine like ourselves (Schol. Prop. 22, and Schol. Prop. 27, pt. 3).

[1] See p. 123, note.

Explanation.—Between commiseration and compassion there seems to be no difference, excepting perhaps that commiseration refers rather to an individual affect and compassion to it as a habit.

XIX. *Favour* is love towards those who have benefited others.

XX. *Indignation* is hatred towards those who have injured others.

Explanation.—I am aware that these names in common bear a different meaning. But my object is not to explain the meaning of words but the nature of things, and to indicate them by words whose customary meaning shall not be altogether opposed to the meaning which I desire to bestow upon them. I consider it sufficient to have said this once for all. As far as the cause of these affects is concerned, see Corol. 1, Prop. 27, pt. 3, and Schol. Prop. 22, pt. 3.

XXI. *Over-estimation* consists in thinking too highly of another person in consequence of our love for him.

XXII. *Contempt* consists in thinking too little of another person in consequence of our hatred for him.

Explanation.—Over-estimation and contempt are therefore respectively effects or properties of love or hatred, and so over-estimation may be defined as love in so far as it affects a man so that he thinks too much of the beloved object; and, on the contrary, contempt may be defined as hatred in so far as it affects a man so that he thinks too little of the object he hates. (See Schol. Prop. 26, pt. 3.)

XXIII. *Envy* is hatred in so far as it affects a man so that he is sad at the good fortune of another person and is glad when any evil happens to him.

Explanation.—To envy is generally opposed compassion (*misericordia*), which may therefore be defined as follows, notwithstanding the usual signification of the word :—

XXIV. *Compassion* is love in so far as it affects a

man so that he is glad at the prosperity of another person and is sad when any evil happens to him.

Explanation.—With regard to the other properties of envy, see Schol. Prop. 24, and Schol. Prop. 32, pt. 3. These are affects of joy and sorrow which are attended by the idea of an external object as their cause, either of itself or accidentally. I pass now to consider other affects which are attended by the idea of something within us as the cause.

XXV. *Self-satisfaction* is the joy which is produced by contemplating ourselves and our own power of action.

XXVI. *Humility* is the sorrow which is produced by contemplating our impotence or helplessness.

Self-satisfaction is opposed to humility in so far as we understand by the former the joy which arises from contemplating our power of action, but in so far as we understand by it joy attended with the idea of something done, which we believe has been done by a free decree of our mind, it is opposed to repentance, which we may thus define :—

XXVII. *Repentance* is sorrow accompanied with the idea of something done which we believe has been done by a free decree of our mind.

Explanation.—We have shown what are the causes of these affects in Schol. Prop. 51, pt. 3, Props. 53 and 54, pt. 3, and Prop. 55, pt. 3, together with its Schol. With regard to a free decree of the mind, see Schol. Prop. 35, pt. 2. Here, however, I must observe, that it is not to be wondered at that sorrow should always follow all those actions which are from custom called wicked, and that joy should follow those which are called good. But that this is chiefly the effect of education will be evident from what we have before said. Parents, by reprobating what are called bad actions, and frequently blaming their children whenever they commit them, while they persuade them to what are called good actions, and praise their children when they perform them, have caused the emotions of sorrow to connect themselves with the former, and those of joy with the latter. Experience proves this, for custom and religion are not the same everywhere; but, on the contrary, things which are sacred to some are profane to others, and what are honourable with some are disgraceful with others. Education alone, therefore, will determine whether a man will repent of any deed or boast of it.

XXVIII. *Pride* is thinking too much of ourselves, through self-love.

Explanation.—Pride differs, therefore, from over-estimation, inasmuch as the latter is related to an external object, but pride to the man himself who thinks of himself too highly. As over-estimation, therefore, is an effect or property of love, so pride is an effect or property of self-love, and it may therefore be defined as love of ourselves or self-satisfaction, in so far as it affects us so that we think too highly of ourselves. (See Schol. Prop. 26, pt. 3.)

To this affect a contrary does not exist, for no one, through hatred of himself, thinks too little of himself; indeed, we may say that no one thinks too little of himself, in so far as he imagines himself unable to do this or that thing. For whatever he imagines that he cannot do, that thing he necessarily imagines, and by his imagination is so disposed that he is actually incapable of doing what he imagines he cannot do. So long, therefore, as he imagines himself unable to do this or that thing, so long is he not determined to do it, and consequently so long it is impossible for him to do it. If, however, we pay attention to what depends upon opinion alone, we shall be able to conceive it possible for a man to think too little of himself, for it may happen that while he sorrowfully contemplates his own weakness he will imagine himself despised by everybody, although nothing could be further from their thoughts than to despise him. A man may also think too little of himself if in the present he denies something of himself in relation to a future time of which he is not sure ; for example, when he denies that he can conceive of nothing with certitude, and that he can desire and do nothing which is not wicked and base. We may also say that a man thinks too little of himself when we see that, from an excess of fear or shame, he does not dare to do what others who are his equals dare to do. This affect, to which I will give the name of Despondency, may therefore be opposed to pride; for as self-satisfaction springs from pride, so despondency springs from humility, and it may therefore be defined thus—

XXIX. *Despondency* is thinking too little of ourselves through sorrow.

Explanation.—We are, nevertheless, often in the habit of opposing humility to pride, but only when we attend to their effects rather than to their nature. For we are accustomed to call a man proud who boasts too much (Schol. Prop. 30, pt. 3), who talks about nothing but his own virtues and other people's vices, who wishes to be preferred to everybody else, and who marches along with that stateliness and pomp which belong to others whose position is far above his. On the other hand, we call a man humble who often blushes, who confesses his own faults and talks about the virtues of others, who yields to every one, who walks with bended head, and who neglects to adorn himself. These affects, humility and despondency, are very rare, for human nature, considered in itself, struggles against them as much as it can (Props. 13 and 54, pt. 3), and hence those who have the most credit for being abject and humble are generally the most ambitious and envious.

XXX. *Self-exaltation* is joy with the accompanying idea of some action we have done, which we imagine people praise.

XXXI. *Shame* is sorrow, with the accompanying idea of some action which we imagine people blame.

Explanation.—With regard to these affects see Schol. Prop. 30, pt. 3. A difference, however, is here to be observed between shame and modesty. Shame is sorrow which follows a deed of which we are ashamed. Modesty is the dread or fear of shame, which keeps a man from committing any disgraceful act. To modesty is usually opposed impudence, which indeed is not an affect, as I shall show in the proper place; but the names of affects, as I have already said, are matters rather of custom than indications of the nature of the affects. I have thus discharged the task which I set myself of explaining the affects of joy and sorrow. I will advance now to those which I ascribe to desire.

XXXII. *Regret* is the desire or longing to possess something, the affect being strengthened by the memory of the object itself, and at the same time being restrained by the memory of other things which exclude the existence of the desired object.

Explanation.—Whenever we recollect a thing, as we have often said, we are thereby necessarily disposed to contemplate it with the same affect as if it were present before us. But this disposition or effort, while we are awake, is generally restrained by the images of things which exclude the existence of the thing which we recollect. Whenever, therefore, we recollect a thing which affects us with any kind of joy, we thereby endeavour to contemplate it with the same affect of joy as if it were present,—an attempt which is, however, immediately restrained by the memory of that which excludes the existence of the thing. Regret, therefore, is really a sorrow which is opposed to the joy which arises from the absence of what we hate. (See Schol. Prop. 47, pt. 3.) But because the name *regret* seems to connect this affect with desire, I therefore ascribe it to desire.

XXXIII. *Emulation* is the desire which is begotten in us of a thing because we imagine that other persons have the same desire.

Explanation.—He who seeks flight because others seek it, he who fears because he sees others fear, or even he who withdraws his hand and moves his body as if his hand were burning because he sees that another person has burnt his hand, such as these, I say, although they may indeed imitate the affect of another, are not said to emulate it; not because we have recognised one cause for emulation and another for imitation, but because it has been the custom to call that man only emulous who imitates what we think noble, useful, or pleasant. With regard to the cause of emulation, see also Prop. 27, pt. 3, with the Schol. For the reason why envy is generally connected with this affect, see Prop. 32, pt. 3, with its Schol.

XXXIV. *Thankfulness* or *gratitude* is the desire or endeavour of love with which we strive to do good to others who, from a similar affect of love, have done good to us (Prop. 39, with Schol. Prop. 41, pt. 3).

XXXV. *Benevolence* is the desire to do good to those whom we pity (Schol. Prop. 27, pt. 3).

XXXVI. *Anger* is the desire by which we are impelled, through hatred, to injure those whom we hate (Prop. 39, pt. 3).

XXXVII. *Vengeance* is the desire which, springing from mutual hatred, urges us to injure those who, from a similar affect, have injured us (Corol. 2, Prop. 40, pt. 3, with Schol.)

XXXVIII. *Cruelty* or *ferocity* is the desire by which a man is impelled to injure any one whom we love or pity.

Explanation.—To cruelty is opposed mercy, which is not a passion, but a power of the mind by which a man restrains anger and vengeance.

XXXIX. *Fear* is the desire of avoiding the greater of two dreaded evils by the less (Schol. Prop. 39, pt. 3).

XL. *Audacity* is the desire by which we are impelled to do something which is accompanied with a danger which our equals fear to meet.

XLI. A person is said to be *pusillanimous* whose desire is restrained by the fear of a danger which his equals dare to meet.

Explanation.—Pusillanimity, therefore, is nothing but the dread of some evil which most persons do not usually fear, and therefore I do not ascribe it to the affects of desire. I wished, notwithstanding, to explain it here, because in so far as we attend to desire, pusillanimity is the true opposite of the affect of audacity.

XLII. *Consternation* is affirmed of the man whose desire of avoiding evil is restrained by astonishment at the evil which he fears.

Explanation.—Consternation is therefore a kind of pusillanimity. But because consternation springs from a double fear, it may be more aptly defined as that dread which holds a man stupefied or vacillating, so that he cannot remove an evil. I say *stupefied*, in so far as we understand his desire of removing the evil to be restrained by his astonishment. I say also *vacillating*, in so far as we conceive the same desire to be restrained by the fear of another evil which equally tortures him, so that he does not know which of the two evils to avoid. See Schol. Prop. 39, and Schol. Prop. 52, pt. 3. With regard to pusillanimity and audacity, see Schol. Prop. 51, pt. 3.

XLIII. *Courtesy* or *moderation* is the desire of doing those things which please men and omitting those which displease them.

XLIV. *Ambition* is the immoderate desire of glory.

Explanation.—Ambition is a desire which increases and strengthens all the affects (Props. 27 and 31, pt. 3), and that is the reason why it can hardly be kept under control. For so long as a man is possessed by any desire, he is necessarily at the same time possessed by this. *Every noble man*, says Cicero, *is led by glory, and even the philosophers who write books about despising glory place their names on the title-page.*[1]

XLV. *Luxuriousness* is the immoderate desire or love of good living.

XLVI. *Drunkenness* is the immoderate desire and love of drinking.

XLVII. *Avarice* is the immoderate desire and love of riches.

XLVIII. *Lust* is the immoderate desire and love of sexual intercourse.

Explanation.—This desire of sexual intercourse is usually called lust, whether it be held within bounds or not. I may add that the five last-mentioned affects (as we have shown in Schol. Prop. 56, pt. 3) have no contraries, for moderation is a kind of ambition (see Schol. Prop. 29, pt. 3), and I have already observed that temperance, sobriety, and chastity show a power and not a passion of the mind. Even supposing that an avaricious, ambitious, or timid man refrains from an excess of eating, drinking, or sexual intercourse, avarice, ambition, and fear are not therefore the opposites of voluptuousness, drunkenness, or lust. For the avaricious man generally desires to swallow as much meat and drink as he can, provided only it belong to another person. The ambitious man, too, if he hopes he can keep it a secret, will restrain himself in nothing, and if he lives amongst drunkards and libertines, will be more inclined to their vices just because he is ambitious. The timid man, too, does what he does not will; and although, in order to avoid death, he may throw his riches into the sea, he remains avaricious; nor does the lascivious man cease to be lascivious because he is sorry that he cannot gratify his desire. Absolutely, therefore, these affects have reference not so much to the acts themselves of eating and drinking as to the appetite and love itself. Consequently nothing can be opposed to these affects but nobility of soul and strength of mind, as we shall see afterwards.

[1] Pro Archia.

The definitions of jealousy and the other vacillations of the mind I pass over in silence, both because they are compounded of the affects which we have already defined, and also because many of them have no names,—a fact which shows that, for the purposes of life, it is sufficient to know these combinations generally. Moreover, it follows from the definitions of the affects which we have explained that they all arise from desire, joy, or sorrow, or rather that there are none but these three, which pass under names varying as their relations and external signs vary. If, therefore, we attend to these primitive affects and to what has been said above about the nature of the mind, we shall be able here to define the affects in so far as they are related to the mind alone.

General definition of the affects.—Affect, which is called *animi pathema*, is a confused idea by which the mind affirms of its body, or any part of it, a greater or less power of existence than before; and this increase of power being given, the mind itself is determined to one particular thought rather than to another.

Explanation.—I say, in the first place, that an affect or passion of the mind *is a confused idea.* For we have shown (Prop. 3, pt. 3) that the mind suffers only in so far as it has inadequate or confused ideas. I say again, *by which the mind affirms of its body, or any part of it, a greater or less power of existence than before.* For all ideas which we possess of bodies indicate the actual constitution of our body rather than the nature of the external body (Corol. 2, Prop. 16, pt. 2); but this idea, which constitutes the form of an affect, must indicate or express the constitution of the body, or of some part of it; which constitution the body or any part of it possesses from the fact that its power of action or force of existence is increased or diminished, helped or limited. But it is to be observed, that when I say *a greater or less power of existence than before,* I do not mean that the mind compares the present with the past constitution of the body, but that the idea which constitutes the form of affect affirms something of the body which actually involves more or less reality than before. Moreover, since the essence of the mind (Props. 11 and 13, pt. 2) consists in its affirmation of the actual existence of its body, and since we understand by perfection the essence itself of the thing, it follows that the mind passes to a greater or less perfection when it is able to affirm of its body, or some part of it, something which involves a greater or less reality than before. When, therefore, I have said that the mind's power of thought is increased or diminished, I have wished to be understood as meaning nothing else than that the mind has formed an idea of its body, or some part of its body, which expresses more or less reality than it had hitherto affirmed of the body. For the value of ideas and the actual power of thought are measured by the value of the object. Finally, I added, *which being given, the mind itself is determined to one particular thought rather than to another*, that I might also express the nature of desire in addition to that of joy and sorrow, which is explained by the first part of the definition.

END OF THE THIRD PART

ETHIC.

𝔉𝔬𝔲𝔯𝔱𝔥 ℘𝔞𝔯𝔱.

OF HUMAN BONDAGE OR OF THE STRENGTH OF THE AFFECTS.

PREFACE.

THE impotence of man to govern or restrain the affects I call bondage, for a man who is under their control is not his own master, but is mastered by fortune, in whose power he is, so that he is often forced to follow the worse, although he sees the better before him. I propose in this part to demonstrate why this is, and also to show what of good and evil the affects possess. But before I begin I should like to say a few words about perfection and imperfection, and about good and evil. If a man has proposed to do a thing and has accomplished it, he calls it perfect, and not only he, but every one else who has really known or has believed that he has known the mind and intention of the author of that work will call it perfect too. For example, having seen some work (which I suppose to be as yet not finished), if we know that the intention of the author of that work is to build a house, we shall call the house imperfect; while, on the other hand, we shall call it perfect as soon as we see the work has been brought to the end which the author had determined for it. But if we see any work such as we have never seen before, and if we do not know the mind of the workman, we shall then not be able to say whether the work is perfect or imperfect.[1] This seems to have been the first signification of these words; but afterwards men began to form universal ideas, to think out for themselves types of houses, buildings, castles, and to prefer some types of things to others; and so it happened that each person called a thing perfect which seemed to agree with the universal idea which he had formed of that thing, and, on the other hand, he called a thing imperfect which seemed to agree less with his typal conception, although, according to the intention of the workman, it had been entirely completed. This appears to be the only reason why the words *perfect* and *imperfect* are commonly applied to natural objects which are not made with human hands; for men are in the habit of forming, both of natural as well as of artificial objects, universal ideas which they regard as types of things, and which they think nature has in view, setting them before herself as types too; it being the common opinion that she does nothing except for the sake of some end. When, therefore, men see something done by nature which does not altogether answer to that typal conception which they have of the thing, they think that nature herself has failed or committed an error, and that she has left the thing imperfect. Thus we see that the custom of applying the words *perfect* and *imperfect* to natural objects has arisen rather from prejudice than from true knowledge of them. For we have shown in the Appendix to the First Part of this work that nature does nothing for the sake of an end, for that eternal and infinite Being whom we call God or Nature acts by the same necessity by which He exists; for we have shown that He acts by the same necessity of nature as that by which He exists (Prop. 16, pt. 1). The reason or cause, therefore, why

---

[1] A translation cannot show the etymology of the word *perfect* as it is shown in the original Latin, so that this passage may perhaps seem rather obscure. It is only necessary, however, to bear in mind that *perfect* and *accomplished* are expressible by the same word in Latin, and that *accomplish* is the primary meaning of *perficere.*—TRANS.

M

God or nature acts and the reason why He exists are one and the same. Since, therefore, He exists for no end, He acts for no end; and since He has no principle or end of existence, He has no principle or end of action. A final cause, as it is called, is nothing, therefore, but human desire, in so far as this is considered as the principle or primary cause of anything. For example, when we say that the having a house to live in was the final cause of this or that house, we merely mean that a man, because he imagined the advantages of a domestic life, desired to build a house. Therefore, having a house to live in, in so far as it is considered as a final cause, is merely this particular desire, which is really an efficient cause, and is considered as primary, because men are usually ignorant of the causes of their desires; for, as I have often said, we are conscious of our actions and desires, but ignorant of the causes by which we are determined to desire anything. As for the vulgar opinion that nature sometimes fails or commits an error, or produces imperfect things, I class it amongst those fictions mentioned in the Appendix to the First Part.

Perfection, therefore, and imperfection are really only modes of thought; that is to say, notions which we are in the habit of forming from the comparison with one another of individuals of the same species or genus, and this is the reason why I have said, in Def. 6, pt. 2, that by reality and perfection I understand the same thing; for we are in the habit of referring all individuals in nature to one genus, which is called the most general; that is to say, to the notion of being, which embraces absolutely all the individual objects in nature. In so far, therefore, as we refer the individual objects in nature to this genus, and compare them one with another, and discover that some possess more being or reality than others, in so far do we call some more perfect than others; and in so far as we assign to the latter anything which, like limitation, termination, impotence, &c., involves negation, shall we call them imperfect, because they do not affect our minds so strongly as those we call perfect, but not because anything which really belongs to them is wanting, or because nature has committed an error. For nothing belongs to the nature of anything excepting that which follows from the necessity of the nature of the efficient cause, and whatever follows from the necessity of the nature of the efficient cause necessarily happens.

With regard to good and evil, these terms indicate nothing positive in things considered in themselves, nor are they anything else than modes of thought, or notions which we form from the comparison of one thing with another. For one and the same thing may at the same time be both good and evil or indifferent. Music, for example, is good to a melancholy person, bad to one mourning, while to a deaf man it is neither good nor bad. But although things are so, we must retain these words. For since we desire to form for ourselves an idea of man upon which we may look as a model of human nature, it will be of service to us to retain these expressions in the sense I have mentioned. By *good*, therefore, I understand in the following pages everything which we are certain is a means by which we may approach nearer and nearer to the model of human nature we set before us. By *evil*, on the contrary, I understand everything which we are certain hinders us from reaching that model. Again, I shall call men more or less perfect or imperfect in so far as they approach more or less nearly to this same model. For it is to be carefully observed, that when I say that an individual passes from a less to a greater perfection and *vice versâ*, I do not understand that from one essence or form he is changed into another (for a horse, for instance, would be as much destroyed if it were changed into a man as if it were changed into an insect), but rather we conceive that his power of action, in so far as it is understood by his own nature, is increased or diminished. Finally, by perfection generally, I understand as I have said, reality; that is to say, the essence of any object in so far as it exists and acts in a certain manner, no regard being paid to its duration. For no individual thing can be said to be more perfect because for a longer time it has persevered in existence; inasmuch as the duration of things cannot be determined by their essence, the essence of things involving no fixed or determined period of existence; any object, whether it be more or less perfect, always being able to persevere in existence with the same force as that with which it commenced existence. All things, therefore, are equal in this respect.

DEFINITIONS.

I.—By good, I understand that which we certainly know is useful to us.

II. By evil, on the contrary, I understand that which we certainly know hinders us from possessing anything that is good.

With regard to these two definitions, see the close of the preceding preface.

III. I call individual things contingent in so far as we discover nothing, whilst we attend to their essence alone, which necessarily posits their existence or which necessarily excludes it.

IV. I call these individual things possible, in so far as we are ignorant, whilst we attend to the causes from which they must be produced, whether these causes are determined to the production of these things. In Schol. 1, Prop. 33, pt. 1, I made no difference between possible and contingent, because there was no occasion there to distinguish them accurately.

V. By contrary affects, I understand in the following pages those which, although they may be of the same kind, draw a man in different directions; such as voluptuousness and avarice, which are both a species of love, and are not contrary to one another by nature, but only by accident.

VI. What I understand by affect towards a thing future, present, and past, I have explained in Schol. 1 and 2, Prop. 18, pt. 3, to which the reader is referred.

Here, however, it is to be observed that it is the same with time as it is with place; for as beyond a certain limit we can form no distinct imagination of distance—that is to say, as we usually imagine all objects to be equally distant from us, and as if they were on the same plane, if their distance from us exceeds 200 feet, or if their distance from the position we occupy is greater than we can distinctly imagine—so we imagine all objects to be equally distant from the present time, and refer them as if to one moment, if the period to which their existence belongs is separated from the present by a longer interval than we can usually imagine distinctly.

VII. By end for the sake of which we do anything, I understand appetite.

VIII. By virtue and power, I understand the same thing; that is to say (Prop. 7, pt. 3), virtue, in so far as it is related to man, is the essence itself or nature of the man in so far as it has the power of effecting certain things which can be understood through the laws of its nature alone.

AXIOM.

There is no individual thing in nature which is not surpassed in strength and power by some other thing, but any individual thing being given, another and a stronger is also given, by which the former can be destroyed.

PROP. I.—*Nothing positive contained in a false idea is removed by the presence of the true in so far as it is true.*

Demonst.—Falsity consists in nothing but the privation of knowledge which inadequate ideas involve (Prop. 35, pt. 2), nor do they possess anything positive on account of which they are called false (Prop. 33, pt. 2); on the

contrary, in so far as they are related to God, they are
true (Prop. 32, pt. 2). If, therefore, anything positive
contained in a false idea were removed by the presence
of the true in so far as it is true, a true idea would be
removed by itself, which (Prop. 4, pt. 3) is absurd. Nothing positive, therefore, &c.—Q.E.D.

Schol. — This proposition can be understood more
clearly from Corol. 2, Prop. 16, pt. 2. For an imagination is an idea which indicates the present constitution
of the human body rather than the nature of an external
body, not indeed distinctly but confusedly, so that the
mind is said to err. For example, when we look at the
sun, we imagine his distance from us to be about 200
feet, and in this we are deceived so long as we remain in
ignorance of the true distance. When this is known, the
error is removed, but not the imagination, that is to say,
the idea of the sun which manifests his nature in so far
only as the body is affected by him; so that although we
know his true distance, we nevertheless imagine him close
to us. For, as we have shown in Schol. Prop. 35, pt. 2,
it is not because we are ignorant of the sun's true distance
that we imagine him to be so close to us, but because
the mind conceives the magnitude of the sun just in so
far as the body is affected by him. So when the rays of
the sun falling upon a surface of water are reflected to
our eyes, we imagine him to be in the water, although his
true place is known to us. So with the other imaginations by which the mind is deceived; whether they indicate the natural constitution of the body or an increase
or diminution in its power of action, they are not opposed
to the truth, nor do they disappear with the presence of
the truth. We know that when we groundlessly fear
any evil, the fear vanishes when we hear correct intelligence; but we also know, on the other hand, that when
we fear an evil which will actually come upon us, the
fear vanishes when we hear false intelligence, so that
the imaginations do not disappear with the presence of

the truth, in so far as it is true, but because other imaginations arise which are stronger, and which exclude the present existence of the objects we imagine, as we have shown in Prop. 17, pt. 2.

PROP. II.—*We suffer in so far as we are a part of nature, which part cannot be conceived by itself nor without the other parts.*

Demonst.—We are said to suffer when anything occurs in us of which we are only the partial cause (Def. 2, pt. 3), that is to say (Def. 1, pt. 3), anything which cannot be deduced from the laws of our own nature alone; we suffer, therefore, in so far as we are a part of nature, which part cannot be conceived by itself nor without the other parts.—Q.E.D.

PROP. III.—*The force by which man perseveres in existence is limited, and infinitely surpassed by the power of external causes.*

Demonst.—This is evident from the Axiom, pt. 4. For any man being given, there is given something else—for example, A—more powerful than he is, and A being given, there is again given something, B, more powerful than A, and so on *ad infinitum.* Hence the power of man is limited by the power of some other object, and is infinitely surpassed by the power of external causes.—Q.E.D.

PROP. IV.—*It is impossible that a man should not be a part of nature, and that he should suffer no changes but those which can be understood through his own nature alone, and of which he is the adequate cause.*

Demonst.—The power by which individual things and consequently man preserve their being is the actual power of God or nature (Corol. Prop. 24, pt. 1), not in so far as it is infinite, but in so far as it can be manifested by the actual essence of man (Prop. 7, pt. 3). The power therefore of man, in so far as it is manifested by his actual essence, is part of the infinite power of God or nature, that is to say (Prop. 34, pt. 1), part of His essence. This was the first thing to be proved. Again, if it were possible that man could suffer no changes but those which can be understood through his nature alone, it would follow (Props. 4 and 6, pt. 3) that he could not perish, but that he would exist for ever necessarily; and this necessary existence must result from a cause whose power is either finite or infinite, that is to say, either from the power of man alone, which would be able to place at a distance from himself all other changes which could take their origin from external causes, or it must result from the infinite power of nature by which all individual things would be so directed that man could suffer no changes but those tending to his preservation. But the first case (by the preceding proposition, whose demonstration is universal and capable of application to all individual objects) is absurd; therefore if it were possible for a man to suffer no changes but those which could be understood through his own nature alone, and consequently (as we have shown) that he should always necessarily exist, this must follow from the infinite power of God; and therefore (Prop. 16, pt. 1) from the necessity of the divine nature, in so far as it is considered as affected by the idea of any one man, the whole order of nature, in so far as it is conceived under the attributes of thought and extension, would have to be deduced. From this it would follow (Prop. 21, pt. 1) that man would be infinite, which (by the first part of this demonstration) is an absurdity. It is impossible, therefore, that a man can suffer no changes but those of which he is the adequate cause. — Q.E.D.

Corol.—Hence it follows that a man is necessarily always subject to passions, and that he follows and obeys the common order of nature, accommodating himself to it as far as the nature of things requires.

PROP. V.—*The force and increase of any passion and its perseverance in existence are not limited by the power by which we endeavour to persevere in existence, but by the power of an external cause compared with our own power.*

Demonst.—The essence of a passion cannot be explained by our essence alone (Defs. 1 and 2, pt. 3); that is to say (Prop. 7, pt. 3), the power of a passion cannot be limited by the power by which we endeavour to persevere in our being, but (as has been shown in Prop. 16, pt. 2) must necessarily be limited by the power of an external cause compared with our own power.—Q.E.D.

PROP. VI.—*The other actions or power of a man may be so far surpassed by force of some passion or affect, that the affect may obstinately cling to him.*

Demonst.—The force and increase of any passion and its perseverance in existence are limited by the power of an external cause compared with our own power (Prop. 5, pt. 4), and therefore (Prop. 3, pt. 4) may surpass the power of man.—Q.E.D.

PROP. VII.—*An affect cannot be restrained nor removed unless by an opposed and stronger affect.*

Demonst.—An affect, in so far as it is related to the mind, is an idea by which the mind affirms a greater or less power of existence for its body than the body possessed before (by the general definition of affects at the end of Third Part). Whenever, therefore, the mind is agitated by any affect, the body is at the same time affected with an affection by which its power of action is increased or diminished. Again, this affection of the body (Prop. 5, pt. 4) receives from its own cause a power to persevere in its own being, a power, therefore, which cannot be restrained nor removed unless by a bodily cause (Prop. 6, pt. 2) affecting the body with an affection contrary to the first (Prop. 5, pt. 3), and stronger than it (Ax. 1, pt. 4). Thus the mind (Prop. 12, pt. 2) is affected by the idea of an affection stronger than the former and contrary to it; that is to say (by the general definition of the affects), it will be affected with an affect stronger than the former and contrary to it, and this stronger affect will exclude the existence of the other or remove it. Thus an affect cannot be restrained nor removed unless by an opposed and stronger affect.— Q.E.D.

Corol.—An affect, in so far as it is related to the mind, cannot be restrained nor removed unless by the idea of a bodily affection opposed to that which we suffer and stronger than it. For the affect which we suffer cannot be restrained nor removed unless by an opposed and stronger affect (Prop. 7, pt. 4); that is to say (by the general definition of the affects), it cannot be removed unless by the idea of a bodily affection stronger than that which affects us, and opposed to it.

PROP. VIII.—*Knowledge of good or evil is nothing but an affect of joy or sorrow in so far as we are conscious of it.*

Demonst.—We call a thing good which contributes to the preservation of our being, and we call a thing evil if it is an obstacle to the preservation of our being (Defs. 1 and 2, pt. 4); that is to say (Prop. 7, pt. 3), a thing is called by us good or evil as it increases or diminishes, helps or restrains, our power of action. In so far, therefore (Defs. of *joy* and *sorrow* in Schol. Prop. 11, pt. 3), as we perceive that any object affects us with joy or sorrow do we call it good or evil, and therefore the knowledge of good or evil is nothing but an idea of joy or sorrow which necessarily follows from the affect itself of joy or sorrow (Prop. 22, pt. 2). But this idea is united to the affect in the same way as the mind is united to the body (Prop. 21, pt. 2), or, in other words (as we have shown in the Schol. to Prop. 21, pt. 2), this idea is not actually distinguished from the affect itself; that is to say (by the general definition of the affects), it is not actually distinguished from the idea of the affection of the body, unless in conception alone. This knowledge, therefore of good and evil is nothing but the affect itself of joy and sorrow in so far as we are conscious of it.—Q.E.D.

PROP. IX.—*If we imagine the cause of an affect to be actually present with us, that affect will be stronger than if we imagined the cause not to be present.*

Demonst.—The imagination is an idea by which the mind contemplates an object as present (see the definition of the imagination in Schol. Prop. 17, pt. 2), an idea which nevertheless indicates the constitution of the human body rather than the nature of the external object (Corol. 2, Prop. 16, pt. 2). Imagination, therefore (by the general definition of the affects), is an affect in so far as it indicates the constitution of the body. But the imagination (Prop. 17, pt. 2) increases in intensity in proportion as we imagine nothing which excludes the present existence of the external object. If, therefore, we imagine the cause of an affect to be actually present with us, that affect will be intenser or stronger than if we imagined the cause not to be present.—Q.E.D.

Schol.—When I said (in Prop. 18, pt. 3) that we are affected by the image of an object in the future or the past with the same affect with which we should be affected if the object we imagined were actually present, I was careful to warn the reader that this was true in so far only as we attend to the image alone of the object itself, for the image is of the same nature whether we have imagined the object or not; but I have not denied that the image becomes weaker when we contemplate as present other objects which exclude the present existence of the future object. This exception I neglected to make, because I had determined to treat in this part of my work of the strength of the affects.

Corol.—The image of a past or future object, that is to say, of an object which we contemplate in relation to the past or future to the exclusion of the present, other things being equal, is weaker than the image of a present object, and consequently the affect towards a future or past object, other things being equal, is weaker then than the affect towards a present object.

PROP. X.—*We are affected with regard to a future object which we imagine will soon be present more powerfully than if we imagine that the time at which it will exist is further removed from the present, and the memory of an object which we imagine has but just passed away also affects us more powerfully than if we imagine the object to have passed away some time ago.*

Demonst.—In so far as we imagine that an object will quickly be present or has not long since passed away, do we imagine something which excludes the presence of the object less than if we imagine that the time of its existence is at a great distance from the present, either in the future or the past (as is self-evident), and therefore (Prop. 9, pt. 4) so far shall we be affected more strongly with regard to it.—Q.E.D.

Schol.—From the observations which we made upon Def. 6, pt. 4, it follows that all objects which are separated from the present time by a longer interval than our imagination has any power to determine affect us equally slightly, although we know them to be separated from one another by a large space of time.

PROP. XI.—*The affect towards an object which we imagine as necessary, other things being equal, is stronger than that towards an object that is possible, contingent, or not necessary.*

Demonst.—In so far as we imagine any object to be necessary do we affirm its existence, and, on the other hand, we deny its existence in so far as we imagine it to be not necessary (Schol. 1, Prop. 33, pt. 1), and therefore (Prop. 9, pt. 4) the affect towards a necessary object, other things being equal, is stronger than that which we feel towards one that is not necessary.

PROP. XII.—*The affect towards an object which we know does not exist in the present, and which we imagine as possible, other things being equal, is stronger than the affect towards a contingent object.*

Demonst.—In so far as we imagine an object as contingent, we are not affected by the image of any other object which posits the existence of the first (Def. 3, pt. 4), but, on the contrary (by hypothesis), we imagine some things which exclude its present existence. But in so far as we imagine any object in the future to be possible do we imagine some things which posit its existence (Def. 4, pt. 4), that is to say (Schol. 2, Prop. 18, pt. 3), things which foster hope or fear, and therefore the affect towards a possible object is stronger, &c. —Q.E.D.

Corol.—The affect towards an object which we know does not exist in the present, and which we imagine as contingent, is much weaker than if we imagined that the object were present to us.

Demonst.—The affect towards an object which we imagine to exist in the present is stronger than if we imagined it as future (Corol. Prop. 9, pt. 4), and is much stronger if we imagine the future to be at a great[1] distance from the present time (Prop. 10, pt. 4). The affect, therefore, towards an object which we imagine will

[1] *Non multum distare*, Ed. Pr. Corrected from Dutch version.—TR.

not exist for a long time is so much feebler than if we imagined it as present, and nevertheless (Prop. 12, pt. 4) is stronger than if we imagined it as contingent; and therefore the affect towards a contingent object is much feebler than if we imagined the object to be present to us.—Q.E.D.

PROP. XIII.—*The affect towards a contingent object which we know does not exist in the present, other things being equal, is much weaker than the affect towards a past object.*

Demonst.—In so far as we imagine an object as contingent, we are affected with no image of any other object which posits the existence of the first (Def. 3, pt. 4). On the contrary, we imagine (by hypothesis) certain things which exclude its present existence. But in so far as we imagine it in relationship to past time are we supposed to imagine something which brings it back to the memory or which excites its image (Prop. 18, pt. 2, with the Schol.), and therefore so far causes us to contemplate it as present (Corol. Prop. 17, pt. 2). Therefore (Prop. 9, pt. 4), the affect towards a contingent object which we know does not exist in the present, other things being equal, will be weaker than the affect towards a past object.—Q.E.D.

PROP. XIV.—*No affect can be restrained by the true knowledge of good and evil in so far as it is true, but only in so far as it is considered as an affect.*

Demonst.—An affect is an idea by which the mind affirms a greater or less power of existence for the body than it possessed before (by the general definition of the affects); and therefore (Prop. 1, pt. 4) this idea has nothing positive which can be removed by the presence of the truth, and consequently the true knowledge

of good and evil, in so far as it is true, can restrain no
affect. But in so far as it is an affect (see Prop. 8, pt.
4) will it restrain any other affect, provided that the
latter be the weaker of the two (Prop. 7, pt. 4).—Q.E.D.

PROP. XV.—*Desire which arises from a true knowledge of
good and evil can be extinguished or restrained by
many other desires which take their origin from the
affects by which we are agitated.*

Demonst.—From the true knowledge of good and evil,
in so far as this (Prop. 8, pt. 4) is an affect, necessarily
arises desire (Def. 1 of the affects, pt. 3), which is greater
in proportion as the affect from which it springs is
greater (Prop. 37, pt. 3). But this desire (by hypothesis),
because it springs from our understanding something
truly, follows therefore in us in so far as we act (Prop.
1, pt. 3), and therefore must be understood through our
essence alone (Def. 2, pt. 3), and consequently its strength
and increase must be limited by human power alone
(Prop. 7, pt. 3). But the desires which spring from the
affects by which we are agitated are greater as the affects
themselves are greater, and therefore their strength and
increase (Prop. 5, pt. 4) must be limited by the power
of external causes, a power which, if it be compared
with our own, indefinitely surpasses it (Prop. 3, pt. 4).
The desires, therefore, which take their origin from such
affects as these may be much stronger than that which
takes its origin from a true knowledge of good and evil,
and the former (Prop. 7, pt. 4) may be able to restrain
and extinguish the latter.—Q.E.D.

PROP. XVI.—*The desire which springs from a knowledge of
good and evil can be easily extinguished or restrained,
in so far as this knowledge is connected with the
future, by the desire of things which in the present are
sweet.*

Demonst.—The affect towards an object which we imagine as future is weaker than towards that which we imagine as present (Corol. Prop. 9, pt. 4). But the desire which springs from a true knowledge of good and evil, even although the knowledge be of objects which are good at the present time, may be extinguished or restrained by any casual desire (Prop. 15, pt. 4, the demonstration of this proposition being universal), and therefore the desire which springs from a knowledge of good and evil, in so far as this knowledge is connected with the future, can be easily restrained or extinguished.—Q.E.D.

PROP. XVII.—*The desire which springs from a true knowledge of good and evil can be still more easily restrained, in so far as this knowledge is connected with objects which are contingent, by the desire of objects which are present.*

Demonst.—This proposition is demonstrated in the same way as the preceding proposition from Corol. Prop. 12, pt. 4.

Schol.—In these propositions I consider that I have explained why men are more strongly influenced by an opinion than by true reason, and why the true knowledge of good and evil causes disturbance in the mind, and often gives way to every kind of lust, whence the saying of the poet, " *Video meliora proboque, deteriora sequor.*" The same thought appears to have been in the mind of the Preacher when he said, " *He that increaseth knowledge increaseth sorrow.*" I say these things not because I would be understood to conclude, therefore, that it is better to be ignorant than to be wise, or that the wise man in governing his passions is nothing better than the fool, but I say them because it is necessary for us to know both the strength and weakness of our nature, so that we may determine what reason can do and what it cannot do in governing our affects. This, moreover, let it be remembered, is the Part in which I meant to treat of human weakness alone, all consideration of the power of reason over the passions being reserved for a future portion of the book.

PROP. XVIII.—*The desire which springs from joy, other things being equal, is stronger than that which springs from sorrow.*

Demonst.—Desire is the very essence of man (Def. 1 of the Affects, pt. 3), that is to say (Prop. 7, pt. 3), the effort by which a man strives to persevere in his being. The desire, therefore, which springs from joy, by that very affect of joy (by the definition of joy in Schol. Prop. 11, pt. 3) is assisted or increased, while that which springs from sorrow, by that very affect of sorrow (by the same Schol.) is lessened or restrained, and so the force of the desire which springs from joy must be limited by human power, together with the power of an external cause, while that which springs from sorrow must be limited by human power alone. The latter is, therefore, weaker than the former.—Q.E.D.

Schol.—I have thus briefly explained the causes of human impotence and want of stability, and why men do not obey the dictates of reason. It remains for me now to show what it is which reason prescribes to us, which affects agree with the rules of human reason, and which, on the contrary, are opposed to these rules. Before, however, I begin to demonstrate these things by our full geometrical method, I should like briefly to set forth here these dictates of reason, in order that what I have in my mind about them may be easily comprehended by all. Since reason demands nothing which is opposed to nature, it demands, therefore, that every person should love himself, should seek his own profit,—what is truly profitable to him,—should desire everything that really

N

leads man to greater perfection, and absolutely that every one should endeavour, as far as in him lies, to preserve his own being.   This is all true as necessarily as that the whole is greater than its part (Prop. 6, pt. 3).   Again, since virtue (Def. 8, pt. 4) means nothing but acting according to the laws of our own nature, and since no one endeavours to preserve his being (Prop. 7, pt. 3) except in accordance with the laws of his own nature, it follows: *Firstly*, That the foundation of virtue is that endeavour itself to preserve our own being, and that happiness consists in this—that a man can preserve his own being.   *Secondly*, It follows that virtue is to be desired for its own sake, nor is there anything more excellent or more useful to us than virtue, for the sake of which virtue ought to be desired.   *Thirdly*, It follows that all persons who kill themselves are impotent in mind, and have been thoroughly overcome by external causes opposed to their nature.   Again, from Post. 4, pt. 2, it follows that we can never free ourselves from the need of something outside us for the preservation of our being, and that we can never live in such a manner as to have no intercourse with objects which are outside us.   Indeed, so far as the mind is concerned, our intellect would be less perfect if the mind were alone, and understood nothing but itself.   There are many things, therefore, outside us which are useful to us, and which, therefore, are to be sought.   Of all these, none more excellent can be discovered than those which exactly agree with our nature.   If, for example, two individuals of exactly the same nature are joined together, they make up a single individual, doubly stronger than each alone. Nothing, therefore, is more useful to man than man. Men can desire, I say, nothing more excellent for the preservation of their being than that all should so agree at every point that the minds and bodies of all should form, as it were, one mind and one body ; that all should together endeavour as much as possible to preserve their being, and that all should together seek the common good of all. From this it follows that men who are governed by reason,—that is to say, men who, under the guidance of reason, seek their own profit,—desire nothing for themselves which they do not desire for other men, and that, therefore, they are just, faithful, and honourable.

These are those dictates of reason which I purposed briefly to set forth before commencing their demonstration by a fuller method, in order that, if possible, I might win the attention of those who believe that this principle,—that every one is bound to seek his own profit,—is the foundation of impiety, and not of virtue and piety. Having now briefly shown that this belief of theirs is the contrary of the truth, I proceed, by the same method as that which we have hitherto pursued, to demonstrate what I have said.

PROP. XIX.—*According to the laws of his own nature each person necessarily desires that which he considers to be good, and avoids that which he considers to be evil.*

Demonst.—The knowledge of good and evil (Prop. 8, pt. 4) is the affect itself of joy or sorrow, in so far as we are conscious of it, and, therefore (Prop. 28, pt. 3), each person necessarily desires that which he considers to be good, and avoids that which he considers to be evil. But this desire is nothing but the essence itself or nature of man (Def. of appetite in Schol. Prop. 9, pt. 3, and Def. 1 of the Affects, pt. 3). Therefore, according to the laws of his own nature alone, he necessarily desires or avoids, &c.—Q.E.D.

PROP. XX.—*The more each person strives and is able to seek his own profit, that is to say, to preserve his being, the more virtue does he possess; on the other hand, in so far as each person neglects his own profit, that is to say, neglects to preserve his own being, is he impotent.*

Demonst.—Virtue is human power itself, which is limited by the essence alone of man (Def. 8, pt. 4), that is to say (Prop. 7, pt. 3), which is limited by the effort alone by which man endeavours to persevere in his being. The more, therefore, each person strives and is able to preserve his being, the more virtue does he possess, and consequently (Props. 4 and 6, pt. 3), in proportion as he neglects to preserve his being is he impotent.

Schol.—No one, therefore, unless defeated by external causes and those which are contrary to his nature, neglects to seek his own profit or preserve his being. No one, I say, refuses food or kills himself from a necessity of his nature, but only when forced by external causes. The compulsion may be exercised in many ways. A man kills himself under compulsion by another when that other turns the right hand, with which the man had by chance laid hold of a sword, and compels him to direct the sword against his own heart; or the command of a tyrant may compel a man, as it did Seneca, to open his own veins, that is to say, he may desire to avoid a greater evil by a less. External and hidden causes also may so dispose his imagination and may so affect his body as to cause it to put on another nature contrary to that which it had at first, and one whose idea cannot exist in the mind (Prop. 10, pt. 3); but a very little reflection will show that it is as impossible that a man, from the necessity of his nature, should endeavour not to exist, or to be changed into some other form, as it is that something should be begotten from nothing.

PROP. XXI.—*No one can desire to be happy, to act well and live well, who does not at the same time desire to be, to act, and to live, that is to say, actually to exist.*

Demonst.—The demonstration of this proposition, or rather the proposition itself, is self-evident, and is also evident from the definition of desire. For desire (Def. 1

of the Affects, pt. 3), whether it be desire of living or acting happily or well, is the very essence of man, that is to say (Prop. 7, pt. 3), the endeavour by which every one strives to preserve his own being. No one, therefore, can desire, &c.—Q.E.D.

PROP. XXII.—*No virtue can be conceived prior to this (the endeavour, namely, after self-preservation).*

Demonst.—The endeavour after self-preservation is the essence itself of a thing (Prop. 7, pt. 3). If, therefore, any virtue could be conceived prior to this of self-preservation, the essence itself of the thing would be conceived (Def. 8, pt. 4) as prior to itself, which (as is self-evident) is absurd. No virtue, therefore, &c.—Q.E.D.

Corol.—The endeavour after self-preservation is the primary and only foundation of virtue. For prior to this principle no other can be conceived (Prop. 22, pt. 4), and without it (Prop. 21, pt. 4) no virtue can be conceived.

PROP. XXIII.—*A man cannot be absolutely said to act in conformity with virtue, in so far as he is determined to any action because he has inadequate ideas, but only in so far as he is determined because he understands.*

Demonst.—In so far as a man is determined to action because he has inadequate ideas (Prop. 1, pt. 3), he suffers, that is to say (Defs. 1 and 2, pt. 3), he does something which through his essence alone cannot be perceived, that is to say (Def. 8, pt. 4), which does not follow from his virtue. But in so far as he is determined to any action because he understands, he acts (Prop. 1, pt. 3), that is to say (Def. 2, pt. 3), he does something which is perceived through his essence alone, or (Def. 8, pt. 4) which adequately follows from his virtue.—Q.E.D.

PROP. XXIV.—*To act absolutely in conformity with virtue is, in us, nothing but acting, living, and preserving our being (these three things have the same meaning) as reason directs, from the ground of seeking our own profit.*

Demonst.—To act absolutely in conformity with virtue is nothing (Def. 8, pt. 4) but acting according to the laws of our own proper nature. But only in so far as we understand do we act (Prop. 3, pt. 3). Therefore, to act in conformity with virtue is nothing but acting, living, and preserving our being as reason directs, and doing so (Corol. Prop. 22, pt. 4) from the ground of seeking our own profit.

PROP. XXV.—*No one endeavours to preserve his own being for the sake of another object.*

Demonst.—The effort by which any object strives to persevere in its own being is limited solely by the essence of the object itself (Prop. 7, pt. 3), and from this given essence alone it necessarily follows (and not from the essence of any other object) (Prop. 6, pt. 3) that each object strives to preserve its being. This proposition is also evident from Corol. Prop. 22, pt. 4. For if a man endeavoured to preserve his being for the sake of any other object, this object would then become the primary foundation of virtue (as is self-evident), which (by the Corol. just quoted) is an absurdity. No one, therefore, endeavours to preserve his being, &c.—Q.E.D.

PROP. XXVI.—*All efforts which we make through reason are nothing but efforts to understand, and the mind, in so far as it uses reason, adjudges nothing as profitable to itself excepting that which conduces to understanding.*

Demonst.—The endeavour after self-preservation is

nothing but the essence of the object itself (Prop. 7, pt. 3), which, in so far as it exists, is conceived to have power to persevere in existence (Prop. 6, pt. 3), and to do those things which necessarily follow from its given nature. (See the definition of desire in Schol. Prop. 9, pt. 3.) But the essence of reason is nothing but our mind, in so far as it clearly and distinctly understands. (See definition of clear and distinct understanding in Schol. 2, Prop. 40, pt. 2.) Therefore (Prop. 40, pt. 2), all efforts which we make through reason are nothing else than efforts to understand. Again, since this effort of the mind, by which the mind, in so far as it reasons, endeavours to preserve its being, is nothing but the effort to understand (by the first part of this demonstration), it follows (Corol. Prop. 22, pt. 4), that this effort to understand is the primary and sole foundation of virtue, and that (Prop. 25, pt. 4) we do not endeavour to understand things for the sake of any end, but, on the contrary, the mind, in so far as it reasons, can conceive nothing as being good for itself except that which conduces to understanding (Def. 1, pt. 4).—Q.E.D.

PROP. XXVII.—*We do not know that anything is certainly good or evil excepting that which actually conduces to understanding, or which can prevent us from understanding.*

Demonst.—The mind, in so far as it reasons, desires nothing but to understand, nor does it adjudge anything to be profitable to itself excepting what conduces to understanding (Prop. 26, pt. 4). But the mind (Props. 41 and 43, pt. 2, with the Schol.) possesses no certitude, unless in so far as it possesses adequate ideas, or (which by Schol. Prop. 40, pt. 2, is the same thing) in so far as it reasons. We do not know, therefore, that anything is certainly good, excepting that which actually conduces to understanding, and, on the other hand, we do not know that anything is evil excepting that which can hinder us from understanding.—Q.E.D.

PROP. XXVIII.—*The highest good of the mind is the knowledge of God, and the highest virtue of the mind is to know God.*

Demonst.—The highest thing which the mind can understand is God, that is to say (Def. 6, pt. 1), Being absolutely infinite, and without whom (Prop. 15, pt. 1) nothing can be nor can be conceived, and therefore (Props. 26 and 27, pt. 4) that which is chiefly profitable to the mind, or (Def. 1, pt. 4) which is the highest good of the mind, is the knowledge of God. Again, the mind acts only in so far as it understands (Props. 1 and 3, pt. 3), and only in so far (Prop. 23, pt. 4) can it be absolutely said to act in conformity with virtue. To understand, therefore, is the absolute virtue of the mind. But the highest thing which the mind can understand is God (as we have already demonstrated), and therefore the highest virtue of the mind is to understand or know God.—Q.E.D.

PROP. XXIX.—*No individual object whose nature is altogether different from our own can either help or restrain our power of acting, and absolutely nothing can be to us either good or evil unless it possesses something in common with ourselves.*

Demonst.—The power of an individual object, and consequently (Corol. Prop. 10, pt. 2) that of man, by which he exists and acts, is determined only by another individual object (Prop. 28, pt. 1), whose nature (Prop. 6, pt. 2) must be understood through the same attribute as that by means of which human nature is conceived. Our power of acting, therefore, in whatever way it may be conceived, can be determined, and consequently helped or restrained, by the power of another individual object possessing something in common with us, and cannot be thus determined by the power of an object whose nature is altogether different from ours. Inasmuch, therefore, as a thing is called good or evil because it is the cause of joy or sorrow (Prop. 8, pt. 4), that is to say (Schol. Prop. 11, pt. 3), because it increases or diminishes, helps or restrains, our power of action ; an object, whose nature is altogether different from our own, cannot be either good or evil to us.—Q.E.D.

PROP. XXX.—*Nothing can be evil through that which it possesses in common with our nature, but in so far as a thing is evil to us is it contrary to us.*

Demonst.—We call that thing evil which is the cause of sorrow (Prop. 8, pt. 4), that is to say (by the definition of sorrow in Schol. Prop. 11, pt. 3), which lessens or restrains our power of action. If, therefore, any object were evil to us through that which it possesses in common with us, it could lessen or restrain what it possesses in common with us, which (Prop. 4, pt. 3) is absurd. Nothing, therefore, through that which it possesses in common with us can be evil to us, but, on the contrary, in so far as it is evil, that is to say (as we have already shown), in so far as it can lessen or restrain our power of action (Prop. 5, pt. 3), is it contrary to us.—Q.E.D.

PROP. XXXI.—*In so far as an object agrees with our nature is it necessarily good.*

Demonst.—In so far as any object agrees with our nature (Prop. 30, pt. 4) it cannot be evil. It must, therefore, necessarily be either good or indifferent. If it be supposed as indifferent, that is to say, as neither good nor evil, nothing (Ax. 3, pt. 1, and Def. 1, pt. 4) will follow from its nature which conduces to the preservation of our nature, that is to say (by hypothesis), which conduces to its own preservation. But this (Prop. 6, pt. 3) is absurd, and, therefore, in so far as the object agrees with our nature, it will necessarily be good.—Q.E.D.

Corol.—Hence it follows that the more an object agrees with our own nature, the more profitable it is to us, that is to say, the better it is for us, and, conversely, the more profitable an object is to us, the more does it agree with our own nature. For in so far as it does not agree with our nature it will necessarily be either diverse from our nature or contrary to it. If diverse, it can (Prop. 29, pt. 4) be neither good nor evil, but if contrary, it will therefore be contrary also to that which agrees with our own nature, that is to say (Prop. 31, pt. 4), contrary to the good, or, in other words, it will be evil. Nothing, therefore, can be good except in so far as it agrees with our nature, and therefore the more an object agrees with our nature the more profitable it will be, and *vice versa.*—Q.E.D.

PROP. XXXII.—*In so far as men are subject to passions, they cannot be said to agree in nature.*

Demonst.—Things which are said to agree in nature are understood to agree in power (Prop. 7, pt. 3), and not in impotence or negation, and consequently (Schol. Prop. 3, pt. 3), not in passion, and therefore men, in so far as they are subject to passion, cannot be said to agree in nature.—Q.E.D.

Schol.—This proposition is self-evident, for he who says that black and white agree solely in the fact that neither of them is red, absolutely affirms that black and white agree in nothing. So also if we say that a stone and a man agree solely in this, that they are both finite or impotent, or do not exist from the necessity of their nature, or are both to an indefinite extent dominated by external causes, we affirm that a stone and a man agree in nothing, for things which agree in negation only, or in that which they have not, really agree in nothing.

PROP. XXXIII.—*Men may differ in nature from one another in so far as they are agitated by affects which are passions, and in so far also as one and the same man is agitated by passions is he changeable and inconstant.*

Demonst.—The nature or essence of the affects cannot be explained through our essence or nature alone (Defs. 1 and 2, pt. 3), but must be determined by the power, that is to say (Prop. 7, pt. 3), the nature of external causes compared with our own nature. Hence it follows that there are as many kinds of each affect as there are kinds of objects by which we are affected (Prop. 56, pt. 3); that men are affected in different ways by one and the same object (Prop. 51, pt. 3), and so far differ in nature; and, finally, that one and the same man (Prop. 51, pt. 3) is affected in different ways towards the same object, and so far is changeable and inconstant.—Q.E.D.

PROP. XXXIV.—*In so far as men are agitated by affects which are passions can they be contrary to one another.*

Demonst.—A man, Peter, for example, may be a cause of sorrow to Paul, because he possesses something resembling that which Paul hates (Prop. 16, pt. 3), or because he alone possesses something which Paul himself also loves (Prop. 32, pt. 3, with its Schol.), or for other reasons (the chief of which are mentioned in Schol. Prop. 55, pt. 3). Hence it will come to pass (Def. 7 of the affects) that Paul hates Peter, and, consequently, it will easily happen (Prop. 40, pt. 3, with its Schol.) that Peter in turn hates Paul, and that they endeavour (Prop. 39, pt. 3) to injure one another, or, in other words

(Prop. 30, pt. 4), that they are contrary to one another. But the affect of sorrow is always a passion (Prop. 59, pt. 3), and therefore men, in so far as they are agitated by affects which are passions, can be contrary to one another.—Q.E.D.

Schol.—I have said that Paul hates Peter because he imagines that Peter possesses something which he himself loves, from which at first sight it appears to follow, that because they both love the same thing, and consequently agree in nature with one another, they are, therefore, injurious to one another; and if this be true, Props. 30 and 31, pt. 4, would be false. But if we will examine the matter impartially, we shall see that all these things are quite in accord. For Peter and Paul are not injurious to one another in so far as they agree in nature, that is to say, in so far as they both love the same object, but in so far as they differ from one another. For in so far as they both love the same object is the love of each strengthened (Prop. 31, pt. 3), that is to say (Def. 6 of the Affects), so far is the joy of both increased. It is far from true, therefore, that in so far as they love the same object and agree in nature they are injurious to one another. They are injurious to one another, on the contrary, as I have said, solely because they are supposed to differ in nature. For we suppose Peter to have an idea of a beloved object which he now possesses, and Paul, on the other hand, to have an idea of a beloved object which he has lost. The former, therefore, is affected with joy, and the latter, on the contrary, with sorrow, and so far they are contrary to one another. In this manner we can easily show that the other causes of hatred depend solely on the fact that men differ by nature and not on anything in which they agree.

PROP. XXXV.—*So far as men live in conformity with the guidance of reason, in so far only do they always necessarily agree in nature.*

Demonst.—In so far as men are agitated by affects

which are passions can they differ in nature (Prop. 33, pt. 4) and be contrary to one another (Prop. 34, pt. 4). But men are said to act only in so far as they live according to the guidance of reason (Prop. 3, pt. 3), and therefore, whatever follows from human nature, in so far as it is determined by reason (Def. 2, pt. 3), must be understood through human nature alone as through its proximate cause. But because every one, according to the laws of his own nature, desires that which he adjudges to be good, and endeavours to remove that which he adjudges to be evil (Prop. 19, pt. 4), and because that which from the dictates of reason we judge to be good or evil is necessarily good or evil (Prop. 41, pt. 2), it follows that men, only in so far as they live according to the guidance of reason, necessarily do those things which are good to human nature, and consequently to each man, that is to say (Corol. Prop. 31, pt. 4), which agree with the nature of each man, and therefore also men necessarily always agree with one another in so far as they live according to the guidance of reason.—Q.E.D.

Corol. 1.—There is no single thing in nature which is more profitable to man than a man who lives according to the guidance of reason. For that is most profitable to man which most agrees with his own nature (Corol. Prop. 31, pt. 4), that is to say, man (as is self-evident). But a man acts absolutely from the laws of his own nature when he lives according to the guidance of reason (Def. 2, pt. 3), and so far only does he always necessarily agree with the nature of another man (Prop. 35, pt. 4); therefore there is no single thing more profitable to a man than man, &c.—Q.E.D.

Corol. 2.—When each man seeks most that which is profitable to himself, then are men most profitable to one another; for the more each man seeks his own profit and endeavours to preserve himself, the more virtue does he possess (Prop. 20, pt. 4), or, in other words (Def. 8, pt. 4), the more power does he possess to act according to the laws of his own nature, that is to say (Prop. 3, pt. 3), to live according to the guidance of reason. But men most agree in nature when they live according to the guidance of reason (Prop. 35, pt. 4), therefore (by the previous Corol.) men will be most profitable to one another when each man seeks most what is profitable to himself.—Q.E.D.

Schol.—To what we have just demonstrated daily experience itself testifies by so many and such striking proofs, that it is in almost everybody's mouth that man is a God to man. It is very seldom indeed that men live according to the guidance of reason; on the contrary, it so happens that they are generally envious and injurious to one another. But, nevertheless, they are scarcely ever able to lead a solitary life, so that to most men the definition of man that he is a social animal entirely commends itself, and indeed it is the case that far more advantages than disadvantages arise from the common society of men. Let satirists therefore scoff at human affairs as much as they please, let theologians denounce them, and let the melancholy praise as much as they can a life rude and without refinement, despising men and admiring the brutes, men will nevertheless find out that by mutual help they can much more easily procure the things they need, and that it is only by their united strength they can avoid the dangers which everywhere threaten them, to say nothing about its being far nobler and worthier of our knowledge to meditate upon the doings of men than upon those of brutes. But more of this elsewhere.

PROP. XXXVI.—*The highest good of those who follow after virtue is common to all, and all may equally enjoy it.*

Demonst.—To act in conformity with virtue is to act according to the guidance of reason (Prop. 24, pt. 4), and every effort which we make through reason is an

effort to understand (Prop. 26, pt. 4), and therefore
(Prop. 28, pt. 4) the highest good of those who follow
after virtue is to know God, that is to say (Prop. 47,
pt. 2, with its Schol.), it is a good which is common to
all men, and can be equally possessed by all men in so
far as they are of the same nature.—Q.E.D.

Schol.—If anybody asks, What if the highest good of
those who follow after virtue were not common to all?
would it not thence follow (as above, see Prop. 34, pt. 4)
that men who live according to the guidance of reason,
that is to say (Prop. 35, pt. 4), men in so far as they
agree in nature, would be contrary to one another? We
reply that it arises from no accident, but from the nature
itself of reason, that the highest good of man is common to all, inasmuch as it is deduced from the human
essence itself, in so far as it is determined by reason, and
also because man could not be nor be conceived if he had
not the power of rejoicing in this highest good. For it
pertains (Prop. 47, pt. 2) to the essence of the human
mind to have an adequate knowledge of the eternal and
infinite essence of God.

PROP. XXXVII.—*The good which every one who follows
after virtue seeks for himself he will desire for other
men; and his desire on their behalf will be greater in
proportion as he has a greater knowledge of God.*

Demonst.—Men are most profitable to man in so far
as they live according to the guidance of reason (Corol. 1,
Prop. 35, pt. 4), and therefore (Prop. 19, pt. 4), according to the guidance of reason, we necessarily endeavour
to cause men to live according to the guidance of reason.
But the good which each person seeks who lives according to the dictates of reason, that is to say (Prop. 24,
pt. 4), who follows after virtue, is to understand (Prop.
26, pt. 4), and therefore the good which each person
seeks who follows after virtue he will also desire for

other men. Again, desire, in so far as it is related to the mind, is the essence itself of the mind (Def. 1 of the Affects). But the essence of the mind consists in knowledge (Prop. 11, pt. 2), which involves the knowledge of God (Prop. 47, pt. 2), and without this knowledge the essence of the mind can neither be nor be conceived (Prop. 15, pt. 1); and therefore the greater the knowledge of God which the essence of the mind involves, the greater will be the desire with which he who follows after virtue will desire for another the good which he seeks for himself.—Q.E.D.

Another Demonstration.—The good which a man seeks for himself and which he loves he will love more unchangeably if he sees that others love it (Prop. 31, pt. 3), and therefore (Corol. Prop. 31, pt. 3) he will endeavour to make others love it; and because this good (Prop. 36, pt. 4) is common to all and all can rejoice in it, he will endeavour (by the same reasoning) to cause all to rejoice in it, and (Prop. 37, pt. 3) he will do so the more the more he rejoices in this good himself.—Q.E.D.

Schol. 1.—He who strives from an affect alone to make others love what he himself loves, and to make others live according to his way of thinking, acts from mere impulse, and is therefore hateful, especially to those who have other tastes, and who therefore also desire, and by the same impulse strive to make others live according to their way of thinking.

Again, since the highest good which men seek from an affect is often such that only one person can possess it, it follows that persons who love are not consistent with themselves, and, whilst they delight to recount the praises of the beloved object, fear lest they should be believed. But he who endeavours to lead others by reason does not act from impulse, but with humanity and kindness, and is always consistent with himself.

Everything which we desire and do, of which we are the cause in so far as we possess an idea of God, or in so far as we know God, I refer to *Religion.* The desire of doing well which is born in us, because we live according to the guidance of reason, I call *Piety.* The desire to join others in friendship to himself, with which a man living according to the guidance of reason is possessed, I call *Honour.* I call that thing *Honourable* which men who live according to the guidance of reason praise; and that thing, on the contrary, I call *Base* which sets itself against the formation of friendship. Moreover, I have also shown what are the foundations of a State.

The difference also between true virtue and impotence may, from what has already been said, be easily seen to be this—that true virtue consists in living according to the guidance of reason alone; and that impotence therefore consists in this alone—that a man allows himself to be led by things which are outside himself, and by them to be determined to such actions as the common constitution of external things demands, and not to such as his own nature considered in itself alone demands. These are the things which I promised in Schol. Prop. 18, pt. 4, I would demonstrate. From them we see that the law against killing animals is based upon an empty superstition and womanish tenderness, rather than upon sound reason. A proper regard, indeed, to one's own profit teaches us to unite in friendship with men, and not with brutes, nor with things whose nature is different from human nature. It teaches us, too, that the same right which they have over us we have over them. Indeed, since the right of any person is limited by his virtue or power, men possess a far greater right over brutes than brutes possess over men. I by no means deny that brutes feel, but I do deny that on this account it is unlawful for us to consult our own profit by using them for our own pleasure and treating them as is most convenient for us, inasmuch as they do not agree in nature with us, and their affects are different from our own (Schol. Prop. 57, pt. 3).

o

It now remains that I should explain what are Justice, Injustice, Crime, and, finally, Merit. With regard to these, see the following scholium.

Schol. 2.—In the Appendix to the First Part I promised I would explain what are praise and blame, merit and crime, justice and injustice. I have already shown what is the meaning of praise and blame in Schol. Prop. 29, pt. 3, and this will be a fitting place for the explanation of the rest. A few words must, however, first be said about the natural and civil state of man.

It is by the highest right of nature that each person exists, and consequently it is by the highest right of nature that each person does those things which follow from the necessity of his nature; and therefore it is by the highest right of nature that each person judges what is good and what is evil, consults his own advantage as he thinks best (Props. 19 and 20, pt. 4), avenges himself (Corol. 2, Prop. 40, pt. 3), and endeavours to preserve what he loves and to destroy what he hates (Prop. 28, pt. 3). If men lived according to the guidance of reason, every one would enjoy this right without injuring any one else (Corol. 1, Prop. 35, pt. 4). But because men are subject to affects (Corol. Prop. 4, pt. 4), which far surpass human power or virtue (Prop. 6, pt. 4), they are often drawn in different directions (Prop. 33, pt. 4), and are contrary to one another (Prop. 34, pt. 4), although they need one another's help (Schol. Prop. 35, pt. 4).

In order, then, that men may be able to live in harmony and be a help to one another, it is necessary for them to cede their natural right, and beget confidence one in the other that they will do nothing by which one can injure the other. In what manner this can be done, so that men who are necessarily subject to affects (Corol. Prop. 4, pt. 4), and are uncertain and changeable (Prop. 33, pt. 4), can beget confidence one in the other and have faith in one another, is evident from Prop. 7, pt. 4, and Prop. 39, pt. 3. It is there shown that no affect can be restrained unless by a stronger and contrary affect, and that every one abstains from doing an injury through fear of a greater injury. By this law, therefore, can society be strengthened, if only it claims for itself the right which every individual possesses of avenging himself and deciding what is good and what is evil, and provided, therefore, that it possess the power of prescribing a common rule of life, of promulgating laws and supporting them, not by reason, which cannot restrain the affects (Schol. Prop. 17, pt. 4), but by penalties.

This society, firmly established by law and with a power of self-preservation, is called a *State*, and those who are protected by its right are called *Citizens*. We can now easily see that in the natural state there is nothing which by universal consent is good or evil, since every one in a natural state consults only his own profit; deciding according to his own way of thinking what is good and what is evil with reference only to his own profit, and is not bound by any law to obey any one but himself. Hence in a natural state sin cannot be conceived, but only in a civil state, where it is decided by universal consent what is good and what is evil, and where every one is bound to obey the State. *Sin*, therefore, is nothing but disobedience, which is punished by the law of the State alone; obedience, on the other hand, being regarded as a *merit* in a citizen, because on account of it he is considered worthy to enjoy the privileges of the State. Again, in a natural state no one by common consent is the owner of anything, nor is there anything in nature which can be said to be the rightful property of this and not of that man, but all things belong to all, so that in a natural state it is impossible to conceive a desire of rendering to each man his own or taking from another that which is his; that is to say, in a natural state there is nothing which can be called just or unjust, but only in a civil state, in which it is decided by universal consent what is one person's and what is another's. Justice and injustice, therefore, sin and merit, are external notions, and not attributes, which manifest the nature of the mind. But enough of these matters.

PROP. XXXVIII.—*That which so disposes the human body that it can be affected in many ways, or which renders it capable of affecting external bodies in many ways, is profitable to man, and is more profitable in proportion as by its means the body becomes better fitted to be affected in many ways, and to affect other bodies ; on the other hand, that thing is injurious which renders the body less fitted to affect or be affected.*

Demonst.—In proportion as the body is rendered more fitted for this is the mind rendered more capable of perception (Prop. 14, pt. 2), and, therefore, whatever disposes the body in this way, and renders it fitted for this, is necessarily good or profitable (Props. 26 and 27, pt. 4), and is more profitable in proportion to its power of rendering the body more fitted for this, while, on the contrary (by Prop. 14, pt. 2, conversely, and Props. 26 and 27, pt. 4), it is injurious if it renders the body less fitted for this.—Q.E.D.

PROP. XXXIX.—*Whatever is effective to preserve the proportion of motion and rest which the parts of the human body bear to each other is good, and, on the contrary, that is evil which causes the parts of the human body to have a different proportion of motion and rest to each other.*

Demonst.—The human body needs for its preservation very many other bodies (Post. 4, pt. 2). But what constitutes the form of the human body is this, that its parts communicate their motions to one another in a certain fixed proportion (Def. preceding Lem. 4, following Prop. 13, pt. 2). Whatever, therefore, is effective to preserve the proportion of motion and rest which the parts of the human body bear to each other, preserves the form of the human body, and, consequently (Posts. 3 and 6, pt. 2), is effective to enable the body to be affected in many ways, and to affect external bodies in many ways, and, therefore (Prop. 38, pt. 4), is good. Again, whatever causes the parts of the human body to get a different proportion of motion and rest (by the definition just quoted), causes the human body to assume another form, that is to say (as is self-evident, and as we observed at the end of the preface to this part), causes the human body to be destroyed, rendering it consequently incapable of being affected in many ways, and is, therefore (Prop. 38, pt. 4.) bad.—Q.E.D.

Schol.—In what degree these things may injure or profit the mind will be explained in the Fifth Part. Here I observe merely that I understand the body to die when its parts are so disposed as to acquire a different proportion of motion and rest to each other. For I dare not deny that the human body, though the circulation of the blood and the other things by means of which it is thought to live be preserved, may, nevertheless, be changed into another nature altogether different from its own. No reason compels me to affirm that the body never dies unless it is changed into a corpse. Experience, indeed, seems to teach the contrary. It happens sometimes that a man undergoes such changes that he cannot very well be said to be the same man, as was the case with a certain Spanish poet of whom I have heard, who was seized with an illness, and although he recovered, remained, nevertheless, so oblivious of his past life that he did not believe the tales and tragedies he had composed were his own, and he might, indeed, have been taken for a grown-up child if he had also forgotten his native tongue. But if this seems incredible, what shall we say of children? The man of mature years believes the nature of children to be so different from his own, that it would be impossible to persuade him he had ever been a child, if he did not conjecture regarding himself from what he sees of others. But in order to avoid giving to the superstitious matter for new questions, I prefer to go no farther in the discussion of these matters.

PROP. XL.—*Whatever conduces to the universal fellowship of men, that is to say, whatever causes men to live in harmony with one another, is profitable, and, on the contrary, whatever brings discord into the State is evil.*

Demonst.—For whatever causes men to live in harmony with one another causes them to live according to the guidance of reason (Prop. 35, pt. 4), and, therefore (Props. 26 and 27, pt. 4), is good, and (by the same reasoning) those things are evil which excite discord.—Q.E.D.

PROP. XLI.—*Joy is not directly evil, but good ; sorrow, on the other hand, is directly evil.*

Demonst.—Joy (Prop. 11, pt. 3, with its Schol.) is an affect by which the body's power of action is increased or assisted. Sorrow, on the other hand, is an affect by which the body's power of action is lessened or restrained, and, therefore (Prop. 38, pt. 4), joy is directly good.—Q.E.D.

PROP. XLII.—*Cheerfulness can never be excessive, but is always good ; melancholy, on the contrary, is always evil.*

Demonst.—Cheerfulness (see its definition in Schol. Prop. 11, pt. 3) is joy, which, in so far as it is related to the body, consists in this, that all the parts of the body are equally affected, that is to say (Prop. 11, pt. 3), the body's power of action is increased or assisted, so that all the parts acquire the same proportion of motion and rest to each other. Cheerfulness, therefore (Prop. 39, pt. 4), is always good, and can never be excessive. But melancholy (see its definition in Schol. Prop. 11, pt. 3) is sorrow, which, in so far as it is related to the body, consists in this, that the body's power of action is absolutely lessened or restrained, and melancholy, therefore (Prop. 38, pt. 4), is always evil.—Q.E.D.

PROP. XLIII.—*Pleasurable excitement may be excessive and an evil, and pain may be good in so far as pleasurable excitement or joy is evil.*

Demonst.—Pleasurable excitement is joy, which, in so far as it is related to the body, consists in this, that one or some of the parts of the body are affected more than others (see Def. in Schol. Prop. 11, pt. 3). The power of this affect may, therefore, be so great as to overcome the other actions of the body (Prop. 6, pt. 4); it may cling obstinately to the body; it may impede the body in such a manner as to render it less capable of being affected in many ways, and therefore (Prop. 38, pt. 4) may be evil. Again, pain, which, on the contrary, is sorrow, considered in itself alone cannot be good (Prop. 41, pt. 4). But because its power and increase is limited by the power of an external cause compared with our own power (Prop. 5, pt. 4), we can therefore conceive infinite degrees of strength of this affect, and infinite kinds of it (Prop. 3, pt. 4), and we can therefore conceive it to be such that it can restrain an excess of pleasurable excitement, and so far (by the first part of this proposition) preventing the body from becoming less capable. So far, therefore, will pain be good.—Q.E.D.

PROP. XLIV.—*Love and desire may be excessive.*

Demonst.—Love is joy (Def. 6 of the Affects) with the

accompanying idea of an external cause. Pleasurable excitement, therefore (Schol. Prop. 11, pt. 3), with the accompanying idea of an external cause, is love, and therefore love (Prop. 43, pt. 4) may be excessive. Again, desire is greater as the affect from which it springs is greater (Prop. 37, pt. 3). Inasmuch, therefore, as an affect (Prop. 6, pt. 4) may overpower the other actions of a man, so also the desire which springs from this affect may also overpower the other desires, and may therefore exist in the same excess which we have shown (in the preceding proposition) that pleasurable excitement possesses.—Q.E.D.

Schol.—Cheerfulness, which I have affirmed to be good, is more easily imagined than observed; for the affects by which we are daily agitated are generally related to some part of the body which is affected more than the others, and therefore it is that the affects exist for the most part in excess, and so hold the mind down to the contemplation of one object alone, that it can think about nothing else; and although men are subject to a number of affects, and therefore few are found who are always under the control of one and the same affect, there are not wanting those to whom one and the same affect obstinately clings. We see men sometimes so affected by one object, that although it is not present, they believe it to be before them; and if this happens to a man who is not asleep, we say that he is delirious or mad. Nor are those believed to be less mad who are inflamed by love, dreaming about nothing but a mistress or harlot day and night, for they excite our laughter. But the avaricious man who thinks of nothing else but gain or money, and the ambitious man who thinks of nothing but glory, inasmuch as they do harm, and are, therefore, thought worthy of hatred, are not believed to be mad. In truth, however, avarice, ambition, lust, &c., are a kind of madness, although they are not reckoned amongst diseases.

Prop. XLV.—*Hatred can never be good.*

Demonst.—The man whom we hate we endeavour to destroy (Prop. 39, pt. 3), that is to say (Prop. 37, pt. 4), we endeavour to do something which is evil. Therefore hatred, &c.—q.e.d.

Schol.—It is to be observed that here and in the following propositions I understand by hatred, hatred towards men only.

Corol. 1.—Envy, mockery, contempt, anger, revenge, and the other affects which are related to hatred or arise from it, are evil. This is also evident from Prop. 39, pt. 3, and Prop. 37, pt. 4.

Corol. 2.—Everything which we desire because we are affected by hatred is base and unjust in the State. This is also evident from Prop. 39, pt. 3, and from the definition in Schol. Prop. 37, pt. 4, of what is base and unjust.

Schol.—I make a great distinction between mockery (which I have said in Corol. 1 of this Prop. is bad) and laughter; for laughter and merriment are nothing but joy, and therefore, provided they are not excessive, are in themselves good (Prop. 41, pt. 4). Nothing but a gloomy and sad superstition forbids enjoyment. For why is it more seemly to extinguish hunger and thirst than to drive away melancholy? My reasons and my conclusions are these :—No God and no human being, except an envious one, is delighted by my impotence or my trouble, or esteems as any virtue in us tears, sighs, fears, and other things of this kind, which are signs of mental impotence; on the contrary, the greater the joy with which we are affected, the greater the perfection to which we pass thereby, that is to say, the more do we necessarily partake of the divine nature. To make use of things, therefore, and to delight in them as much as possible (provided we do not disgust ourselves with them, which is not delighting in them), is the part of a wise man. It is the part of a wise man, I say, to refresh and invigorate himself with moderate and pleasant eating and drinking, with sweet scents and the beauty of green plants, with ornament, with music, with sports, with the theatre, and with all things of this kind which one man can enjoy without hurting another. For the human body is composed of a great number of parts of diverse nature, which constantly need new and varied nourishment, in order that the whole of the body may be equally fit for everything which can follow from its nature, and consequently that the mind may be equally fit to understand many things at once. This mode of living best of all agrees both with our principles and with common practice; therefore this mode of living is the best of all, and is to be universally commended. There is no need, therefore, to enter more at length into the subject.

PROP. XLVI.—*He who lives according to the guidance of reason strives as much as possible to repay the hatred, anger, or contempt of others towards himself with love or generosity.*

Demonst.—All affects of hatred are evil (Corol. 1, Prop. 45, pt. 4), and, therefore, the man who lives according to the guidance of reason will strive as much as possible to keep himself from being agitated by the affects of hatred (Prop. 19, pt. 4), and, consequently (Prop. 37, pt. 4), will strive to keep others from being subject to the same affects. But hatred is increased by reciprocal hatred, and, on the other hand, can be extinguished by love (Prop. 43, pt. 3), so that hatred passes into love (Prop. 44, pt. 3). Therefore he who lives according to the guidance of reason will strive to repay the hatred of another, &c., with love, that is to say, with generosity (see definition of generosity in Schol. Prop. 59, pt. 3).—Q.E.D.

Schol.—He who wishes to avenge injuries by hating in return does indeed live miserably. But he who, on the contrary, strives to drive out hatred by love, fights joyfully and confidently, with equal ease resisting one man or a number of men, and needing scarcely any assistance from fortune. Those whom he conquers yield gladly, not from defect of strength, but from an increase of it. These truths, however, all follow so plainly from the definitions alone of love and the intellect, that there is no need to demonstrate them singly.

PROP. XLVII.—*The affects of hope and fear cannot be good of themselves.*

Demonst.—The affects of hope and fear cannot exist without sorrow; for fear (Def. 13 of the Affects) is sorrow, and hope (see the explanation of Defs. 12 and 13 of the Affects) cannot exist without fear. Therefore (Prop. 41, pt. 4) these affects cannot be good of themselves, but only in so far as they are able to restrain the excesses of joy (Prop. 43, pt. 4).—Q.E.D.

Schol.—We may here add that these affects indicate want of knowledge and impotence of mind, and, for the same reason, confidence, despair, gladness, and remorse [1] are signs of weakness of mind. For although confidence and gladness are affects of joy, they nevertheless suppose that sorrow has preceded them, namely, hope or fear. In proportion, therefore, as we endeavour to live according to the guidance of reason, shall we strive as much as possible to depend less on hope, to liberate ourselves from fear, to rule fortune, and to direct our actions by the sure counsels of reason.

PROP. XLVIII.—*The affects of over-estimation and contempt are always evil.*

Demonst.—These affects (Defs. 21 and 22 of the Affects) are opposed to reason, and therefore (Props. 26 and 27, pt. 4) are evil.—Q.E.D.

[1] See p. 123, note.

PROP. XLIX.—*Over-estimation easily renders the man who is over-estimated proud.*

Demonst.—If we see that a person, through love, thinks too much of us, we shall easily glorify ourselves (Schol. 41, pt. 3), or, in other words, be affected with joy (Def. 30 of the Affects), and easily believe the good which we hear others affirm of us (Prop. 25, pt. 3), and consequently, through self-love, we shall think too much of ourselves, that is to say (Def. 28 of the Affects), we shall easily grow proud.—Q.E.D.

PROP. L.—*Pity in a man who lives according to the guidance of reason is in itself evil and unprofitable.*

Demonst.—Pity (Def. 18. of the Affects) is sorrow, and therefore (Prop. 41, pt. 4) is in itself evil. The good, however, which issues from pity, namely, that we endeavour to free from misery the man we pity (Corol. 3, Prop. 27, pt. 3), we desire to do from the dictate of reason alone (Prop. 37, pt. 4); nor can we do anything except by the dictate of reason alone, which we are sure is good (Prop. 27, pt. 4). Pity, therefore, in a man who lives according to the guidance of reason is in itself bad and unprofitable.—Q.E.D.

Corol.—Hence it follows that a man who lives according to the dictates of reason endeavours as much as possible to prevent himself from being touched by pity.

Schol.—The man who has properly understood that everything follows from the necessity of the divine nature, and comes to pass according to the eternal laws and rules of nature, will in truth discover nothing which is worthy of hatred, laughter, or contempt, nor will he pity any one, but, so far as human virtue is able, he will endeavour to *do well*, as we say, and to *rejoice*. We must add also, that a man who is easily touched by the affect of pity, and is moved by the misery or tears of another, often does something of which he afterward repents, both because from an affect we do nothing which we certainly know to be good, and also because we are so easily deceived by false tears. But this I say expressly of the man who lives according to the guidance of reason. For he who is moved neither by reason nor pity to be of any service to others is properly called inhuman; for (Prop. 27, pt. 3) he seems to be unlike a man.

PROP. LI.—*Favour is not opposed to reason, but agrees with it, and may arise from it.*

Demonst.—Favour is love towards him who does good to another (Def. 19 of the Affects), and therefore can be related to the mind in so far as it is said to act (Prop. 59, pt. 3), that is to say (Prop. 3, pt. 3), in so far as it understands, and therefore favour agrees with reason.—Q.E.D.

Another Demonstration.—If we live according to the guidance of reason, we shall desire for others the good which we seek for ourselves (Prop. 37, pt. 4). Therefore if we see one person do good to another, our endeavour to do good is assisted, that is to say (Schol. Prop. 11, pt. 3), we shall rejoice, and our joy (by hypothesis) will be accompanied with the idea of the person who does good to the other, that is to say (Def. 19 of the Affects), we shall favour him.—Q.E.D.

Schol.—Indignation, as it is defined by us (Def. 20 of the Affects), is necessarily evil (Prop. 45, pt. 4); but it is to be observed that when the supreme authority, constrained by the desire of preserving peace, punishes a citizen who injures another, I do not say that it is indignant with the citizen, since it is not excited by hatred to destroy him, but punishes him from motives of piety.

PROP. LII.—*Self-satisfaction may arise from reason, and the self-satisfaction alone which arises from reason is the highest which can exist.*

Demonst.—Self-satisfaction is the joy which arises from a man's contemplating himself and his power of action (Def. 25 of the Affects). But man's true power of action or his virtue is reason itself (Prop. 3, pt. 3), which he contemplates clearly and distinctly (Props. 40 and 43, pt. 2). Self-satisfaction therefore arises from reason. Again, man, when he contemplates himself, perceives nothing clearly and distinctly or adequately, excepting those things which follow from his power of action (Def. 2, pt. 3), that is to say (Prop. 3, pt. 3), those things which follow from his power of understanding; and therefore from this contemplation alone the highest satisfaction which can exist arises.—Q.E.D.

Schol.—Self-satisfaction is indeed the highest thing for which we can hope, for (as we have shown in Prop. 25, pt. 4) no one endeavours to preserve his being for the sake of any end. Again, because this self-satisfaction is more and more nourished and strengthened by praise (Corol. Prop. 53, pt. 3), and, on the contrary (Corol. Prop. 55, pt. 3), more and more disturbed by blame, therefore we are principally led by glory, and can scarcely endure life with disgrace.

PROP. LIII.—*Humility is not a virtue, that is to say, it does not spring from reason.*

Demonst.—Humility is sorrow, which springs from this, that a man contemplates his own weakness (Def. 26 of the Affects). But in so far as a man knows himself by true reason is he supposed to understand his essence, that is to say (Prop. 7, pt. 3), his power. If, therefore, while contemplating himself, he perceives any impotence of his, this is not due to his understanding himself, but, as we have shown (Prop. 55, pt. 3), to the fact that his

power of action is restrained. But if we suppose that
he forms a conception of his own impotence because he
understands something to be more powerful than himself, by the knowledge of which he limits his own power
of action, in this case we simply conceive that he understands himself distinctly (Prop. 26, pt. 4), and his
power of action is increased. Humility or sorrow, therefore, which arises because a man contemplates his own
impotence, does not spring from true contemplation or
reason, and is not a virtue, but a passion.—Q.E.D.

PROP. LIV.—*Repentance is not a virtue, that is to say, it
does not spring from reason ; on the contrary, the man
who repents of what he has done is doubly wretched or
impotent.*

Demonst.—The first part of this proposition is demonstrated in the same manner as the preceding proposition. The second part follows from the definition alone
of this affect (Def. 27 of the Affects). For, in the first
place, we allow ourselves to be overcome by a depraved
desire, and, in the second place, by sorrow.

Schol.—Inasmuch as men seldom live as reason dictates, therefore these two affects, humility and repentance, together with hope and fear, are productive of more
profit than disadvantage, and therefore, since men must
sin, it is better that they should sin in this way.
For if men impotent in mind were all equally proud,
were ashamed of nothing, and feared nothing, by what
bonds could they be united or constrained ? The multitude becomes a thing to be feared if it has nothing to
fear. It is not to be wondered at, therefore, that the
prophets, thinking rather of the good of the community
than of a few, should have commended so greatly
humility, repentance, and reverence. Indeed, those who
are subject to these affects can be led much more easily
than others, so that, at last, they come to live accord-

ing to the guidance of reason, that is to say, become free men, and enjoy the life of the blessed.

PROP. LV.—*The greatest pride or the greatest despondency is the greatest ignorance of one's self.*

Demonst.—This is evident from Defs. 28 and 29 of the Affects.

PROP. LVI.—*The greatest pride or despondency indicates the greatest impotence of mind.*

Demonst.—The primary foundation of virtue is the preservation of our being (Corol. Prop. 22, pt. 4) according to the guidance of reason (Prop. 24, pt. 4). The man, therefore, who is ignorant of himself is ignorant of the foundation of all the virtues, and consequently is ignorant of all the virtues. Again, to act in conformity with virtue is nothing but acting according to the guidance of reason (Prop. 24, pt. 4), and he who acts according to the guidance of reason must necessarily know that he acts according to the guidance of reason (Prop. 43, pt. 2). He, therefore, who is ignorant of himself, and consequently (as we have just shown) altogether ignorant of all the virtues, cannot in any way act in conformity with virtue, that is to say (Def. 8, pt. 4), is altogether impotent in mind. Therefore (Prop. 55, pt. 4), the greatest pride or despondency indicates the greatest impotence of mind.—Q.E.D.

Corol.—Hence follows, with the utmost clearness, that the proud and the desponding are above all others subject to affects.

Schol.—Despondency, nevertheless, can be corrected more easily than pride, since the former is an affect of sorrow, while the latter is an affect of joy, and is, therefore (Prop. 18, pt. 4), stronger than the former.

PROP. LVII.—*The proud man loves the presence of parasites or flatterers, and hates that of the noble-minded.*

Demonst.—Pride is joy arising from a man's having too high an opinion of himself (Defs. 28 and 6 of the Affects). This opinion a proud man will endeavour, as much as he can, to cherish (Schol. Prop. 13, pt. 3), and, therefore, will love the presence of parasites or flatterers (the definitions of these people are omitted, because they are too well known), and will shun that of the noble-minded who think of him as is right.—Q. E. D.

Schol.—It would take too much time to enumerate here all the evils of pride, for the proud are subject to all affects, but to none are they less subject than to those of love and pity. It is necessary, however, to observe here that a man is also called proud if he thinks too little of other people, and so, in this sense, pride is to be defined as joy which arises from the false opinion that we are superior to other people, while despondency, the contrary to this pride, would be defined as sorrow arising from the false opinion that we are inferior to other people. This being understood, it is easy to see that the proud man is necessarily envious (Schol. Prop. 55, pt. 3), and that he hates those above all others who are the most praised on account of their virtues. It follows, too, that his hatred of them is not easily overcome by love or kindness (Schol. Prop. 41, pt. 3), and that he is delighted by the presence of those only who humour his weakness, and from a fool make him a madman. Although despondency is contrary to pride, the despondent man is closely akin to the proud man. For since the sorrow of the despondent man arises from his judging his own impotence by the power or virtue of others, his sorrow will be mitigated, that is to say, he will rejoice, if his imagination be occupied in contemplating the vices of others. Hence the proverb—It is a consolation to the wretched to have had

P

companions in their misfortunes. On the other hand, the more the despondent man believes himself to be below other people, the more will he sorrow; and this is the reason why none are more prone to envy than the despondent; and why they, above all others, try to observe men's actions with a view to finding fault with them rather than correcting them, so that at last they praise nothing but despondency and glory in it; but in such a manner, however, as always to seem despondent.

These things follow from this affect as necessarily as it follows from the nature of a triangle that its three angles are equal to two right angles. It is true, indeed, that I have said that I call these and the like affects evil, in so far as I attend to human profit alone; but the laws of nature have regard to the common order of nature of which man is a part—a remark I desired to make in passing, lest it should be thought that I talk about the vices and absurdities of men rather than attempt to demonstrate the nature and properties of things. As I said in the Preface to the Third Part, I consider human affects and their properties precisely as I consider other natural objects; and, indeed, the affects of man, if they do not show his power, show, at least, the power and workmanship of nature, no less than many other things which we admire and delight to contemplate. I proceed, however, to notice those things connected with the affects which are productive either of profit or loss to man.

PROP. LVIII.—*Self-exaltation is not opposed to reason, but may spring from it.*

Demonst.—This is plain from Def. 30 of the Affects, and also from the definition of honour in Schol. 1, Prop. 37, pt. 4.

Schol.—What is called vainglory is self-satisfaction, nourished by nothing but the good opinion of the multitude, so that when that is withdrawn, the satisfaction, that is to say (Schol. Prop. 52, pt. 4), the chief good which every one loves, ceases. For this reason those who glory in the good opinion of the multitude anxiously and with daily care strive, labour, and struggle to preserve their fame. For the multitude is changeable and fickle, so that fame, if it be not preserved, soon passes away. As every one, moreover, is desirous to catch the praises of the people, one person will readily destroy the fame of another; and, consequently, as the object of contention is what is commonly thought to be the highest good, a great desire arises on the part of every one to keep down his fellows by every possible means, and he who at last comes off conqueror boasts more because he has injured another person than because he has profited himself. This glory of self-satisfaction, therefore, is indeed vain, for it is really no glory. What is worthy of notice with regard to shame may easily be gathered from what has been said about compassion and repentance. I will only add that pity, like shame, although it is not a virtue, is nevertheless good, in so far as it shows that a desire of living uprightly is present in the man who is possessed with shame, just as pain is called good in so far as it shows that the injured part has not yet putrefied. A man, therefore, who is ashamed of what he has done, although he is sorrowful, is nevertheless more perfect than the shameless man who has no desire of living uprightly. These are the things which I undertook to establish with regard to the affects of joy and sorrow. With reference to the desires, these are good or evil as they spring from good or evil affects. All of them, however, in so far as they are begotten in us of affects which are passions, are blind (as may easily be inferred from what has been said in Schol. Prop. 44, pt. 4), nor would they be of any use if men could be easily persuaded to live according to the dictates of reason alone, as I shall show in a few words.

Prop. LIX.—*To all actions to which we are determined by an affect which is a passion we may, without the affect, be determined by reason.*

Demonst.—To act according to reason is nothing (Prop. 3, and Def. 2, pt. 3) but to do those things which follow from the necessity of our nature considered in itself alone. But sorrow is evil so far as it lessens or restrains this power of action (Prop. 41, pt. 4); therefore we can be determined by this affect to no action which we could not perform if we were led by reason. Again, joy is evil so far only as it hinders our fitness for action (Props. 41 and 43, pt. 4); and therefore also we can so far be determined to no action which we could not do if we were led by reason. Finally, in so far as joy is good, so far it agrees with reason (for it consists in this, that a man's power of action is increased or assisted), and it is not a passion unless in so far as man's power of action is not increased sufficiently for him to conceive adequately himself and his actions (Prop. 3, pt. 3, with its Schol.) If, therefore, a man affected with joy were led to such perfection as to conceive adequately himself and his actions, he would be fitted—better even than before—for the performance of those actions to which he is now determined by the affects which are passions. But all the affects are related to joy, sorrow, or desire (see the explanation of Def. 4 of the Affects), and desire (Def. 1 of the Affects) is nothing but the endeavour itself to act; therefore to all actions to which we are determined by an affect which is a passion we may without the affect be determined by reason alone.—Q.E.D.

Another Demonstration.—Any action is called evil in so far as it arises from our being affected with hatred or some evil affect (Corol. 1, Prop. 45, pt. 4). But no action considered in itself alone is either good or evil (as we have already shown in the preface to this part), but one and the same action is sometimes good and sometimes evil. Therefore we may be led by reason (Prop. 19, pt. 4) to that same action which is sometimes evil, or which arises from some evil affect.—Q.E.D.

Schol.—This can be explained more clearly by an example. The action of striking, for instance, in so far as it is considered physically, and we attend only to the fact that a man raises his arm, closes his hand, and forcibly moves the whole arm downwards, is a virtue which is conceived from the structure of the human body. If, therefore, a man agitated by anger or hatred is led to close the fist or move the arm, this comes to pass, as we have shown in the Second Part, because one and the same action can be joined to different images of things, and therefore we may be led to one and the same action as well by the images of things which we conceive confusedly as by those which we conceive clearly and distinctly. It appears, therefore, that every desire which arises from an affect which is a passion would be of no use if men could be led by reason. We shall now see why a desire which arises from an affect which is a passion is called blind.

PROP. LX.—*The desire which arises from joy or sorrow, which is related to one or to some, but not to all, the parts of the body, has no regard to the profit of the whole man.*

Demonst.—Let it be supposed that a part of the body —A, for example—is so strengthened by the force of some external cause that it prevails over the others (Prop. 6, pt. 4). It will not endeavour, therefore, to lose its strength in order that the remaining parts of the body may perform their functions, for in that case it would have a force or power of losing its strength, which (Prop. 6, pt. 3) is absurd. It will endeavour, therefore, and consequently (Props. 7 and 12, pt. 3) the mind also will endeavour, to preserve this same state; and so the desire which arises from such an affect of joy has no regard to the whole man. If, on the other hand, it be supposed that the part A is restrained so that the other parts prevail, it can be demonstrated in the same way that the desire which springs from sorrow has no regard to the whole man.

Schol.—Since, therefore, joy is most frequently related to one part of the body (Schol. Prop. 44, pt. 4), we generally desire to preserve our being without reference to our health as a whole; and, moreover, the desires by which we are chiefly controlled (Corol. Prop. 9, pt. 4) have regard to the present only, and not to the future.

PROP. LXI.—*A desire which springs from reason can never be in excess.*

Demonst.—Desire (Def. 1 of the Affects), absolutely considered, is the very essence of man, in so far as he is conceived as determined in any way whatever to any action, and therefore the desire which springs from reason, that is to say (Prop. 3, pt. 3), which is begotten in us in so far as we act, is the very essence or nature of man in so far as it is conceived as determined to actions which are adequately conceived by the essence of man alone (Def. 2, pt. 3). If, therefore, this desire could be in excess, it would be possible for human nature, considered in itself alone, to exceed itself, or, in other words, more would be possible to it than is possible, which is a manifest contradiction, and therefore this desire can never be in excess.—Q.E.D.

PROP. LXII.—*In so far as the conception of an object is formed by the mind according to the dictate of reason, the mind is equally affected, whether the idea be that of something future, past, or present.*

Demonst.—Everything which the mind, under the guidance of reason, conceives, it conceives under the same form of eternity or necessity (Corol. 2, Prop. 44, pt. 2), and it is affected with the same certainty (Prop. 43, pt. 2, and its Schol.) Therefore, whether the idea be one of a future, past, or present object, the mind conceives the object with the same necessity, and is affected with the same certainty; and whether the idea be that of a future, past, or present object, it will nevertheless be equally true (Prop. 41, pt. 2), that is to say (Def. 4, pt. 2), it will always have the same properties of an adequate idea. Therefore, in so far as the conception of an object is formed by the mind according to the dictates of reason, the mind will be affected in the same way whether the idea be that of something future, past, or present.—Q.E.D.

Schol.—If it were possible for us to possess an adequate knowledge concerning the duration of things, and to determine by reason the periods of their existence, we should contemplate with the same affect objects future and present, and the good which the mind conceived to be future, it would seek just as it would seek the present good. Consequently it would necessarily neglect the present good for the sake of a greater future good, and would, as we shall presently show, be very little disposed to seek a good which was present, but which would be a cause of any future evil. But it is not possible for us to have any other than a very inadequate knowledge of the duration of things (Prop. 31, pt. 2), and we determine (Schol. Prop. 44, pt. 2) the periods of the existence of objects by the imagination alone, which is not affected by the image of a present object in the same way as it is by that of a future object. Hence it comes to pass that the true knowledge of good and evil which we possess is only abstract or universal, and the judgment we pass upon the order of things and the connection of causes, so that we may determine what is good for us in the present and what is evil, is rather imaginary than real. It is not, therefore, to be wondered at if the desire which arises from a knowledge of good and evil, in so far as this knowledge has regard to the future, is capable of being easily restrained by the desire of objects which are sweet to us at the present moment. (See Prop. 16, pt. 4.)

PROP. LXIII.—*He who is led by fear, and does what is good in order that he may avoid what is evil, is not led by reason.*

Demonst.—All the affects which are related to the mind, in so far as it acts, that is to say (Prop. 3, pt. 3), which are related to reason, are no other than affects of joy and desire (Prop. 59, pt. 3); and therefore (Def. 13 of the Affects), he who is led by fear and does good through fear of evil is not led by reason.—Q.E.D.

Schol.—The superstitious, who know better how to rail at vice than to teach virtue, and who study not to lead man by reason, but to hold him in through fear, in order that he may shun evil rather than love virtue, aim at nothing more than that others should be as miserable as themselves, and, therefore, it is not to be wondered at if they generally become annoying and hateful to men.

Corol.—By the desire which springs from reason we follow good directly and avoid evil indirectly.

Demonst.—For the desire which springs from reason cannot spring from sorrow, but only from an affect of joy, which is not a passion (Prop. 59, pt. 3), that is to say, from joy which cannot be in excess (Prop. 61, pt. 4). This desire springs, therefore (Prop. 8, pt. 4), from the knowledge of good, and not from the knowledge of evil, and therefore, according to the guidance of reason, we seek what is good directly, and so far only do we shun what is evil.—Q.E.D.

Schol.—This corollary is explained by the example of a sick man and a healthy man. The sick man, through fear of death, eats what he dislikes; the healthy man takes a pleasure in his food, and so enjoys life more than if he feared death and directly desired to avoid it. So also the judge who condemns a guilty man to death, not from hatred or anger, but solely from love for the public welfare, is led by reason alone.

PROP. LXIV.—*The knowledge of evil is inadequate knowledge.*

Demonst.—The knowledge of evil (Prop. 8, pt. 4) is sorrow itself, in so far as we are conscious of it. But sorrow is the passage to a less perfection (Def. 3 of the Affects), and it cannot, therefore, be understood through the essence itself of man (Props. 6 and 7, pt. 3). It is, therefore (Def. 2, pt. 3), a passion which (Prop. 3, pt. 3) depends upon inadequate ideas, and consequently (Prop. 29, pt. 2) the knowledge of sorrow, that is to say, the knowledge of evil, is inadequate.—Q.E.D.

Corol.—Hence it follows that if the human mind had none but adequate ideas, it would form no notion of evil.

PROP. LXV.—*According to the guidance of reason, of two things which are good, we shall follow the greater good, and of two evils, we shall follow the less.*

Demonst.—The good which hinders us from enjoying a greater good is really an evil, for good and evil (as we have shown in the preface to this part) are affirmed of things in so far as we compare them with one another. By the same reasoning a less evil is really a good, and therefore (Corol. Prop. 63, pt. 4), according to the guidance of reason, we shall seek or follow the greater good only and the lesser evil.—Q.E.D.

Corol.—According to the guidance of reason, we shall follow a lesser evil for the sake of a greater good, and a lesser good which is the cause of a greater evil we shall neglect. For the evil which we here call less is really a good, and the good, on the other hand, is evil; and therefore (Corol. Prop. 63, pt. 4) we shall seek the former and neglect the latter.—Q.E.D.

PROP. LXVI.—*According to the guidance of reason, we shall seek the greater future good before that which is less and present, and we shall seek also the less and present evil before that which is greater and future.*

Demonst.—If it were possible for the mind to have an adequate knowledge of a future object, it would be affected by the same affect towards the future object as towards a present object (Prop. 62, pt. 4). Therefore, in so far as we attend to reason itself, as we are supposing in this proposition that we do, it is the same thing whether the greater good or evil be supposed to be future or present, and therefore (Prop. 65, pt. 4) we shall seek the greater future good before that which is less and present, &c.—Q.E.D.

Corol.—According to the guidance of reason, we shall seek the lesser present evil which is the cause of the greater future good, and the lesser present good which is the cause of a greater future evil we shall neglect. This corollary is connected with the foregoing proposition in the same way as Corol. Prop. 65 is connected with Prop. 65.

Schol.—If what has been said here be compared with what has been demonstrated about the strength of the passions in the first eighteen Props. pt. 4, and in Schol. Prop. 18, pt. 4, it will easily be seen in what consists the difference between a man who is led by affect or opinion alone and one who is led by reason. The former, whether he wills it or not, does those things of which he is entirely ignorant, but the latter does the will of no one but himself, and does those things only which he knows are of greatest importance in life, and which he therefore desires above all things. I call the former, therefore, a slave, and the latter free.

I will add here a few words concerning the character of the free man and his manner of life.

PROP. LXVII.—*A free man thinks of nothing less than of death, and his wisdom is not a meditation upon death but upon life.*

Demonst.—A free man, that is to say, a man who lives according to the dictates of reason alone, is not led by the fear of death (Prop. 63, pt. 4), but directly desires the good (Corol. Prop. 63, pt. 4); that is to say (Prop. 24, pt. 4), desires to act, to live, and to preserve his being in accordance with the principle of seeking his own profit. He thinks, therefore, of nothing less than of death, and his wisdom is a meditation upon life.—Q.E.D.

PROP. LXVIII.—*If men were born free, they would form no conception of good and evil so long as they were free.*

Demonst.—I have said that that man is free who is led by reason alone. He, therefore, who is born free and remains free has no other than adequate ideas, and therefore has no conception of evil (Corol. Prop. 64, pt. 4), and consequently (as good and evil are correlative) no conception of good.—Q.E.D.

Schol.—It is clear from Prop. 4, pt. 4, that the hypothesis of this proposition is false, and cannot be conceived unless in so far as we regard human nature alone, or rather God, not in so far as He is infinite, but in so far only as He is the cause of man's existence. This (together with the other things we have before demonstrated) appears to have been what was meant by Moses in that history of the first man. In that history no other power of God is conceived excepting that by which He created man; that is to say, the power with which He considered nothing but the advantage of man. There-

fore we are told that God forbad free man to eat of the
tree of knowledge of good and evil, and warned him that
as soon as he ate of it he would immediately dread death
rather than desire to live. Afterwards we are told that
when man found a wife who agreed entirely with his
nature, he saw that there could be nothing in nature
which could be more profitable to him than his wife.
But when he came to believe that the brutes were like
himself, he immediately began to imitate their affects
(Prop. 27, pt. 3), and to lose his liberty, which the Patriarchs afterwards recovered, being led by the spirit of
Christ, that is to say, by the idea of God, which alone
can make a man free, and cause him to desire for other
men the good he desires for himself, as (Prop. 37, pt. 4)
we have already demonstrated.

PROP. LXIX.—*The virtue of a free man is seen to be as
great in avoiding danger as in overcoming it.*

Demonst.—An affect cannot be restrained or removed
unless a contrary and stronger affect restrains it (Prop.
7, pt. 4); but blind audacity and fear are affects which
may be conceived as being equally great (Props. 5 and
3, pt. 4). The virtue or strength of mind, therefore
(for the definition of this, see Schol. Prop. 59, pt. 3),
which is required to restrain audacity must be equally
great with that which is required to restrain fear; that
is to say (Defs. 40 and 41 of the Affects), a free man
avoids danger by the same virtue of the mind as that
by which he seeks to overcome it.—Q.E.D.

Corol.—Flight at the proper time, just as well as
fighting, is to be reckoned, therefore, as showing strength
of mind in a man who is free; that is to say, a free man
chooses flight by the same strength or presence of mind
as that by which he chooses battle.

Schol.—What strength of mind is, or what I understand by it, I have explained in Schol. Prop. 59, pt. 3.

By danger, I understand anything which may be the cause of sorrow, hatred, discord, or any other evil like them.

LXX.—*The free man who lives amongst those who are igno-rant strives as much as possible to avoid their favours.*

Demonst.—Every one, according to his own disposition, judges what is good (Schol. Prop. 39, pt. 3). The igno-rant man, therefore, who has conferred a favour on another person, will value it according to his own way of think-ing, and he will be sad if a less value seems to be placed upon it by the person who has received it (Prop. 42, pt. 3). But a free man strives to unite other men with himself by friendship (Prop. 37, pt. 4), and not to return to them favours which they, according to their affects, may consider to be equal to those which they have bestowed. He desires rather to govern himself and others by the free decisions of reason, and to do those things only which he has discovered to be of the first importance. A free man, therefore, in order that he may not be hated by the ignorant, nor yet yield to their appe-tites, but only to reason, will endeavour as much as pos-sible to avoid their favours.—Q.E.D.

Schol.—I say *as much as possible.* For although men are ignorant, they are nevertheless men, who, when we are in straits, are able to afford us human assistance—the best assistance which man can receive. It is often necessary, therefore, to receive a favour from the ignorant, and to thank them for it according to their taste; and besides this, care must be used, even in declining favours, not to seem either to despise the givers or through avarice to dread a return, so that we may not, while striving to escape their hatred, by that very act incur their displea-sure. In avoiding favours, therefore, we must be guided by a consideration of what is profitable and honourable.

PROP. LXXI.—*None but those who are free are very grate-*
ful to one another.

Demonst.—None but those who are free are very profitable to one another, or are united by the closest bond
of friendship (Prop. 35, pt. 4, and Corol. 1), or with
an equal zeal of love strive to do good to one another
(Prop. 37, pt. 4), and therefore (Def. 34 of the Affects)
none but those who are free are very grateful to one another.—Q.E.D.

Schol.—The gratitude to one another of men who are
led by blind desire is generally a matter of business or a
snare rather than gratitude. Ingratitude, it is to be observed, is not an affect. It is nevertheless base, because
it is generally a sign that a man is too much affected by
hatred, anger, pride, or avarice. For he who through
stupidity does not know how to return a gift is not
ungrateful; and much less is he ungrateful who is not
moved by the gifts of a harlot to serve her lust, nor by
those of a thief to conceal his thefts, nor by any other
gifts of a similar kind. On the contrary, a man shows
that he possesses a steadfast mind if he does not suffer
himself to be enticed by any gifts to his own or the
common ruin.

PROP. LXXII.—*A free man never acts deceitfully, but*
always honourably.

Demonst.—If a free man did anything deceitfully, in
so far as he is free, he would do it at the bidding of
reason (for so far only do we call him free); and therefore to act deceitfully would be a virtue (Prop. 24, pt. 4),
and consequently (by the same proposition) it would be
more advantageous to every one, for the preservation of
his being, to act deceitfully; that is to say (as is self-
evident), it would be more advantageous to men to agree
only in words and to be opposed in reality, which (Corol.

Prop. 31, pt. 4) is absurd. A free man, therefore, &c.—Q.E.D.

Schol.—If it be asked whether, if a man by breach of faith could escape from the danger of instant death, reason does not counsel him, for the preservation of his being, to break faith; I reply in the same way, that if reason gives such counsel, she gives it to all men, and reason therefore generally counsels men to make no agreements for uniting their strength and possessing laws in common except deceitfully, that is to say, to have in reality no common laws, which is absurd.

PROP. LXXIII.—*A man who is guided by reason is freer in a State where he lives according to the common laws than he is in solitude, where he obeys himself alone.*

Demonst.—A man who is guided by reason is not led to obey by fear (Prop. 63, pt. 4), but in so far as he endeavours to preserve his being in accordance with the bidding of reason, that is to say (Schol. Prop. 66, pt. 4), in so far as he endeavours to live in freedom, does he desire to have regard for the common life and the common profit (Prop. 37, pt. 4), and consequently (as we have shown in Schol. 2, Prop. 37, pt. 4) he desires to live according to the common laws of the State. A man, therefore, who is guided by reason desires, in order that he may live more freely, to maintain the common rights of the State.—Q.E.D.

Schol.—These, and the like things which we have demonstrated concerning the true liberty of man, are related to fortitude, that is to say (Schol. Prop. 59, pt. 3), to strength of mind and generosity. Nor do I think it worth while to demonstrate here, one by one, all the properties of fortitude, and still less to show how its possessor can hate no one, be angry with no one, can neither envy, be indignant with, nor despise anybody, and can least of all be proud. For all this, together with truths

of a like kind which have to do with the true life and
religion, are easily deduced from Props. 37 and 46, pt. 4,
which show that hatred is to be overcome by love, and
that every one who is guided by reason desires for
others the good which he seeks for himself. In addition,
we must remember what we have already observed in
Schol. Prop. 50, pt. 4, and in other places, that the brave
man will consider above everything that all things follow
from the necessity of the divine nature; and that, consequently, whatever he thinks injurious and evil, and, moreover, whatever seems to be impious, dreadful, unjust,
or wicked, arises from this, that he conceives things in a
disturbed, mutilated, and confused fashion. For this reason, his chief effort is to conceive things as they are in
themselves, and to remove the hindrances to true knowledge, such as hatred, anger, envy, derision, pride, and
others of this kind which we have before noticed ; and so
he endeavours, as we have said, as much as possible to
do well and rejoice. How far human virtue reaches in
the attainment of these things, and what it can do, I shall
show in the following part.

APPENDIX.

My observations in this part concerning the true
method of life have not been arranged so that they could
be seen at a glance, but have been demonstrated here
and there according as I could more easily deduce one
from another. I have determined, therefore, here to collect them, and reduce them under principal heads.

I.

All our efforts or desires follow from the necessity of
our nature in such a manner that they can be understood
either through it alone as their proximate cause, or in so
far as we are a part of nature, which part cannot be ade-

quately conceived through itself and without the other individuals.

II.

The desires which follow from our nature in such a manner that they can be understood through it alone, are those which are related to the mind, in so far as it is conceived to consist of adequate ideas. The remaining desires are not related to the mind, unless in so far as it conceives things inadequately, whose power and increase cannot be determined by human power, but by the power of objects which are without us. The first kind of desires, therefore, are properly called actions, but the latter passions; for the first always indicate our power, and the latter, on the contrary, indicate our impotence and imperfect knowledge.

III.

Our actions, that is to say, those desires which are determined by man's power or reason, are always good; the others may be good as well as evil.

IV.

It is therefore most profitable to us in life to make perfect the intellect or reason as far as possible, and in this one thing consists the highest happiness or blessedness of man ; for blessedness is nothing but the peace of mind which springs from the intuitive knowledge of God, and to perfect the intellect is nothing but to understand God, together with the attributes and actions of God, which flow from the necessity of His nature. The final aim, therefore, of a man who is guided by reason, that is to say, the chief desire by which he strives to govern all his other desires, is that by which he is led adequately to conceive himself and all things which can be conceived by his intelligence.

V.

There is no rational life therefore, without intelligence,

Q

and things are good only in so far as they assist man to enjoy that life of the mind which is determined by intelligence. Those things alone, on the other hand, we call evil which hinder man from perfecting his reason and enjoying a rational life.

VI.

But because all those things of which man is the efficient cause are necessarily good, it follows that no evil can happen to man except from external causes, that is to say, except in so far as he is a part of the whole of nature, whose laws human nature is compelled to obey—compelled also to accommodate himself to this whole of nature in almost an infinite number of ways.

VII.

It is impossible that a man should not be a part of nature and follow her common order; but if he be placed amongst individuals who agree with his nature, his power of action will by that very fact be assisted and supported. But if, on the contrary, he be placed amongst individuals who do not in the least agree with his nature, he will scarcely be able without great change on his part to accommodate himself to them.

VIII.

Anything that exists in nature which we judge to be evil or able to hinder us from existing and enjoying a rational life, we are allowed to remove from us in that way which seems the safest; and whatever, on the other hand, we judge to be good or to be profitable for the preservation of our being or the enjoyment of a rational life, we are permitted to take for our use and use in any way we may think proper; and absolutely, every one is allowed by the highest right of nature to do that which he believes contributes to his own profit.

IX.

Nothing, therefore, can agree better with the nature of any object than other individuals of the same kind, and so (see § 7) there is nothing more profitable to man for the preservation of his being and the enjoyment of a rational life than a man who is guided by reason. Again, since there is no single thing we know which is more excellent than a man who is guided by reason, it follows that there is nothing by which a person can better show how much skill and talent he possesses than by so educating men that at last they will live under the direct authority of reason.

X.

In so far as men are carried away by envy or any affect of hatred towards one another, so far are they contrary to one another, and consequently so much the more are they to be feared, as they have more power than other individuals of nature.

XI.

Minds, nevertheless, are not conquered by arms, but by love and generosity.

XII.

Above all things is it profitable to men to form communities and to unite themselves to one another by bonds which may make all of them as one man; and absolutely, it is profitable for them to do whatever may tend to strengthen their friendships.

XIII.

But to accomplish this skill and watchfulness are required; for men are changeable (those being very few who live according to the laws of reason), and nevertheless generally envious and more inclined to vengeance than pity. To bear with each, therefore, according to his disposition and to refrain from imitating his affects requires a singular power of mind. But those, on the contrary, who know how to revile men, to denounce vices rather than teach virtues, and not to strengthen men's minds but to weaken them, are injurious both to themselves and others, so that many of them through an excess of impatience and a false zeal for religion prefer living with brutes rather than amongst men; just as boys or youths, unable to endure with equanimity the rebukes of their parents, fly to the army, choosing the discomforts of war and the rule of a tyrant rather than the comforts of home and the admonitions of a father, suffering all kinds of burdens to be imposed upon them in order that they may revenge themselves upon their parents.

XIV.

Although, therefore, men generally determine everything by their pleasure, many more advantages than disadvantages arise from their common union. It is better, therefore, to endure with equanimity the injuries inflicted by them, and to apply our minds to those things which subserve concord and the establishment of friendship.

XV.

The things which beget concord are those which are related to justice, integrity, and honour; for besides that which is unjust and injurious, men take ill also anything which is esteemed base, or that any one should despise the received customs of the State. But in order to win love, those things are chiefly necessary which have reference to religion and piety. (See Schols. 1 and 2, Prop. 37, Schol. Prop. 46, and Schol. Prop. 73, pt. 4.)

XVI.

Concord, moreover, is often produced by fear, but it is without good faith. It is to be observed, too, that fear arises from impotence of mind, and therefore is of no service to reason; nor is pity, although it seems to present an appearance of piety.

XVII.

Men also are conquered by liberality, especially those who have not the means wherewith to procure what is necessary for the support of life. But to assist every one who is needy far surpasses the strength or profit of a private person, for the wealth of a private person is altogether insufficient to supply such wants. Besides, the power of any one man is too limited for him to be able to unite every one with himself in friendship. The care, therefore, of the poor is incumbent on the whole of society and concerns only the general profit.

XVIII.

In the receipt of benefits and in returning thanks, care altogether different must be taken—concerning which see Schol. Prop. 70, and Schol. Prop. 71, pt. 4.

XIX.

The love of a harlot, that is to say, the lust of sexual intercourse, which arises from mere external form, and absolutely all love which recognises any other cause than the freedom of the mind, easily passes into hatred, unless, which is worse, it becomes a species of delirium, and thereby discord is cherished rather than concord (Corol. Prop. 31, pt. 3).

XX.

With regard to marriage, it is plain that it is in accordance with reason, if the desire of connection is engendered not merely by external form, but by a love of begetting children and wisely educating them; and if, in addition, the love both of the husband and wife has for its cause not external form merely, but chiefly liberty of mind.

XXI.

Flattery, too, produces concord, but only by means of the disgraceful crime of slavery or perfidy; for there are none who are more taken by flattery than the proud, who wish to be first and are not so.

XXII.

There is a false appearance of piety and religion in dejection; and although dejection is the opposite of pride, the humble dejected man is very near akin to the proud (Schol. Prop. 57, pt. 4).

XXIII.

Shame also contributes to concord, but only with regard to those matters which cannot be concealed. Shame, too, inasmuch as it is a kind of sorrow, does not belong to the service of reason.

XXIV.

The remaining affects of sorrow which have man for their object are directly opposed to justice, integrity, honour, piety, and religion; and although indignation may seem to present an appearance of equity, yet there is no law where it is allowed to every one to judge the deeds of another, and to vindicate his own or another's right.

XXV.

Affability, that is to say, the desire of pleasing men, which is determined by reason, is related to piety (Schol. Prop. 37, pt. 4). But if affability arise from an affect, it is ambition or desire, by which men, generally under a false pretence of piety, excite discords and seditions. For he who desires to assist other people, either by advice or by deed, in order that they may together enjoy the highest good, will strive, above all things, to win their love, and not to draw them into admiration, so that a doctrine may be named after him, nor absolutely to give any occasion for envy. In common conversation, too, he will avoid referring to the vices of men, and will take care only sparingly to speak of human impotence, while he will talk largely of human virtue or power, and of the way by which it may be made perfect, so that men being moved not by fear or aversion, but solely by the affect of joy, may endeavour as much as they can to live under the rule of reason.

XXVI.

Excepting man, we know no individual thing in nature in whose mind we can take pleasure, nor anything which we can unite with ourselves by friendship or any kind of intercourse, and therefore regard to our own profit does not demand that we should preserve anything which exists in nature excepting men, but teaches us to preserve it or destroy it in accordance with its varied uses, or to adapt it to our own service in any way whatever.

XXVII.

The profit which we derive from objects without us, over and above the experience and knowledge which we obtain because we observe them and change them from their existing forms into others, is chiefly the preservation of the body, and for this reason those objects are the most profitable to us which can feed and nourish the body, so that all its parts are able properly to perform their functions. For the more capable the body is of being affected in many ways, and affecting external bodies in many ways, the more capable of thinking is the mind (Props. 38 and 39, pt. 4). But there seem to be very few things in nature of this kind, and it is consequently necessary for the requisite nourishment of the body to use many different kinds of food; for the human body is composed of a great number of parts of different nature, which need constant and varied food in order that the whole of the body may be equally adapted for all those things which can follow from its nature, and consequently that the mind also may be equally adapted to conceive many things.

XXVIII.

The strength of one man would scarcely suffice to obtain these things if men did not mutually assist one another. As money has presented us with an abstract of everything, it has come to pass that its image above every other usually occupies the mind of the multitude, because they can imagine hardly any kind of joy without the accompanying idea of money as its cause.

XXIX.

This, however, is a vice only in those who seek money not from poverty or necessity, but because they have learnt the arts of gain, by which they keep up a grand appearance. As for the body itself, they feed it in accordance with custom, but sparingly, because they believe that they lose so much of their goods as they spend upon the preservation of their body. Those, however, who know the true use of money, and regulate the measure of wealth according to their needs, live contented with few things.

XXX.

Since, therefore, those things are good which help the parts of the body to perform their functions, and since joy consists in this, that the power of man, in so far as he is made up of mind and body, is helped or increased, it follows that all those things which bring joy are good. But inasmuch as things do not work to this end—that they may affect us with joy—nor is their power of action guided in accordance with our profit, and finally, since joy is generally related chiefly to some one part of the body, it follows that generally the affects of joy (unless reason and watchfulness be present), and consequently the desires which are begotten from them, are excessive. It is to be added, that an affect causes us to put that thing first which is sweet to us in the present, and that we are not able to judge the future with an equal affect of the mind (Schol. Prop. 44, and Schol. Prop. 60, pt. 4).

XXXI.

Superstition, on the contrary, seems to affirm that what brings sorrow is good, and, on the contrary, that what brings joy is evil. But, as we have already said (Schol. Prop. 45, pt. 4), no one excepting an envious man is delighted at my impotence or disadvantage, for the greater the joy with which we are affected, the greater the perfection to which we pass, and consequently the more do we participate in the divine nature; nor can joy ever be evil which is controlled by a true consideration for our own profit. On the other hand, the man who is led by fear, and does what is good that he may avoid what is evil, is not guided by reason.

XXXII.

But human power is very limited, and is infinitely surpassed by the power of external causes, so that we do not possess an absolute power to adapt to our service the things which are without us. Nevertheless we shall bear with equanimity those things which happen to us contrary to what a consideration of our own profit demands, if we are conscious that we have performed our duty, that the power we have could not reach so far as to enable us to avoid those things, and that we are a part of the whole of nature, whose order we follow. If we clearly and distinctly understand this, the part of us which is determined by intelligence, that is to say, the better part of us, will be entirely satisfied therewith, and in that satisfaction will endeavour to persevere; for, in so far as we understand, we cannot desire anything excepting what is necessary, nor, absolutely, can we be satisfied with anything but the truth. Therefore in so far as we understand these things properly will the efforts of the better part of us agree with the order of the whole of nature.

ETHIC.

Fifth Part.

OF THE POWER OF THE INTELLECT, OR OF HUMAN LIBERTY.

PREFACE.

I PASS at length to the other part of Ethic which concerns the method or way which leads to liberty. In this part, therefore, I shall treat of the power of reason, showing how much reason itself can control the affects, and then what is freedom of mind or blessedness. Thence we shall see how much stronger the wise man is than the ignorant. In what manner and in what way the intellect should be rendered perfect, and with what art the body is to be cared for in order that it may properly perform its functions, I have nothing to do with here; for the former belongs to logic, the latter to medicine. I shall occupy myself here, as I have said, solely with the power of the mind or of reason, first of all showing the extent and nature of the authority which it has over the affects in restraining them and governing them; for that we have not absolute authority over them we have already demonstrated. The Stoics indeed thought that the affects depend absolutely on our will, and that we are absolutely masters over them; but they were driven, by the contradiction of experience, though not by their own principles, to confess that not a little practice and study are required in order to restrain and govern the affects. This one of them attempted to illustrate, if I remember rightly, by the example of two dogs, one of a domestic and the other of a hunting breed; for he was able by habit to make the house-dog hunt, and the hunting dog, on the contrary, to desist from running after hares. To the Stoical opinion Descartes much inclines. He affirms that the soul or mind is united specially to a certain part of the brain called the pineal gland, which the mind by the mere exercise of the will is able to move in different ways, and by whose help the mind perceives all the movements which are excited in the body and external objects. This gland he affirms is suspended in the middle of the brain in such a manner that it can be moved by the least motion of the animal spirits. Again, he affirms that any variation in the manner in which the animal spirits impinge upon this gland is followed by a variation in the manner in which it is suspended in the middle of the brain, and moreover that the number of different impressions on the gland is the same as that of the different external objects which propel the animal spirits towards it. Hence it comes to pass that if the gland, by the will of the soul moving it in different directions, be afterwards suspended in this or that way in which it had once been suspended by the spirits agitated in this or that way, then the gland itself will propel and determine the animal spirits themselves in the same way as that in which they had before been repelled by a similar suspension of the gland. Moreover, he affirmed that each volition of the mind is united in nature to a certain motion of the gland. For example, if a person wishes to behold a remote object, this volition will cause the pupil of the eye to dilate, but if he thinks merely of the dilation of the pupil, to have that volition will profit him nothing, because nature has not connected a motion of the gland which serves to impel the animal spirits towards the optic nerve in a way suitable for dilation or contraction of the pupil with the volition of dilation or contraction, but only with the volition of beholding objects afar off or close at hand. Finally, he maintained that although each motion of this gland appears to be connected by nature from the commencement of our life with an individual thought, these motions can nevertheless be connected by habit with other thoughts, a proposition which he attempts to demonstrate in his " Passions of the Soul," art. 50, pt. 1.

From this he concludes that there is no mind so feeble that it cannot, when properly directed, acquire absolute power over its passions ; for passions, as defined by him, are " perceptions, or sensations, or emotions of the soul which are related to it specially, and which (N.B.) are produced,[1] preserved, and strengthened by some motion of the spirits." (See the " Passions of the Soul," art. 27, pt. 1.) But since it is possible to join to a certain volition any motion of the gland, and consequently of the spirits, and since the determination of the will depends solely on our power, we shall be able to acquire absolute mastery over our passions provided only we determine our will by fixed and firm decisions by which we desire to direct our actions and bind with these decisions the movements of the passions we wish to have. So far as I can gather from his own words, this is the opinion of that distinguished man, and I could scarcely have believed it possible for one so great to have put it forward if it had been less subtle. I can hardly wonder enough that a philosopher who firmly resolved to make no deduction except from self-evident principles, and to affirm nothing but what he clearly and distinctly perceived, and who blamed all the schoolmen because they desired to explain obscure matters by occult qualities, should accept a hypothesis more occult than any occult quality. What does he understand, I ask, by the union of the mind and body? What clear and distinct conception has he of thought intimately connected with a certain small portion of matter? I wish that he had explained this union by its proximate cause. But he

---

[1] After "quæque," the corrigenda to the Ed. Pr. add "ita Auctor scripserat, N.B." The Dutch version omits the "ita Auctor scripserat," but retains the " N.B." —TR.

conceived the mind to be so distinct from the body that he was able to assign no single cause of this union, nor of the mind itself, but was obliged to have recourse to the cause of the whole universe, that is to say, to God. Again, I should like to know how many degrees of motion the mind can give to that pineal gland, and with how great a power the mind can hold it suspended. For I do not understand whether this gland is acted on by the mind more slowly or more quickly than by the animal spirits, and whether the movements of the passions, which we have so closely bound with firm decisions, might not be separated from them again by bodily causes, from which it would follow that although the mind had firmly determined to meet danger, and had joined to this decision the motion of boldness, the sight of the danger might cause the gland to be suspended in such a manner that the mind could think of nothing but flight. Indeed, since there is no relation between the will and motion, so there is no comparison between the power or strength of the body and that of the mind, and consequently the strength of the body can never be determined by the strength of the mind. It is to be remembered also that this gland is not found to be so situated in the middle of the brain that it can be driven about so easily and in so many ways, and that all the nerves are not extended to the cavities of the brain. Lastly, I omit all that Descartes asserts concerning the will and the freedom of the will, since I have shown over and over again that it is false. Therefore, inasmuch as the power of the mind, as I have shown above, is determined by intelligence alone, we shall determine by the knowledge of the mind alone the remedies against the affects—remedies which every one, I believe, has experienced, although there may not have been any accurate observation or distinct perception of them, and from this knowledge of the mind alone shall we deduce everything which relates to its blessedness.

Axioms.

1. If two contrary actions be excited in the same subject, a change must necessarily take place in both, or in one alone, until they cease to be contrary.

2. The power of an affect is limited by the power of its cause, in so far as the essence of the affect is manifested or limited by the essence of the cause itself.

This axiom is evident from Prop. 7, pt. 3.

PROP. I.—*As thoughts and the ideas of things are arranged and connected in the mind, exactly so are the affections of the body or the images of things arranged and connected in the body.*

Demonst.—The order and connection of ideas is the same (Prop. 7, pt. 2) as the order and connection of things, and *vice versa*, the order and connection of things is the same (Corol. Props. 6 and 7, pt. 2) as the order and connection of ideas. Therefore, as the order and connection of ideas in the mind is according to the order and connection of the affections of the body (Prop. 18, pt. 2), it follows, *vice versa* (Prop. 2, pt. 3), that the order and connection of the affections of the body is according to the order and connection in the mind of the thoughts and ideas of things.—Q.E.D.

PROP. II.—*If we detach an emotion of the mind or affect from the thought of an external cause and connect it with other thoughts, then the love or hatred towards the external cause and the fluctuations of the mind which arise from these affects will be destroyed.*

Demonst.—That which constitutes the form of love or hatred is joy or sorrow, accompanied with the idea of an external cause (Defs. 6 and 7 of the Affects). If this idea therefore be taken away, the form of love or hatred is also removed, and therefore these affects and any others which arise from them are destroyed.—Q.E.D.

PROP. III.—*An affect which is a passion ceases to be a passion as soon as we form a clear and distinct idea of it.*

Demonst.—An affect which is a passion is a confused idea (by the general definition of the Affects). If, therefore, we form a clear and distinct idea of this affect, the idea will not be distinguished—except by reason—from this affect, in so far as the affect is related to the mind alone (Prop. 21, pt. 2, with its Schol.), and therefore (Prop. 3, pt. 3) the affect will cease to be a passion.—Q.E.D.

Corol.—In proportion, then, as we know an affect better is it more within our control, and the less does the mind suffer from it.

PROP. IV.——*There is no affection of the body of which we cannot form some clear and distinct conception.*

Demonst.—Those things which are common to all cannot be otherwise than adequately conceived (Prop. 38, pt. 2), and therefore (Prop. 12, and Lem. 2, following Schol. Prop. 13, pt. 2) there is no affection of the body of which we cannot form some clear and distinct conception.—Q.E.D.

Corol.—Hence it follows that there is no affect of which we cannot form some clear and distinct conception. For an affect is an idea of an affection of the body (by the general definition of the Affects), and this idea therefore (Prop. 4, pt. 5) must involve some clear and distinct conception.

Schol.—Since nothing exists from which some effect does not follow (Prop. 36, pt. 1), and since we understand clearly and distinctly everything which follows from an idea which is adequate in us (Prop. 40, pt. 2), it is a necessary consequence that every one has the power, partly at least, if not absolutely, of understanding clearly and distinctly himself and his affects, and consequently of bringing it to pass that he suffers less from them. We have therefore mainly to strive to acquire a clear and distinct knowledge as far as possible of each affect, so that the mind may be led to pass from the affect to think those things which it perceives clearly and distinctly, and with which it is entirely satisfied, and to strive also that the affect may be separated from the thought of an external cause and connected with true thoughts. Thus not only love, hatred, &c., will be destroyed (Prop. 2, pt. 5), but also the appetites or desires to which the affect gives rise cannot be excessive (Prop. 61, pt. 4). For it is above everything to be observed that the appetite by which a man is said to act is one and the same appetite as that by which he is said to suffer. For example, we have shown that human nature is so constituted that every one desires that other people should live according to his way of thinking (Schol. Prop. 31, pt. 3), a desire which in a man who is not guided by reason is a passion which is called ambition, and is not very different from pride; while, on the other hand, in a man who lives according to the dictates of reason it is an action or virtue which is called piety (Schol. 1, Prop. 37, pt. 4, and Demonst. 2 of the same Prop.) In the same manner, all the appetites or desires are passions only in so far as they arise from inadequate ideas, and are classed among the virtues whenever they are excited or begotten by adequate ideas; for all the desires by which we are determined to any action may arise either from adequate or inadequate ideas (Prop. 59, pt. 4). To return, therefore, to the point from which we set out: there is no remedy within our power which can be conceived more excellent for the affects than that which consists in a true knowledge of them, since the mind possesses no other power than that of thinking and forming adequate ideas, as we have shown above (Prop. 3, pt. 3).

PROP. V.—*An affect towards an object which we do not imagine as necessary, possible, or contingent, but which we simply imagine, is, other things being equal, the greatest of all.*

Demonst.—The affect towards an object which we imagine to be free is greater than towards one which is necessary (Prop. 49, pt. 3), and consequently still greater than towards one which we imagine as possible or contingent (Prop. 11, pt. 4). But to imagine an object as free can be nothing else than to imagine it simply, while we know not the causes by which it was determined to action. (See Schol. Prop. 35, pt. 2.) An affect, therefore, towards an object which we simply imagine is, other things being equal, greater than towards one which we imagine as necessary, possible, or contingent, and consequently greatest of all.—Q.E.D.

PROP. VI.—*In so far as the mind understands all things as necessary, so far has it greater power over the affects, or suffers less from them.*

Demonst.—The mind understands all things to be necessary (Prop. 29, pt. 1), and determined by an infinite chain of causes to existence and action (Prop. 28, pt. 1), and therefore (Prop. 5, pt. 5) so far enables itself to suffer less from the affects which arise from these things, and (Prop. 48, pt. 3) to be less affected towards them. —Q.E.D.

Schol.—The more this knowledge that things are necessary is applied to individual things which we imagine more distinctly and more vividly, the greater is this power of the mind over the affects,—a fact to which experience also testifies. For we see that sorrow for the loss of anything good is diminished if the person who has lost it considers that it could not by any possibility have been preserved. So also we see that nobody pities

R

an infant because it does not know how to speak, walk,
or reason, and lives so many years not conscious, as it
were, of itself; but if a number of human beings were
born adult, and only a few here and there were born
infants, every one would pity the infants, because we
should then consider infancy not as a thing natural and
necessary, but as a defect or fault of nature. Many
other facts of a similar kind we might observe.

PROP. VII.—*The affects which spring from reason or which
are excited by it are, if time be taken into account, more
powerful than those which are related to individual
objects which we contemplate as absent.*

Demonst.—We do not contemplate an object as absent
by reason of the affect by which we imagine it, but by
reason of the fact that the body is affected with another
affect, which excludes the existence of that object (Prop.
17, pt. 2). The affect, therefore, which is related to an
object which we contemplate as absent, is not of such a
nature as to overcome the other actions and power of
man (concerning these things see Prop. 6, pt. 4), but,
on the contrary, is of such a nature that it can in some
way be restrained by those affections which exclude the
existence of its external cause (Prop. 9, pt. 4). But the
affect which arises from reason is necessarily related to
the common properties of things (see the definition of
reason in Schol. 2, Prop. 40, pt. 2), which we always contemplate as present (for nothing can exist which excludes
their present existence), and which we always imagine
in the same way (Prop. 38, pt. 2). This affect, therefore, always remains the same. and consequently (Ax. 1,
pt. 5), the affects which are contrary to it, and which are
not maintained by their external cause, must more and
more accommodate themselves to it until they are no
longer contrary to it. So far, therefore, the affect which
springs from reason is the stronger.—Q.E.D.

PROP. VIII.—*The greater the number of the causes which simultaneously concur to excite any affect, the greater it will be.*

Demonst.—A number of simultaneous causes can do more than if they were fewer (Prop. 7, pt. 3), and therefore (Prop. 5, pt. 4) the greater the number of the simultaneous causes by which an affect is excited, the greater it is.—Q.E.D.

Schol.—This proposition is also evident from Ax. 2, pt. 5.

PROP. IX.—*If we are affected by an affect which is related to many and different causes, which the mind contemplates at the same time with the affect itself, we are less injured, suffer less from it, and are less affected therefore towards each cause than if we were affected by another affect equally great which is related to one cause only or to fewer causes.*

Demonst.—An affect is bad or injurious only in so far as it hinders the mind from thinking (Props. 26 and 27, pt. 4), and therefore that affect by which the mind is determined to the contemplation of a number of objects at the same time is less injurious than another affect equally great which holds the mind in the contemplation of one object alone or of a few objects, so that it cannot think of others. This is the first thing we had to prove. Again, since the essence of the mind, that is to say (Prop. 7, pt. 3), its power, consists in thought alone (Prop. 11, pt. 2), the mind suffers less through an affect by which it is determined to the contemplation of a number of objects at the same time than through an affect equally great which holds it occupied in the contemplation of one object alone or of a few objects. This is the second thing we had to prove. Finally, this affect (Prop. 48, pt. 3), in so far as it is related to a number of external causes, is therefore less towards each.—Q.E.D.

PROP. X.—*So long as we are not agitated by affects which are contrary to our nature do we possess the power of arranging and connecting the affections of the body according to the order of the intellect.*

Demonst.—The affects which are contrary to our nature, that is to say (Prop. 30, pt. 4), which are evil, are evil so far as they hinder the mind from understanding (Prop. 27, pt. 4). So long, therefore, as we are not agitated by affects which are contrary to our nature, so long the power of the mind by which it endeavours to understand things (Prop. 26, pt. 4) is not hindered, and therefore so long does it possess the power of forming clear and distinct ideas, and of deducing them the one from the other (see Schol. 2, Prop. 40, and Schol. Prop. 47, pt. 2). So long, consequently (Prop. 1, pt. 5), do we possess the power of arranging and connecting the affections of the body according to the order of the intellect.—Q.E.D.

Schol.—Through this power of properly arranging and connecting the affections of the body we can prevent ourselves from being easily affected by evil affects. For (Prop. 7, pt. 5) a greater power is required to restrain affects which are arranged and connected according to the order of the intellect than is required to restrain those which are uncertain and unsettled. The best thing, therefore, we can do, so long as we lack a perfect knowledge of our affects, is to conceive a right rule of life, or sure maxims (*dogmata*) of life,—to commit these latter to memory, and constantly to apply them to the particular cases which frequently meet us in life, so that our imagination may be widely affected by them, and they may always be ready to hand. For example, amongst the maxims of life we have placed this (see Prop. 46, pt. 4, with its Schol.), that hatred is to be conquered by love or generosity, and is not to be met with hatred in return. But in order that we may always have this prescript of reason in readiness whenever it will be of service, we must think over and often meditate upon the common injuries inflicted by men, and consider how and in what way they may best be repelled by generosity; for thus we shall connect the image of injury with the imagination of this maxim, and (Prop. 18, pt. 2) it will be at hand whenever an injury is offered to us. If we also continually have regard to our own true profit, and the good which follows from mutual friendship and common fellowship, and remember that the highest peace of mind arises from a right rule of life (Prop. 52, pt. 4), and also that man, like other things, acts according to the necessity of nature, then the injury or the hatred which usually arises from that necessity will occupy but the least part of the imagination, and will be easily overcome: or supposing that the anger which generally arises from the greatest injuries is not so easily overcome, it will nevertheless be overcome, although not without fluctuation of mind, in a far shorter space of time than would have been necessary if we had not possessed those maxims on which we had thus meditated beforehand. This is evident from Props. 6, 7, and 8, pt. 5.

Concerning strength of mind, we must reflect in the same way for the purpose of getting rid of fear, that is to say, we must often enumerate and imagine the common dangers of life, and think upon the manner in which they can best be avoided and overcome by presence of mind and courage. It is to be observed, however, that in the ordering of our thoughts and images we must always look (Corol. Prop. 63, pt. 4, and Prop. 59, pt. 3) to those qualities which in each thing are good, so that we may be determined to action always by an affect of joy.

For example, if a man sees that he pursues glory too eagerly, let him think on its proper use, for what end it is to be followed, and by what means it can be obtained; but let him not think upon its abuse and vanity, and on the inconstancy of men and things of this sort, about which no one thinks unless through disease of mind; for with such thoughts do those who are ambitious greatly torment themselves when they despair of obtaining the honours for which they are striving; and while they vomit forth rage, wish to be thought wise. Indeed it is certain that those covet glory the most who are loudest in declaiming against its abuse and the vanity of the world. Nor is this a peculiarity of the ambitious, but is common to all to whom fortune is adverse and who are impotent in mind; for we see that a poor and avaricious man is never weary of speaking about the abuse of money and the vices of the rich, thereby achieving nothing save to torment himself and show to others that he is unable to bear with equanimity not only his own poverty but also the wealth of others. So also a man who has not been well received by his mistress thinks of nothing but the fickleness of women, their faithlessness, and their other oft-proclaimed failings,—all of which he forgets as soon as he is taken into favour by his mistress again. He, therefore, who desires to govern his affects and appetites from a love of liberty alone will strive as much as he can to know virtues and their causes, and to fill his mind with that joy which springs from a true knowledge of them. Least of all will he desire to contemplate the vices of men and disparage men, or to delight in a false show of liberty. He who will diligently observe these things (and they are not difficult), and will continue to practise them, will assuredly in a short space of time be able for the most part to direct his actions in accordance with the command of reason.

PROP. XI.—*The greater the number of objects to which an image is related, the more constant is it, or the more frequently does it present itself, and the more does it occupy the mind.*

Demonst.—The greater the number of objects to which

an image or affect is related, the greater is the number of causes by which it can be excited and cherished. All these causes the mind contemplates simultaneously by means of the affect (by hypothesis), and therefore the more constant is the affect, or the more frequently does it present itself, and the more does it occupy the mind (Prop. 8, pt. 5).—Q.E.D.

PROP. XII.—*The images of things are more easily connected with those images which are related to things which we clearly and distinctly understand than with any others.*

Demonst.—Things which we clearly and distinctly understand are either the common properties of things or what are deduced from them (see the definition of reason in Schol. 2, Prop. 40, pt. 2), and consequently (Prop. 11, pt. 5) are more frequently excited in us ; and therefore it is easier for us to contemplate other things together with these which we clearly and distinctly understand than with any others, and consequently (Prop. 18, pt. 2), it is easier to connect things with these which we clearly and distinctly understand than with any others.

PROP. XIII.—*The greater the number of other things with which any image is connected, the more frequently does it present itself.*

Demonst.—For the greater the number of other things with which an image is connected, the greater is the number of causes (Prop. 18, pt. 2) by which it may be excited.—Q.E.D.

PROP. XIV.—*The mind can cause all the affections of the body or the images of things to be related to the idea of God (ideam Dei).* [1]

---

[1] See note, p. 24.—TR.

Demonst.—There is no affection of the body of which the mind cannot form some clear and distinct conception (Prop. 4, pt. 5), and therefore (Prop. 15, pt. 1) it can cause all the affections of the body to be related to the idea of God.—Q.E.D.

PROP. XV.—*He who clearly and distinctly understands himself and his affects loves God, and loves Him better the better he understands himself and his affects.*

Demonst.—He who clearly and distinctly understands himself and his affects rejoices (Prop. 53, pt. 3), and his joy is attended with the idea of God (Prop. 14, pt. 5) therefore (Def. 6 of the Affects) he loves God, and (by the same reasoning) loves Him better the better he understands himself and his affects.—Q.E.D.

PROP. XVI.—*This love to God above everything else ought to occupy the mind.*

Demonst.—For this love is connected with all the affections of the body (Prop. 14, pt. 5), by all of which it is cherished (Prop. 15, pt. 5), and therefore (Prop. 11, pt. 5) above everything else ought to occupy the mind.—Q.E.D.

PROP. XVII.—*God is free from passions, nor is He affected with any affect of joy or sorrow.*

Demonst.—All ideas, in so far as they are related to God, are true (Prop. 32, pt. 2); that is to say (Def. 4, pt. 2), are adequate, and therefore (by the general definition of the Affects) God is free from passions. Again, God can neither pass to a greater nor to a less perfection (Corol. 2, Prop. 20, pt. 1), and therefore (Defs. 2 and 3 of the Affects) He cannot be affected with any affect of joy or sorrow.—Q.E.D.

Corol.—Properly speaking, God loves no one and hates no one; for God (Prop. 17, pt. 5) is not affected with any affect of joy or sorrow, and consequently (Defs. 6 and 7 of the Affects) He neither loves nor hates any one.

PROP. XVIII.—*No one can hate God.*

Demonst.—The idea of God which is in us is adequate and perfect (Props. 46 and 47, pt. 2), and therefore in so far as we contemplate God do we act (Prop. 3, pt. 3), and consequently (Prop. 59, pt. 3) no sorrow can exist with the accompanying idea of God; that is to say (Def. 7 of the Affects), no one can hate God.—Q.E.D.

Corol.—Love to God cannot be turned into hatred.

Schol.—But some may object, that if we understand God to be the cause of all things, we do for that very reason consider Him to be the cause of sorrow. But I reply, that in so far as we understand the causes of sorrow, it ceases to be a passion (Prop. 3, pt. 5), that is to say (Prop. 59, pt. 3), it ceases to be sorrow; and therefore in so far as we understand God to be the cause of sorrow do we rejoice.

PROP. XIX.—*He who loves God cannot strive that God should love him in return.*

Demonst.—If a man were to strive after this, he would desire (Corol. Prop. 17, pt. 5) that God, whom he loves, should not be God, and consequently (Prop. 19, pt. 3) he would desire to be sad, which (Prop. 28, pt. 3) is absurd. Therefore he who loves God, &c.—Q.E.D.

PROP. XX.—*This love to God cannot be defiled either by the affect of envy or jealousy, but is the more strengthened the more people we imagine to be connected with God by the same bond of love.*

Demonst.—This love to God is the highest good which

we can seek according to the dictate of reason (Prop. 28, pt. 4); is common to all men (Prop. 36, pt. 4); and we desire that all may enjoy it (Prop. 37, pt. 4). It cannot, therefore (Def. 23 of the Affects), be sullied by the affect of envy, nor (Prop. 18, pt. 5, and Def. of Jealousy in Schol. Prop. 35, pt. 3) by that of jealousy, but, on the contrary (Prop. 31, pt. 3), it must be the more strengthened the more people we imagine to rejoice in it.—Q.E.D.

Schol.—It is possible to show in the same manner that there is no affect directly contrary to this love and able to destroy it, and so we may conclude that this love to God is the most constant of all the affects, and that, in so far as it is related to the body, it cannot be destroyed unless with the body itself. What its nature is, in so far as it is related to the mind alone, we shall see hereafter.

I have, in what has preceded, included all the remedies for the affects, that is to say, everything which the mind, considered in itself alone, can do against them. It appears therefrom that the power of the mind over the affects consists—

1. In the knowledge itself of the affects. (See Schol. Prop. 4, pt. 5.)

2. In the separation by the mind of the affects from the thought of an external cause, which we imagine confusedly. (See Prop. 2, pt. 5, and Schol. Prop. 4, pt. 5.)

3. In duration, in which the affections * which are related to objects we understand surpass those related to objects conceived in a mutilated or confused manner. (Prop. 7, pt. 5.)

4. In the multitude of causes by which the affections * which are related to the common properties of things or to God are nourished. (Props. 9 and 11, pt. 5.)

5. In the order in which the mind can arrange its affects and connect them one with the other. (Schol. Prop. 10, pt. 5, and see also Props. 12, 13, and 14, pt. 5.)

But that this power of the mind over the affects may

* *Affectiones.* Probably a misprint, however, for *Affectus* (Tr.).

be better understood, it is to be carefully observed that
we call the affects great when we compare the affect of
one man with that of another, and see that one man is
agitated more than another by the same affect, or when
we compare the affects of one and the same man with
one another, and discover that he is affected or moved
more by one affect than by another.

For (Prop. 5, pt. 4) the power of any affect is limited
by the power of the external cause as compared with our
own power. But the power of the mind is limited solely
by knowledge, whilst impotence or passion is estimated
solely by privation of knowledge, or, in other words, by
that through which ideas are called inadequate; and it
therefore follows that that mind suffers the most whose
largest part consists of inadequate ideas, so that it is
distinguished rather by what it suffers than by what it
does, while, on the contrary, that mind acts the most
whose largest part consists of adequate ideas, so that
although it may possess as many inadequate ideas as the
first, it is nevertheless distinguished rather by those which
belong to human virtue than by those which are a sign
of human impotence. Again, it is to be observed that
our sorrows and misfortunes mainly proceed from too
much love towards an object which is subject to many
changes, and which we can never possess. For no one
is troubled or anxious about any object he does not love,
neither do wrongs, suspicions, hatreds, &c., arise except
from love towards objects of which no one can be truly
the possessor.

From all this we easily conceive what is the power
which clear and distinct knowledge, and especially that
third kind of knowledge (see Schol. Prop. 47, pt. 2)
whose foundation is the knowledge itself of God, possesses
over the affects; the power, namely, by which it is able,
in so far as they are passions, if not actually to destroy
them (see Prop. 3, pt. 5, with the Schol. to Prop. 4, pt.
5), at least to make them constitute the smallest part of

the mind (see Prop. 14, pt. 5). Moreover, it begets a love towards an immutable and eternal object (see Prop. 15, pt. 5) of which we are really partakers (see Prop. 45, pt. 2); a love which therefore cannot be vitiated by the defects which are in common love, but which can always become greater and greater (Prop. 15, pt. 5), occupy the largest part of the mind (Prop. 16, pt. 5), and thoroughly affect it.

I have now concluded all that I had to say relating to this present life. For any one who will attend to what has been urged in this scholium, and to the definition of the mind and its affects, and to Props. 1 and 3, pt. 3, will easily be able to see the truth of what I said in the beginning of the scholium, that in these few words all the remedies for the affects are comprehended. It is time, therefore, that I should now pass to the consideration of those matters which appertain to the duration of the mind without relation to the body.

PROP. XXI.—*The mind can imagine nothing, nor can it recollect anything that is past, except while the body exists.*

Demonst.—The mind does not express the actual existence of its body, nor does it conceive as actual the affections of the body, except while the body exists (Corol. Prop. 8, pt. 2), and consequently (Prop. 26, pt. 2) it conceives no body as actually existing except while its own body exists. It can therefore imagine nothing (see the definition of Imagination in Schol. Prop. 17, pt. 2), nor can it recollect anything that is past, except while the body exists (see the definition of Memory in Schol. Prop. 18, pt. 2).—Q.E.D.

PROP. XXII.—*In God, nevertheless, there necessarily exists an idea which expresses the essence of this or that human body under the form of eternity.*

Demonst.—God is not only the cause of the existence of this or that human body, but also of its essence (Prop. 25, pt. 1), which therefore must necessarily be conceived through the essence of God itself (Ax. 4, pt. 1) and by a certain eternal necessity (Prop. 16, pt. 1). This conception, moreover, must necessarily exist in God (Prop. 3, pt. 2).—Q.E.D.

PROP. XXIII.—*The human mind cannot be absolutely destroyed with the body, but something of it remains which is eternal.*

Demonst.—In God there necessarily exists a conception or idea which expresses the essence of the human body (Prop. 22, pt. 5). This conception or idea is therefore necessarily something which pertains to the essence of the human mind (Prop. 13, pt. 2). But we ascribe to the human mind no duration which can be limited by time, unless in so far as it expresses the actual existence of the body, which is manifested through duration, and which can be limited by time, that is to say (Corol. Prop. 8, pt. 2), we cannot ascribe duration to the mind except while the body exists.

But nevertheless, since this something is that which is conceived by a certain eternal necessity through the essence itself of God (Prop. 22, pt. 5), this something which pertains to the essence of the mind will necessarily be eternal.—Q.E.D.

Schol.—This idea which expresses the essence of the body under the form of eternity is, as we have said, a certain mode of thought which pertains to the essence of the mind, and is necessarily eternal. It is impossible, nevertheless, that we should recollect that we existed before the body, because there are no traces of any such existence in the body, and also because eternity cannot be defined by time, or have any relationship to it. Nevertheless we feel and know by experience that we are eternal. For the mind is no less sensible of those things which it conceives through intelligence than of those which it remembers, for demonstrations are the eyes of the mind by which it sees and observes things.

Although, therefore, we do not recollect that we existed before the body, we feel that our mind, in so far as it involves the essence of the body under the form of eternity, is eternal, and that this existence of the mind cannot be limited by time nor manifested through duration. Only in so far, therefore, as it involves the actual existence of the body can the mind be said to possess duration, and its existence be limited by a fixed time, and so far only has it the power of determining the existence of things in time, and of conceiving them under the form of duration.

PROP. XXIV.—*The more we understand individual objects, the more we understand God.*

Demonst.—This is evident from Corol. Prop. 25, pt. 1.

PROP. XXV.—*The highest effort of the mind and its highest virtue is to understand things by the third kind of knowledge.*

Demonst.—The third kind of knowledge proceeds from an adequate idea of certain attributes of God to an adequate knowledge of the essence of things (see its definition in Schol. 2, Prop. 40, pt. 2); and the more we understand things in this manner (Prop. 24, pt. 5), the more we understand God; and therefore (Prop. 28, pt. 4) the highest virtue of the mind, that is to say (Def. 8, pt. 4), the power or nature of the mind, or (Prop. 7, pt. 3) its highest effort, is to understand things by the third kind of knowledge.—Q.E.D.

PROP. XXVI.—*The better the mind is adapted to under-*

stand things by the third kind of knowledge, the more it desires to understand them by this kind of knowledge.

Demonst.—This is evident; for in so far as we conceive the mind to be adapted to understand things by this kind of knowledge, do we conceive it to be determined to understand things by this kind of knowledge, and consequently (Def. 1 of the Affects) the better the mind is adapted to this way of understanding things, the more it desires it.—Q.E.D.

PROP. XXVII.—*From this third kind of knowledge arises the highest possible peace of mind.*

Demonst.—The highest virtue of the mind is to know God (Prop. 28, pt. 4), or to understand things by the third kind of knowledge (Prop. 25, pt. 5). This virtue is greater the more the mind knows things by this kind of knowledge (Prop. 24, pt. 5), and therefore he who knows things by this kind of knowledge passes to the highest human perfection, and consequently (Def. 2 of the Affects) is affected with the highest joy, which is accompanied with the idea of himself and his own virtue (Prop. 43, pt. 2); and therefore (Def. 25 of the Affects) from this kind of knowledge arises the highest possible peace of mind.—Q.E.D.

PROP. XXVIII.—*The effort or the desire to know things by the third kind of knowledge cannot arise from the first kind, but may arise from the second kind of knowledge.*

Demonst.—This proposition is self-evident; for everything that we clearly and distinctly understand, we understand either through itself or through something which is conceived through itself; or, in other words, ideas which are clear and distinct in us, or which are related to the third kind of knowledge (Schol. 2, Prop. 40, pt. 2), cannot follow from mutilated and confused ideas, which (by the same scholium) are related to the first kind of knowledge, but from adequate ideas, that is to say (by the same scholium), from the second and third kinds of knowledge. Therefore (Def. 1 of the Affects) the desire of knowing things by the third kind of knowledge cannot arise from the first kind, but may arise from the second.—Q.E.D.

PROP. XXIX.—*Everything which the mind understands under the form of eternity, it understands not because it conceives the present actual existence of the body, but because it conceives the essence of the body under the form of eternity.*

Demonst.—In so far as the mind conceives the present existence of its body does it conceive duration which can be determined in time, and so far only has it the power of conceiving things in relation to time (Prop. 21, pt. 5, and Prop. 26, pt. 2). But eternity cannot be manifested through duration (Def. 8, pt. 1, and its explanation; therefore the mind so far has not the power of conceiving things under the form of eternity: but because it is the nature of reason to conceive things under the form of eternity (Corol. 2, Prop. 44, pt. 2), and because it also pertains to the nature of the mind to conceive the essence of the body under the form of eternity (Prop. 23, pt. 5), and excepting these two things nothing else pertains to the nature of the mind (Prop. 13, pt. 2), therefore this power of conceiving things under the form of eternity does not pertain to the mind except in so far as it conceives the essence of the body under the form of eternity. —Q.E.D.

Schol.—Things are conceived by us as actual in two ways; either in so far as we conceive them to exist with relation to a fixed time and place, or in so far as we conceive them to be contained in God, and to follow from the necessity of the divine nature. But those things which are conceived in this second way as true or real we conceive under the form of eternity, and their ideas involve the eternal and infinite essence of God, as we have shown in Prop. 45, pt. 2, to the scholium of which proposition the reader is also referred.

PROP. XXX.—*Our mind, in so far as it knows itself and the body under the form of eternity, necessarily has a knowledge of God, and knows that it is in God and is conceived through Him.*

Demonst.—Eternity is the very essence of God, in so far as that essence involves necessary existence (Def. 8, pt. 1). To conceive things therefore under the form of eternity, is to conceive them in so far as they are conceived through the essence of God as actually existing things, or in so far as through the essence of God they involve existence. Therefore our mind, in so far as it conceives itself and its body under the form of eternity, necessarily has a knowledge of God, and knows, &c. —Q.E.D.

PROP. XXXI.—*The third kind of knowledge depends upon the mind as its formal cause, in so far as the mind itself is eternal.*

Demonst.—The mind conceives nothing under the form of eternity, unless in so far as it conceives the essence of its body under the form of eternity (Prop. 29, pt. 5), that is to say (Props. 21 and 23, pt. 5), unless in so far as it is eternal. Therefore (Prop. 30, pt. 5) in so far as the mind is eternal it has a knowledge of God, which is necessarily adequate (Prop. 46, pt. 2), and therefore in so far as it is eternal it is fitted to know all those

S

things which can follow from this knowledge of God
(Prop. 40, pt. 2), that is to say it is fitted to know things
by the third kind of knowledge (see the definition of this
kind of knowledge in Schol. 2, Prop. 40, pt. 2), of which
(Def. 1, pt. 3), in so far as the mind is eternal, it is the
adequate or formal cause.—Q.E.D.

Schol.—As each person therefore becomes stronger in
this kind of knowledge, the more is he conscious of himself and of God; that is to say, the more perfect and the
happier he is, a truth which will still more clearly appear
from what follows.   Here, however, it is to be observed,
that although we are now certain that the mind is eternal
in so far as it conceives things under the form of eternity,
yet, in order that what we wish to prove may be more
easily explained and better understood, we shall consider
the mind, as we have hitherto done, as if it had just
begun to be, and had just begun to understand things
under the form of eternity.   This we can do without
any risk of error, provided only we are careful to conclude
nothing except from clear premisses.

PROP. XXXII.—*We delight in whatever we understand by
the third kind of knowledge, and our delight is accompanied with the idea of God as its cause.*

Demonst.—From this kind of knowledge arises the
highest possible peace of mind, that is to say (Def. 25 of
the Affects), the highest joy, attended moreover with the
idea of one's self (Prop. 27, pt. 5), and consequently
(Prop. 30, pt. 5) attended with the idea of God as its
cause.—Q.E.D.

Corol.—From the third kind of knowledge necessarily
springs the intellectual love of God.   For from this kind
of knowledge arises (Prop. 32, pt. 5) joy attended with
the idea of God as its cause, that is to say (Def. 6 of the
Affects), the love of God, not in so far as we imagine Him
as present (Prop. 29, pt. 5), but in so far as we under-

stand that He is eternal; and that is what I call the intellectual love of God.

PROP. XXXIII.—*The intellectual love of God which arises from the third kind of knowledge is eternal.*

Demonst.—The third kind of knowledge (Prop. 31, pt. 5, and Ax. 3, pt. 1) is eternal, and therefore (by the same axiom) the love which springs from it is necessarily eternal.—Q.E.D.

Schol.—Although this love to God has no beginning (Prop. 33, pt. 5), it nevertheless has all the perfections of love, just as if it had originated;—as we supposed in the corollary of Prop. 32, pt. 5. Nor is there here any difference, excepting that the mind has eternally possessed these same perfections which we imagined as now accruing to it, and has possessed them with the accompanying idea of God as the eternal cause. And if joy consist in the passage to a greater perfection, blessedness must indeed consist in this, that the mind is endowed with perfection itself.

PROP. XXXIV.—*The mind is subject to affects which are related to passions only so long as the body exists.*

Demonst.—An imagination is an idea by which the mind contemplates any object as present (see its definition in Schol. Prop. 17, pt. 2). This idea nevertheless indicates the present constitution of the human body rather than the nature of the external object (Corol. 2, Prop. 16, pt. 2). An affect, therefore (by the general definition of the Affects), is an imagination in so far as it indicates the present constitution of the body, and therefore (Prop. 21, pt. 5) the mind, only so long as the body exists, is subject to affects which are related to passions.—Q.E.D.

Corol.—Hence it follows that no love except intellectual love is eternal.

Schol.—If we look at the common opinion of men, we shall see that they are indeed conscious of the eternity of their minds, but they confound it with duration, and attribute it to imagination or memory, which they believe remain after death.

PROP. XXXV.—*God loves Himself with an infinite intellectual love.*

God is absolutely infinite (Def. 6, pt. 1), that is to say (Def. 6, pt. 2), the nature of God delights in infinite perfection accompanied (Prop. 3, pt. 2) with the idea of Himself, that is to say (Prop. 11, and Def. 1, pt. 1), with the idea of Himself as cause, and this is what, in Corol. Prop. 32, pt. 5, we have called intellectual love.

PROP. XXXVI.—*The intellectual love of the mind towards God is the very love with which He loves Himself, not in so far as He is infinite, but in so far as He can be manifested through the essence of the human mind, considered under the form of eternity ; that is to say, the intellectual love of the mind towards God is part of the infinite love with which God loves Himself.*

Demonst.—This love of the mind must be related to the actions of the mind (Corol. Prop. 32, pt. 5, and Prop. 3, pt. 3), and it is therefore an action by which the mind contemplates itself; and which is accompanied with the idea of God as cause (Prop. 32, pt. 5, with the Corol.); that is to say (Corol. Prop. 25, pt. 1, and Corol. Prop. 11, pt. 2), it is an action by which God, in so far as He can be manifested through the human mind, contemplates Himself, the action being accompanied with the idea of Himself; and therefore (Prop. 35, pt. 5), this love of the mind is part of the infinite love with which God loves Himself.—Q.E.D.

Corol.—Hence it follows that God, in so far as He

loves Himself, loves men, and consequently that the love of God towards men and the intellectual love of the mind towards God are one and the same thing.

Schol.—Hence we clearly understand that our salvation, or blessedness, or liberty consists in a constant and eternal love towards God, or in the love of God towards men. This love or blessedness is called Glory in the sacred writings, and not without reason. For whether it be related to God or to the mind, it may properly be called repose of mind, which (Defs. 25 and 30 of the Affects) is, in truth, not distinguished from glory. For in so far as it is related to God, it is (Prop. 35, pt. 5) joy (granting that it is allowable to use this word), accompanied with the idea of Himself, and it is the same thing when it is related to the mind (Prop. 27, pt. 5). Again, since the essence of our mind consists in knowledge alone, whose beginning and foundation is God (Prop. 15, pt. 1, and Schol. Prop. 47, pt. 2), it is clear to us in what manner and by what method our mind, with regard both to essence and existence, follows from the divine nature, and continually depends upon God. I thought it worth while for me to notice this here, in order that I might show, by this example, what that knowledge of individual objects which I have called intuitive or of the third kind (Schol. 2, Prop. 40, pt. 2) is able to do, and how much more potent it is than the universal knowledge, which I have called knowledge of the second kind. For although I have shown generally in the First Part that all things, and consequently also the human mind, depend upon God both with regard to existence and essence, yet that demonstration, although legitimate, and placed beyond the possibility of a doubt, does not, nevertheless, so affect our mind as a proof from the essence itself of any individual object which we say depends upon God.

PROP. XXXVII.—*There is nothing in nature which is contrary to this intellectual love, or which can negate it.*

This intellectual love necessarily follows from the nature of the mind, in so far as it is considered, through the nature of God, as an eternal truth (Props. 33 and 29, pt. 5). If there were anything, therefore, contrary to this love, it would be contrary to the truth, and consequently whatever might be able to negate this love would be able to make the true false, which (as is self-evident) is absurd. There exists, therefore, nothing in nature, &c.—Q.E.D.

Schol.—The axiom of the Fourth Part refers only to individual objects, in so far as they are considered in relation to a fixed time and place. This, I believe, no one can doubt.

PROP. XXXVIII.—*The more objects the mind understands by the second and third kinds of knowledge, the less it suffers from those affects which are evil, and the less it fears death.*

Demonst.—The essence of the mind consists in knowledge (Prop. 11, pt. 2). The more things, therefore, the mind knows by the second and third kinds of knowledge, the greater is that part which abides (Props. 29 and 23, pt. 5), and consequently (Prop. 37, pt. 5) the greater is that part which is not touched by affects which are contrary to our nature, that is to say (Prop. 30, pt. 4), which are evil. The more things, therefore, the mind understands by the second and third kinds of knowledge, the greater is that part which remains unharmed, and the less consequently does it suffer from the affects.

Schol.—We are thus enabled to understand that which I touched upon in Schol. Prop. 39, pt. 4, and which I promised to explain in this part, namely, that death is by so much the less injurious to us as the clear and distinct knowledge of the mind is greater, and consequently as the mind loves God more. Again, since (Prop. 27, pt. 5) from the third kind of knowledge there arises the highest possible peace, it follows that it is possible for the human mind to be of such a nature that that part of it which we have shown perishes with its body (Prop. 21, pt. 5), in comparison with the part of it which remains, is of no consequence. But more fully upon this subject presently.

PROP. XXXIX.—*He who possesses a body fit for many things possesses a mind of which the greater part is eternal.*

Demonst.—He who possesses a body fitted for doing many things is least of all agitated by those affects which are evil (Prop. 38, pt. 4), that is to say (Prop. 30, pt. 4), by affects which are contrary to our nature, and therefore (Prop. 10, pt. 5) he possesses the power of arranging and connecting the affections of the body according to the order of the intellect, and consequently (Prop. 14, pt. 5) of causing all the affections of the body to be related to the idea of God (Prop. 15, pt. 5); in consequence of which he is affected with a love to God, which (Prop. 16, pt. 5) must occupy or form the greatest part of his mind, and therefore (Prop. 33, pt. 5) he possesses a mind of which the greatest part is eternal.

Schol.—Inasmuch as human bodies are fit for many things, we cannot doubt the possibility of their possessing such a nature that they may be related to minds which have a large knowledge of themselves and of God, and whose greatest or principal part is eternal, so that they scarcely fear death. To understand this more clearly, it is to be here considered that we live in constant change, and that according as we change for the better or the worse we are called happy or unhappy. For he who passes from infancy or childhood to death is called unhappy, and, on the other hand, we consider ourselves happy if we can pass through the whole period of life with a sound mind in a sound body. Moreover, he who, like an infant or child, possesses a body fit for very few things, and almost altogether dependent on external causes, has a mind which, considered in itself alone, is almost entirely unconscious of itself, of God, and of objects. On the other hand, he who possesses a body fit for many things possesses a mind which, considered in itself alone, is largely conscious of itself, of God, and of objects. In this life, therefore, it is our chief endeavour to change the body of infancy, so far as its nature permits and is conducive thereto, into another body which is fitted for many things, and which is related to a mind conscious as much as possible of itself, of God, and of objects; so that everything which is related to its memory or imagination, in comparison with the intellect is scarcely of any moment, as I have already said in the scholium of the preceding proposition.

PROP. XL.—*The more perfection a thing possesses, the more it acts and the less it suffers, and conversely the more it acts the more perfect it is.*

Demonst.—The more perfect a thing is, the more reality it possesses (Def. 6, pt. 2), and consequently (Prop. 3, pt. 3, with the Schol.) the more it acts and the less it suffers. Inversely also it may be demonstrated in the same way that the more a thing acts the more perfect it is.—Q.E.D.

Corol.—Hence it follows that that part of the mind which abides, whether great or small, is more perfect than the other part. For the part of the mind which is eternal (Props. 23 and 29, pt. 5) is the intellect, through which alone we are said to act (Prop. 3, pt. 3), but that part which, as we have shown, perishes, is the imagination itself (Prop. 21, pt. 5), through which alone we are said to suffer (Prop. 3, pt. 3, and the general definition of the affects). Therefore (Prop. 40, pt. 5) that part which abides, whether great or small, is more perfect than the latter.—Q.E.D.

Schol.—These are the things I proposed to prove concerning the mind, in so far as it is considered without relation to the existence of the body, and from these, taken together with Prop. 21, pt. 1, and other propositions, it is evident that our mind, in so far as it understands, is an eternal mode of thought, which is determined by another eternal mode of thought, and this again by another, and so on *ad infinitum*, so that all taken together form the eternal and infinite intellect of God.

PROP. XLI.—*Even if we did not know that our mind is eternal, we should still consider as of primary importance Piety and Religion, and absolutely everything which in the Fourth Part we have shown to be related to strength of mind and generosity.*

Demonst.—The primary and sole foundation of virtue or of the proper conduct of life (by Corol. Prop. 22, and Prop. 24, pt. 4) is to seek our own profit. But in order to determine what reason prescribes as profitable, we had no regard to the eternity of the mind, which we did not recognise till we came to the Fifth Part. Therefore, although we were at that time ignorant that the mind is eternal, we considered as of primary importance those things which we have shown are related to strength of mind and generosity; and therefore, even if we were now ignorant of the eternity of the mind, we should consider those commands of reason as of primary importance.—Q.E.D.

Schol.—The creed of the multitude seems to be different from this; for most persons seem to believe that they are free in so far as it is allowed them to obey their lusts, and that they give up a portion of their rights, in so far as they are bound to live according to the commands of divine law. Piety, therefore, and religion, and absolutely all those things that are related to greatness of soul, they believe to be burdens which they hope to be able to lay aside after death; hoping also to receive some reward for their bondage, that is to say, for their piety and religion. It is not merely this hope, however, but also and chiefly fear of dreadful punishments after death, by which they are induced to live according to the commands of divine law, that is to say, as far as their feebleness and impotent mind will permit; and if this hope and fear were not present to them, but if they, on the contrary, believed that minds perish with the body, and that there is no prolongation of life for miserable creatures exhausted with the burden of their piety, they would return to ways of their own liking; they would prefer to let everything be controlled by their own passions, and to obey fortune rather than themselves.

This seems to me as absurd as if a man, because he does not believe that he will be able to feed his body with good food to all eternity, should desire to satiate himself with poisonous and deadly drugs; or as if, because he sees that the mind is not eternal or immortal, he should therefore prefer to be mad and to live without reason,—absurdities so great that they scarcely deserve to be repeated.

PROP. XLII.—*Blessedness is not the reward of virtue, but is virtue itself; nor do we delight in blessedness because we restrain our lusts; but, on the contrary, because we delight in it, therefore are we able to restrain them.*

Demonst.—Blessedness consists in love towards God (Prop. 36, pt. 5, and its Schol.), which arises from the third kind of knowledge (Corol. Prop. 32, pt. 5), and this love, therefore (Props. 59 and 3, pt. 3), must be related to the mind in so far as it acts. Blessedness, therefore (Def. 8, pt. 4), is virtue itself, which was the first thing to be proved. Again, the more the mind delights in this divine love or blessedness, the more it understands (Prop. 32, pt. 5), that is to say (Corol. Prop. 3, pt. 5), the greater is the power it has over its affects, and (Prop. 38, pt. 5) the less it suffers from affects which are evil. Therefore, it is because the mind delights in this divine love or blessedness that it possesses the power of restraining the lusts; and because the power of man to restrain the affects is in the intellect alone, no one, therefore, delights in blessedness because he has restrained his affects, but, on the contrary, the power of restraining his lusts springs from blessedness itself.—Q.E.D.

Schol.—I have finished everything I wished to explain concerning the power of the mind over the affects and concerning its liberty. From what has been said we see what is the strength of the wise man, and how much he surpasses the ignorant who is driven forward by lust alone. For the ignorant man is not only agitated by external causes in many ways, and never enjoys true peace of soul, but lives also ignorant, as it were, both of God and of things, and as soon as he ceases to suffer ceases also to be. On the other hand, the wise man, in so far as he is considered as such, is scarcely ever moved in his mind, but, being conscious by a certain eternal necessity of himself, of God, and of things, never ceases to be, and always enjoys true peace of soul. If the way which, as I have shown, leads hither seem very difficult, it can nevertheless be found. It must indeed be difficult since it is so seldom discovered; for if salvation lay ready to hand and could be discovered without great labour, how could it be possible that it should be neglected almost by everybody? But all noble things are as difficult as they are rare.

FINIS.

INDEX.

T

Presence of mind is strength of mind, 159.

Present objects, affect towards them, 122, 123, 187, 188, 189, 190, 191, 192, 230, 231, 234.

Preservation of being foundation of virtue, 194, 195, 196, 197, 198.

—— of being, no object superior to it, 198.

—— of being, no one neglects it, 196.

—— of being, same as happiness, 194.

—— of being with reference to health as a whole, 230.

Pride, definition, 168, 225.

—— encourages flattery, 225, 246.

—— ignorance of one's self and impotence, 224.

Profit, agreement with our nature, 202.

—— capacity of body for affecting and being affected is true profit, 212, 247.

—— everybody has the right to seek his own, 242.

—— man under guidance of reason is chief profit to man, 205, 243.

—— no one neglects to seek his own, 196.

—— of the whole man, partial joy or sorrow has no regard to it, 229.

—— seeking our own profit is the foundation of virtue, 195, 198.

—— what is the profit of one's self is that of others, 205.

—— what the law of our own profit demands, 247.

Property, rights of it, 211.

Punishment by supreme authority, 221.

Pusillanimity, definition, 149, 172.

QUANTITY, existence in imagination distinguished from existence in intellect, 17.

REALITY, connection between it and attributes, 8.

—— identical with perfection, 48, 179, 180.

Reason, affects which spring from it, 258, 266.

—— conception of objects by it, 230.

—— conformity of men to it is agreement of nature, 204.

—— considers things as necessary, 90.

Reason counsels life under common laws, 239.

—— definition, 86.

—— desire springing from it, 230.

—— directs repayment of hatred, &c., with love, 218.

—— distinguishes truth from falsity, 87.

—— follows greater good and lesser evil, 233.

—— guidance by it as compared with that by affects, 234.

—— knowledge from it is necessarily true, 87.

—— man under guidance of it profitable to man, 205.

—— may determine to actions to which passion determines us, 228.

—— perceives things under form of eternity, 91.

—— perfection of it is our sole profit, 241.

—— seeks greater future good, 234.

—— teaches direct pursuit of good and indirect avoidance of evil, 232.

Recollection, cause of desire, 137.

Regret, definition, 170.

Religion, definition, 209.

—— importance of it, 281.

—— what it is generally thought to be, 282.

Remorse, definition, 123, 165.

—— sign of weakness, 219.

Repentance, definition, 132, 149, 167.

—— not a virtue, 223.

Repose of mind, definition, 277.

Resemblance, connection with love and hatred, 121.

Rest, preservation of proportion of motion and rest, 212.

Right, natural, 210.

SALVATION, in what it consists, 277.

Science, intuitive. See "Intuitive science."

Scorn, definition, 151.

Self-approval, definition, 149, 153.

Self-exaltation, definition, 132, 169.

—— how caused, 135, 226.

Self-love, definition, 153.

Self-preservation. See "Preservation of Being."

Self-satisfaction arising from reason, 222, 249.

—— definition, 167.

THE END.

Printed in the United States
65652LVS00005B/19

9 781564 596253